QUALITY CONTROL IN THE PHARMACEUTICAL INDUSTRY

Volume 1

CONTRIBUTORS

R. BANZIGER
JOAN A. BORICK
PAUL M. BORICK
WILLIAM E. HASSAN, JR.
DONALD JACONIA
AMIEL KIRSHBAUM
A. G. MATHEWS
THOMAS MEDWICK
G. BRIGGS PHILLIPS
W. POOL
ROBERT S. RUNKLE

QUALITY CONTROL IN THE PHARMACEUTICAL INDUSTRY

Edited by Murray S. Cooper

Lederle Laboratories
Pearl River, New York

VOLUME 1

Academic Press New York and London 1972

ACADEMIC PRESS, INC.
111 Fifth Avenue, New York, New York 10003

United Kingdom Edition published by
ACADEMIC PRESS, INC. (LONDON) LTD.
24/28 Oval Road, London NW1

LIBRARY OF CONGRESS CATALOG CARD NUMBER: 79-187248

PRINTED IN THE UNITED STATES OF AMERICA

CONTENTS

Quality-Control Education in the College of Pharmacy

Thomas Medwick

The Role of the World Health Organization in the Quality Control of Biological and Pharmaceutical Products

A. G. Mathews

LIST OF CONTRIBUTORS

Numbers in parentheses indicate the pages on which the authors' contributions begin.

R. Banziger (155), Research Division, Hoffmann-La Roche, Inc., Nutley, New Jersey

Joan A. Borick (1), Union College, Cranford, New Jersey

Paul M. Borick (1), Ethicon, Inc., Somerville, New Jersey

William E. Hassan, Jr., (129), Peter Bent Brigham Hospital, Boston, Massachusetts

Donald Jaconia (101), Research Department, CIBA-GEIGY Pharmaceutical Company, Summit, New Jersey

Amiel Kirshbaum* (39), National Center for Antibiotic Analysis, United States Food and Drug Administration, Washington, D.C.

A. G. Mathews (193), Commonwealth Serum Laboratories, Melbourne, Australia

Thomas Medwick (177), College of Pharmacy, Rutgers University, University Heights Campus, New Brunswick, New Jersey

G. Briggs Phillips (73), Becton, Dickinson Research Center, Raleigh, North Carolina

*Present address: 11013 Gainsborough Road, Potomac, Maryland 20854.

W. Pool (155), Research Division, Hoffmann-La Roche, Inc., Nutley, New Jersey

Robert S. Runkle* (73), Becton, Dickinson Research Center, Raleigh, North Carolina

*Present address: Research Triangle Park, North Carolina 27709.

PREFACE

Development, production, and testing for the quality assurance of pharmaceutical products are each important segments of one of the most sophisticated and advanced industries in the world. The skills necessary to optimally maintain these functions require advanced training in several technical and scientific disciplines.

Although numerous publications deal in part or exclusively with various aspects of pharmaceutical science, no major work has been devoted entirely to the area of quality control or quality assurance of pharmaceutical products. This treatise, when complete, will include at least 25 chapters in three or four volumes, each dealing in depth with a distinct aspect of the subject. The authors who have contributed chapters to this series are eminently qualified for their chosen tasks and, in most instances, are reviewing subjects which are in their primary fields of interest and professional activity.

It was not feasible to group the chapters according to associated subject matters, since they could not be prepared for uniform delivery dates. We believe, however, that this is only a minor disadvantage, since the series ultimately will encompass all of the important areas of quality assurance.

The present series is geared to the needs of the scientist or administrator in the pharmaceutical industry or allied fields wishing to gain additional knowledge of the quality assurance function. These volumes should also prove useful to those who are specialists in one aspect of quality assurance, but have not had the opportunity to deal in depth with the other important areas of this broad function.

MURRAY S. COOPER

STERILITY TESTING OF PHARMACEUTICALS, COSMETICS, AND MEDICAL DEVICES

Paul M. Borick and Joan A. Borick

Ethicon, Inc.,
Somerville, New Jersey, and
Union College,
Cranford, New Jersey

I. Introduction

Major emphasis is being placed today on the sterility of products in the pharmaceutical, cosmetic, and medical device areas. Manufacturers, realizing the necessity for the elimination of microorganisms from their products and environment to protect the public welfare, are spending millions of dollars to eradicate these contaminants. In order to achieve sterility, microorganisms need to be excluded from the desired materials or environment and a means of determining the effectiveness of the sterilization process must be provided. This requires technical competence and knowledge, combined with adept physical manipulations, in order to produce the desired end result. It is our purpose to discuss these factors and to present information which will be of value in achieving this goal, i.e., the assurance of sterility which will ultimately result in safe and pure products for consumer use.

Although sterility implies the absence of all microorganisms and is frequently considered in absolute terms, a more meaningful definition may be expressed as freedom from living microorganisms achieved by the application of a process in which microbial cells or their components are removed or killed to the extent that they are no longer detectable in standard culture media in which they have previously been found to proliferate (Gaughran and Borick, 1972).

Each beginning student in bacteriology is taught the basic tenet that bacteria are ubiquitous. He then immediately learns to appreciate the fact that many of these microorganisms are pathogenic and are potentially harmful or dangerous. Insufficient time, however, is devoted to sterilization and sterility practices during training; hence the novice bacteriologist has only a limited knowledge in this field and must learn through a series of experiences that he frequently has insufficient information to perform the job satisfactorily.

One of us (P. M. B.) holds an Air Force Reserve assignment at the Armed Forces Institute of Pathology in Washington, D.C. Recently, during one of the active duty tours, a series of experiments was performed with a resistant *Bacillus subtilis* culture in various autoclaves routinely employed in bacteriology and virology. It is interesting to note that the autoclave recording the highest temperature, 124°C, was the least effective. Recovery of the test organism was accomplished after 5- and 10-minute exposures in small vials using an inoculum of approximately 2×10^4 spores of *B. subtilis* var. *niger* on paper discs. It was surprising to find that this autoclave failed in performance in spite of the higher temperature recording, while the others performed well at lower temperatures. The point being made here is that, although heat is generally accepted as being extremely effective in the destruction of bacteria, all situations cannot be taken for granted in achieving sterility. One must first be assured that the sterilization process was functioning properly, and, secondly, that sterility was, in fact, achieved.

How is this accomplished? The simplest way, of course, is immersion of the product into the desired culture medium and after sufficient incubation, examination of the culture tube for the presence or absence of microbial growth. In essence, this is how sterility tests are conducted.

Why, then, is so much time and effort devoted to sterility testing and why do manufacturers spend such large sums of money to ensure that their products are sterile? Macek (1970), in reviewing sterility controls, examines some of the reasons in his statement that sterility, like quality, cannot be tested into a product; it can only be built in and its adequacy determined by process controls throughout. Olson (1970) states that efforts to control microbiological health hazards constitute one of the major consumer protection programs of the Food and Drug Administration and that the magnitude of these efforts is justified in that some ten million cases of foodborne diseases occur annually in this country; this does not include infections caused by cosmetics and pharmaceutical products.

Kallings *et al.* (1966), in performing sterility tests on products manufactured in Europe, reported that heavy contamination was present in various products and attributed many human infections to contaminated drugs.

Sterility could be assured if bacteriologists were able to test every product under optimum conditions. Obviously, it is not possible to test every single item for sterility as the manufacturer would then have nothing to sell. Furthermore, our present methods of performing sterility tests have limitations with regard to technique and interpretation. Laboratories performing large numbers of sterility tests soon realize that contamination occurs during testing in spite of all attempts to prevent its occurrence. As an example, Borick (1969) reported that two types of test tubes, with an orifice diameter of 2.2 and 4.7 cm, were employed for the sterility testing of sutures and packets. Although every possible precaution had been taken to maintain asepsis, it was found that contamination occurred much more frequently with the larger size (4.7 cm) tube, where there is approximately a fourfold increase in the surface area of the tubes. This occurred despite a 15-minute surgical scrub-up of personnel, use of sterile caps, gowns and masks, positive pressure in the rooms, disinfection of the test rooms after each operation, use of UV light during the absence of personnel, presence of transfer cabinets, and the installation of laminar-flow units. At this point, the question arises as to how one knows that the contaminant was not derived from the product. These data were obtained from mock sterility tests, the technicians performing all the mechanical manipulations of sterility testing without actually incorporating the product into the test media.

Heat with moist and dry air is without doubt a very common and extremely effective means of achieving sterility. Certain conditions must be satisfied before this can be accomplished. Because situations prevail in which proper sterilization is not achieved, a reliable means of checking the sterility of the product must be established. Shotton (1961) claimed that, in order to obtain sterile products, the proper packing of containers in autoclaves was essential and the location of vent holes or the use of porous materials was of paramount importance. Bowie (1961) further advocated that it was necessary to have adequate contact between the microorganisms and steam or solution at the selected temperature. The problem here is that it is not always possible to know that all of these conditions are satisfied; hence, it is vital to have some means of checking on the reliability of the process. Sterility tests with regular samples or use of biological indicators serve this purpose. The latter will be discussed in greater detail later.

In order to achieve sterility, all parameters must be considered. Moisture, for example, can be an important factor even in dry heat sterilization. Drummond and Pflug (1970) presented data which suggest that if objects to be dry-heat sterilized are conditioned in a low-humidity environment prior to treatment, the probability of achieving sterility is increased and that a further increase can be obtained by lowering the relative humidity of the treatment environment.

Numerous investigators (Artandi and Van Winkle, 1959; Borick and Fogarty, 1967; Pepper *et al.*, 1956; Van Winkle *et al.*, 1967) have shown that irradiation is an extremely effective method of obtaining sterile products. Because of its high degree of reliability, some countries in Europe feel that sterility checks on items sterilized by this means are unnecessary. In the United States, Great Britain, and other countries, sterility tests are performed on all materials without regard to the sterilization process.

According to Opfell and Miller (1965), cold sterilization processes are those effective below temperatures where heat alone can sterilize. They are important for sterility as they can be applied to objects which are destroyed by heat. The use of liquids to effect sterilization has limited use commercially.

Gaseous ethylene oxide is now universally employed in the pharmaceutical, cosmetic, and medical device industries to achieve sterility. One need merely examine the literature to gain some idea of its many and diversified applications. Reviews on this subject include work by Bruch (1961), Bruch and Bruch (1970), Ernst and Doyle (1968), Lloyd (1963), Mayr (1961), Phillips (1961), and Stierli *et al.* (1962). Some of the restrictions in its applications were discussed by Borick (1968).

Microbiologists working in this area are generally agreed that various parameters must be controlled to achieve sterility with this mode of sterilization. One must not only be familiar with the underlying principles of sterilization, but should take into account those factors which make sterility difficult to obtain. Although vegetative bacterial cells may be readily destroyed under certain circumstances, the more resistant bacterial spores may well remain. Even worse, they may be imbedded in a crystalline matrix, or contained in that portion of the product which is difficult to test for sterility. For example, nonsterile powders may produce clumps which would protect the bacterial cell and prevent germination on subsequent incubation, or a contaminant present in a syringe in the area of the inner plunger, covered by a rubber or plastic cap, may be inaccessible for sterilization. Ernst *et al.* (1969), in discussing some of the hazards and uncertainties involved in product testing, claim that a knowledge of the process, avoidance of unfavorable environmental conditions and the education of personnel in testing procedures will alleviate many of the difficult conditions normally associated with sterility testing.

Tests for sterility are of vital importance where sterilization is accomplished by sterile filtration or aseptic transfers. Here it is practically impossible to know how effectively the desired end result has been achieved without examination of the final product or a portion thereof. This means of acquiring sterility is without doubt one of the most difficult. The advisory panel on sterilization and sterility recognized this and recommended a larger sampling plan than for any of the other methods. Consequently, as may be seen in the "United States Pharmacopeia XVIII" (USP, 1970) and "National Formulary XIII" (NF, 1970), more sterility tests are required for sterile items obtained by filtration.

One other factor which should be taken into consideration regarding sterility is the nature of the product to be tested. A highly viscous material, or one which is bacteriostatic or bactericidal, can present additional problems in testing for sterility. Awe *et al.* (1963) studied methyl 2-cyanoacrylate and concluded that this biological adhesive was bacteriostatic and bactericidal. Because microorganisms were not recovered with the normal sterility tests and the chemical showed antimicrobial activity, Lehman *et al.* (1966) concluded that it was self-sterilizing. Page and Borick (1967) were able to demonstrate that when the compound was vigorously shaken to disperse the polymer throughout the test solution, bacterial spores were recovered under normal test conditions after inoculation with three organisms that included aerobic and anaerobic spore-formers.

Filtration has been widely used as a method of attaining sterility for certain products. This process is dependent upon the physical removal of microorganisms by adsorption on the filter medium or by a sieving mechanism, and is commonly used for the sterilization of heat-labile chemicals, e.g., antibiotics or oily solutions.

Sterilizing filters are classified as depth filters and screen filters. Depth filters depend upon random entrapment and adsorption of particles or microorganisms throughout the filter material. Several types of depth filters are asbestos pads, ceramic candles, sintered glass, porous stainless steel, and the complex laminates. The two most commonly used depth filters are the asbestos pad-type and the unglazed porcelain candle.

Screen filters, unlike depth filters, retain on their surface all particles larger than the filter pore. Screen filters act as mechanical sieves. The membrane filter furnishes the most practical method for screen filtration. Membrane filters are thin, porous membranes of biologically inert materials such as cellulose esters and other polymeric materials. Filters of this type are currently produced in a wide range of pore sizes from 10 mμ up to 14 μ.

Membrane filters have found wide application as a simple, accurate method for isolating and identifying bacterial contaminants. Microbes larger than the pore are trapped on the filter surface and may be examined under a microscope or cultured to form viable colonies. Consequently, membrane filters offer a convenient means of testing products containing inhibitory or interfering substances such as preparations in oils and formulations that emulsify or develop turbidity in solution.

Holdowsky (1957) proposed the use of membrane filters for sterility testing of antibiotics. Subsequent studies by other investigators (Bowman and Holdowsky, 1959; Sykes and Hooper, 1959; Bowman, 1966) presented additional evidence confirming the usefulness of this method. The membrane filtration method for testing antibacterial substances is now employed routinely. In 1970, the USP XVIII and the NF XIII, First Supplement, adopted membrane filtration sterility tests as official tests for nonantibiotics as well as antibiotic drugs.

Membrane filter techniques have found wide application for sterility testing of oils and ointments. A detailed method for the sterility testing of oils was described by Russomano and Wollish (1964). The procedure is a simple, rapid method useful for the detection of contamination of oils (except those of high viscosity) with viable organisms, even at low counts. An improved viable counting method for petrolatum-based ointments was developed by Sokolski and Chidester (1964). Advantages of this method are that all the microorganisms in the ointment sample are concentrated on the filter pad, and the filter pad can be rinsed to remove antibacterial agents and traces of petrolatum. A more sensitive sterility test was developed by Tsuji *et al.* (1970) for the detection of microbial contamination in petrolatum-based ointments. The method involves dissolving the ointment in filter-sterilized isopropyl myristate and filtering through a membrane filter.

A method for testing nonsterile aqueous pharmaceutical preparations for their microbial content by membrane filter techniques is described by Buhlmann (1968). This method is applicable for finished products, bulk products, raw materials, and active ingredients.

Sterility tests, then, can be a vital tool in ascertaining not only the effectiveness of the sterilization process, but in showing that the final product is indeed sterile, thus assuring a pure and safe pharmaceutical, cosmetic, or medical device. Details of the various factors involved will be discussed in this article.

II. Sterility Test Procedures: Microscopic and Macroscopic

Present methods of sterilization, with the exception of microbial filtration, deal with the destruction of microorganisms rather than their complete omission from products. For this reason, microscopic examinations to determine sterility are not employed routinely. Although microorganisms or their cellular components may be physically present in products for all practical purposes, if they have been killed, they are considered harmless. It should be borne in mind that certain types can produce pyrogenicity, which is discussed in another chapter of this text. We do not wish to imply that microscopic examination has no value, but rather that it may be necessary in follow-up situations where a readout of culture tubes is doubtful after incubation.

Neither has the use of agar plates for sterility tests gained wide acceptance because the test procedure may be impractical. Agar plates can be advantageously employed, however, in testing of ointments or waxes which have low melting points as the test material may then be distributed throughout the liquid agar and incubated after solidification of the medium. The temperature of the agar must not be too high since heat can cause destruction of viable cells, hence, false sterility readings would be obtained. An added advantage may result with this method in that the number of colonies present on the plates indicates the degree of contamination in the product.

Sterility tests generally in use today for the testing of pharmaceuticals, cosmetics, and medical devices are dependent on the presence of viable microorganisms in the product which consists of bacteria, yeasts, and fungi. Specific tests for viruses are not utilized, but it is assumed that the detection of other microbial forms will also indicate the presence of viruses. Techniques for the cultivation of viruses are still cumbersome and are limited to the detection of specific viruses. Thus, for all practical purposes, the absence of bacteria, yeasts, or fungi implies the absence of viruses.

It is not the intent here to give specific instructions on the various types of sterility tests as this information can be obtained from the official compendia. Rather, those factors will be presented which are involved in the performance of sterility tests, aseptic techniques necessary for their successful accomplishment, the materials and media employed, and the interpretation of the test results.

One of the first considerations of sterility testing is the sample itself. Some products require little, if any, preparation for testing, whereas others require considerable attention. Parenteral drugs or biologicals are normally packaged in ampuls or bottles with tightly fitting rubber or plastic stoppers enclosed with a metal cap. In order to test the solution, either the covered enclosures can be removed and the material tested aseptically by withdrawing the solution with a sterile pipette, or, if preferred, the inner contents may be removed aseptically with a sterile needle and syringe. In either case, it is usually unnecessary to treat the sample package to obtain the inner contents.

On the other hand, when testing products such as sutures contained in glass or aluminum-foil enclosures, it is necessary to decontaminate the outer package to avoid exposure to microorganisms when the product is removed from its container. The recommended procedure is to place the package into a chemical sterilizing solution, such as aqueous glutaraldehyde or alcoholic formaldehyde. Time and concentration (Borick, 1965) must be adequate to assure the destruction of microbial spores on the package in addition to the less-resistant vegetative cells. This presents another problem which the tester must consider. Improper or weak seals can allow penetration of the chemosterilizer into the container and effect subsequent sterilization of the product which would then result in false or misleading information. For this reason, the incorporation of a dye, e.g., methylene blue or safranin, is recommended to detect leakers. The presence of a blue or red color on the product signals that leakage did, in fact, occur.

Testing of small items or low-volume solutions presents little difficulty in contrast to large bulk items. In the former case, the entire material or a portion thereof can be added to the test medium with adequate ease and control. This is not so in the testing of a large package containing, for example, cotton or other bulky material. Here it may be necessary to remove the outer portion of the material, discard it and test the inner contents for sterility. In other instances, it may be necessary to design an outer wrap to prevent contamination of the product on removal from its package. This is done frequently in the case of ethylene oxide gaseous sterilization where gas-permeable paper bags on paper overwraps are used to protect the inner contents after removal from the autoclaves. Belson (1969), in discussing quality control in the manufacture of sterile products, points out that problems related to the above could have been prevented by well-understood and generally accepted quality-control procedures, supplemented by carefully chosen and well-tested materials combined with soundly engineered package design. Halleck (1969) feels that the package is an integral part of the finished product and should be so treated, especially if it also functions in maintenance of sterility. Although the package may be designed to maintain the sterility of the product indefinitely, it is obviously of no value if the inner contents cannot be removed without contamination of the product. This handicap can be overcome in most instances with proper sample preparation prior to performance of sterility tests.

Microbiologists are generally agreed that sterility tests are dependent on culture media and the sensitivity of the test is greatly influenced by the types of culture media employed. Although many kinds of media are available today, the two most generally accepted for sterility testing are thioglycollate and soybean casein digest broths. In spite of the fact that fluid thioglycollate is used extensively, Bowman (1969) and Doyle *et al.* (1968) have cautioned that this medium does not support growth of *B. subtilis* spores when they are entrapped or held so that the organisms cannot be released into an environment of high oxygen tension.

Sabouraud's broth was widely employed in the past to detect yeasts and molds in sterility tests. The latest United States editions of official compendia have omitted this medium from these tests as it is more desirable to use a general-purpose medium such as the soybean casein digest medium to recover as many different kinds of microorganisms as possible.

Since it was recognized that there were limitations in the use of Sabouraud's broth, which ultimately resulted in its elimination from the compendia, it may be that a more desirable medium than that presently employed will be acceptable in the future. It must be a general-purpose medium rather than a selective one, and must promote growth of aerobic and anaerobic bacteria as well as allow growth of yeasts and molds.

Pittman (1946) discussed various factors involved in the employment of media for sterility tests, and advocated the use of pancreatic digest casein because there is adequate peptone for the sterility test medium. A water-soluble extract of yeast was also recommended for promoting bacterial growth. Insofar as pH is concerned, this author recommended a neutral pH which is now generally accepted for sterility tests. The addition of 0.25% sodium chloride seems to provide suitable conditions for the development of both the bacteria that prefer a low pH and no sodium chloride, and those that prefer a higher pH and 0.5% sodium chloride. Cook (1961) indicated that there is no such thing as an ideal or universal medium for sterility testing and regular investigations should be carried out to ensure that false negative results in a sterility test are not covering up nonsterile batches or faulty testing techniques.

Time and temperature of incubation are also important considerations in sterility testing. Bacteria have a wide range of growth, e.g., psychrophils, which live at low temperatures in contrast to the thermophils, which prefer temperatures in excess of 40°C. Obviously, manufacturers would prefer not to maintain a series of varied temperature incubators to cover these wide ranges, consequently, some compromise situation must be provided. The main concern in sterility testing is the detection of pathogenic microorganisms or potential pathogens which favor body temperature. Present methods employ temperatures of 30°C–35°C which are suitable for a wide variety of microorganisms and offer a favorable area for the detection of those microbes generally present as contaminants.

Mold growth occurs readily at room temperature and, for this reason, the accepted temperature of incubation is 20°C–25°C. Thus, sterility tests can be performed with the use of two incubators, except where biological indicators are used in the test procedure when a singular incubator will suffice. This will be discussed later in this chapter.

Bacterial growth in the presence of regularly employed media normally can be detected by a visual macroscopic examination of the tubes after 18–24 hours of incubation. It has been our experience that most microorganisms can be detected after 48–72 hours of incubation. A slow grower, in a single instance, was observed when testing antimicrobial agents on *Lactobacillus*. Very faint pinpoint colonies appeared after 3 days of incubation on agar plates. Where inadequate or sublethal conditions are used in sterilization, prolonged incubation times may be required. However, when sterilization accompanied by adequate controls is assured, a minimum of 7 days of incubation is adequate to detect the presence of microorganisms; this includes the slower growing fungi. Growth during incubation can be expedited by aeration of the test tubes. However, the air supplied to the tubes must be made sterile by employing appropriate filters, and adequate steps must be taken to avoid contamination at the junction of the enclosures. Shake cultures further expedite microbial growth. Where large numbers of sterility tests are performed, these procedures are generally not recommended since they would prove to be too cumbersome.

Aeration may also be useful where the product shows bacteriostasis due to the presence of ethylene oxide or propylene oxide residues after gaseous sterilization. This introduces the condition of bacteriostatic and bactericidal effects in various items.

When testing products such as antibiotics, which themselves have antimicrobial properties, it is necessary to perform tests using methods which overcome the inherent inhibitory properties of the compound. If membrane filtration is not used, dilutions of the product beyond the bactericidal or bacteriostatic range are recommended. It should be borne in mind that dilution to avoid inhibition can also result in dilution or omission of potential microbial contamination; hence, it would become difficult if not impossible to detect a low level of contamination in the product. Under these circumstances, it is appropriate to use neutralizers to eliminate the bacteriostatic or bactericidal effect. This may require the combined talents of the chemist and microbiologist working in a cooperative effort to explore new systems to neutralize the many new drugs which are constantly being introduced into world markets. The chemist, working with the new drug, is obviously the person most familiar with the product and he is the person to be consulted for potential inactivators. It will, then, be necessary for the microbiologist to perform experiments to determine the combined biological effects of the chemical and its potential neutralizing agent.

In some instances, it is possible to use a neutralizing medium which will inactivate the chemicals. Engley (1970) devised a universal neutralizing medium effective against common antimicrobial agents such as phenolics, quaternaries, halogens, and formaldehyde. The data presented showed that neutralization of these chemicals was improved and a better indication of bactericidal and bacteriostatic activities was obtained.

Media used in sterility testing should also be examined to make certain that they are not bacteriostatic or bactericidal per se. This can be done by inoculating with standard cultures of *Staphylococcus aureus* or *Candida albicans* and incubating at the optimum temperature for an appropriate time to determine if there is any inhibition of the inoculated organism.

One further precaution involves the use of potentially contaminated media. It is deemed advisable to hold the media for 1 or 2 days after preparation to make certain that they are, in fact, sterile. A precursory examination may be made prior to use to detect possible growth of microorganisms. The medium should not be kept for any prolonged period of time, should preferably be used within a week, and always be stored in a clean area free from gross contamination.

The single most important factor in sterility testing is the person or people performing the test. It is claimed that sterility tests can be performed under extremely poor conditions if the tester knows what he is doing. The more competent the technician who performs the test, the more reliable the results which can be expected. Testers should not make excess movements, nor should they converse during testing, as aerosolized droplets can be emitted into the environment even though sterile masks are worn. In keeping plate counts of various technicians, it was found that one of the ladies whom we considered a "talker" showed consistently high plate counts. Suitable garments should be worn and aseptic conditions maintained to keep contamination to a minimum (Fig. 1).

Records were kept during sterility testing of various combinations of

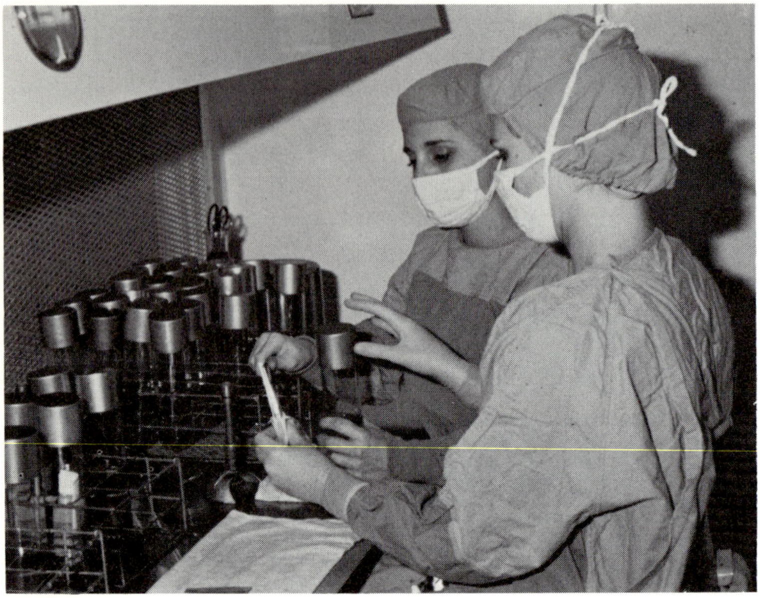

Fig. 1. *Sterility tests performed in a laminar-flow unit under controlled conditions to minimize extraneous contamination.*

technicians, with a team of two persons working in the sterility laboratory. If four technicians are employed, it is possible to have six combinations of employees working in pairs, and records can be maintained on the frequency of contamination during the test period for the best-tester combinations. These teams can be utilized during critical test periods (see Table I).

Frequency of contamination may be influenced by such factors as the length of time of the test, the condition of the rooms, the physical conditions of the technicians (people in poor health should not be utilized), and the expertise of the testers.

Although great importance is attached to the technician for the performance of sterility tests, the responsibility for the interpretation of the results should be that of the microbiologist. Education, combined with sound background experience, is a major requirement for the evaluation of data obtained from the tests performed. In some instances, macroscopic evaluation of certain products for sterility can give the appearance of microbial growth. This may be similar to turbidity due to microbial growth. When this occurs, it may be necessary to perform microscopic examination of the test material to ensure that it is indeed sterile, unless prior experience has shown that this type of result is to be expected. It may be further necessary to sub-

TABLE I

Incidence of Contaminants Recovered When Four Technicians in Differently Paired Combinations Performed Sterility Tests

Technician combination	Number of times in testing	Number of contaminants	Percentage of contamination	Best technician combination
1–2	17	1	5.9	x
1–3	55	12	21.8	
1–4	36	10	27.8	
2–3	30	4	13.3	x
2–4	42	9	21.4	
3–4	30	6	20.0	

culture the medium into an additional medium to assure sterility. Since microscopic examination may reveal only dead microorganisms and the sterilization process may have had no observable physical effect on the cells, subculture may be the only means of determining the sterility of the product.

Kelsey (1969) reported that it is probable that few surgical operations take place in which the occasional microbe does not find its way into a forbidden site so that the most elaborate precautions must still be regarded as being supported by the body's natural defenses. This being the case, why do manufacturers take such elaborate precautions to assure sterility of their product? The principal reason is to prevent infection as any form of possible contamination, even a very low level, is particularly important where resistance to infection is low such as in the case of joint cavities, or meninges, or in the aged, or debilitated. It is now felt that serious sepsis can be caused by lowly organisms such as *Serratia* or *Pseudomonas* which were previously considered to be nonpathogenic. Microbiologists, then, must regard the sterility of a product such as an adhesive bandage used for a minor cut or a bruise as important as that of a suture which is deeply embedded in human tissue or of intravenous drugs which are carried throughout the circulatory system.

After completion of the sterility tests, there are times when a positive culture is present and has occurred in a relatively large sampling plan so that there is some doubt regarding its derivation from the product. It may be that the microorganism appears as a surface contaminant apparently totally unrelated to the product if the product is completely immersed in the test solution at the bottom of the tube. Under these circumstances, the microbiologist must be assured that this was indeed an extraneous contaminant before final release of the product. The many factors involved in sterility testing must, therefore, always be taken into account.

Microbiologists are further aware that climatic conditions have a great deal of influence on microbial contamination. Mold growth, for example, is minimal during the cold winter months, begins to appear in the spring, and reaches a peak during the summer months of July and August. This is especially noticeable in the case of manufacturers located in rural areas. Where there is a serious doubt in the mind of the microbiologist regarding the origin of the culture, he is required to retest the product using regular samples. The accepted procedure is to double the sample size and repeat the tests. However, with each increase in sample size, there is also the probability of increased contamination. Under these circumstances, the chances of showing a sterile product are diminished despite the fact that the actual product may indeed be sterile. This can be further complicated by the demands of production, which should not be taken into consideration and should have no influence on the decision of the microbiologist.

The final responsibility for sterility release of the product rests solely with the microbiologist. A thorough familiarization with the sterilization process as well as the intricacies involved in achieving and maintaining sterility of the product will aid in arriving at a final decision on the test results. This means that we will not only be familiar with the final result of sterility, but have a knowledge of the precontamination levels as well. Knowing the microbial flora and contamination levels of the product can be most helpful in obtaining a sterile object more readily and rapidly. Many products manufactured under clean conditions with germ-killing processes such as heat or drying may have a good history of sterility prior to the sterilization process. This is not to imply that sterilization should be avoided here, but, rather, that the ease with which a sample is sterilized may be greater than when a sample has been grossly contaminated. Similarly, surface contamination of a material can be more easily eliminated than contamination of a product with microorganisms deeply embedded in the interior. Thus, a thorough knowledge of the sterilization process can be a tremendous aid in arriving at a final decision as to whether contamination observed during sterility testing originated in external sources, or was a true indication of a lack of sterility of the product.

III. Official Compendia

A. Biological Indicators vs. Use of Regular Test Samples

Both the "United States Pharmacopeia" and the "National Formulary" are recognized as official compendia by the Federal Food, Drug and Cosmetic Act. USP and NF definitions and standards have been acknowledged as basic and authoritative, and used as guidelines throughout the pharmaceutical, cosmetic, and medical device industries. Sterility tests were first introduced into the USP and NF in 1936. From that time to the present, various changes have been made to improve sterility test methods in an attempt to assure sterile products. According to Chapman (1969), Canadian Drug Regulations also cite specific requirements in relation to microbes in drugs and cosmetics. It is required that drugs be prepared under sanitary conditions and that drugs prepared for parenteral use, with the exception of live vaccines, be sterile.

The most recent revisions of United States compendia were promulgated in the 1970 editions. One of the more significant changes enacted by the Advisory Panel on Sterilization Procedures involved the use of biological indicators in sterility testing.

Prior discussions in this presentation have dealt with the use of regular samples, except in those instances where the conditions may also be applicable to the use of biological indicators. Biological indicators (BI) or inoculated controls as they are sometimes called, are here defined as resistant microorganisms employed in or on various materials which serve to demonstrate the efficacy of the sterilization process, i.e., they indicate the presence of sterility in the products. Although greater difficulty may be encountered in the preparation and sterilization of biological indicators than for regular samples, there is a decided advantage in that a single culture is employed and, thus, can be more readily identified at the termination of the test. Common contaminants, recovered during testing, can be ignored. Since a more resistant, known microorganism is employed, which can be identified if present after incubation, other microbes are presumed to be of a lesser resistance and it can be assumed they were derived as contaminants. When resistant spore-formers are employed, one may further assume other bacterial spores to be of the same order of resistance and reject the product on this basis. In these tests, vegetative bacterial or fungal cells are generally not a criterion for sterility failure. The process can subsequently be examined by challenging it with microorganisms recovered during testing. It is usually unnecessary to resubmit the vegetative cells to the process, but those spore-formers which show characteristics different from the ones used as BI's may be investigated further. Where the microorganism demonstrates a far greater degree of resistance than the inoculum employed, it may be desirable to use the new culture. This can be expected to occur infrequently and the microbiologist need not fear that he may be changing his cultures on a monthly or even yearly basis.

During the USP Open Conference on Biological Indicators for Sterility Assurance (USP, 1970b), questions were raised regarding the use of biological indicators. Christiansen (1970) presented inactivation curves of a number of microorganisms which showed a high degree of resistance to the various sterilization processes. These included various strains of both spore-forming, e.g., *Bacillus sphaericus*, as well as nonsporing bacteria, e.g., *Micrococcus radiodurans*, *Streptococcus faecium*, and *Bacterium antitratum*. Nor was this resistance limited to bacteria alone as *coli* phage T1 was included among the resistant cultures.

Use of *B. sphaericus* may present its own unique problem as there was difficulty in inducing spores. In discussing this situation with Wood (1971), works performed by him indicated that the addition of iron salts to the medium induced spore formation by this microorganism.

Although a single microorganism may be used to monitor different sterilization cycles, the selection of the microorganism is dependent on the process employed to achieve sterility. Those microorganisms now generally accepted and utilized as biological indicators are shown in Table II.

Table II does not imply that one in necessarily restricted to the use of the organisms listed. The investigator may discover that an indicator organism adequately suits the needs of a particular operation and find its use advantageous. In this case, the microorganism which fulfills the requirements of the process is utilized. Brewer and Arnsberger (1966) employed *Bacillus globigii* and *Bacillus stearothermophilus* as spore controls. These scientists found the thermophilic organism much more satisfactory. They felt that this type of organism is not likely to be encountered as a laboratory contaminant in the sterility test. They also recommended the use of a combined biological–chemical indicator for ethylene oxide sterilization as this system affords an immediate visible indication of gas penetration into the materials during the sterilization cycle and further serves as a biological (spore) control. Brewer and McLaughlin (1961) had previously reported that the microorganism is nonpathogenic, nontoxic, nonpyrogenic, and is esthetically acceptable as a bacterial control.

TABLE II

Microorganisms Recommended as Biological Indicators in Sterilization Processes Shown

Process	Microorganism
Dry heat	*B. subtilis* var. *niger*
Moist heat	*Bacillus stearothermophilus*
Irradiation	*Bacillus pumilus*
Ethylene oxide	*B. subtilis* var. *niger*
Liquids	*B. subtilis* or *Clostridium sporogenes*

It is pointed out that the selection of the indicator microorganism is of major significance and its use should be based upon results attained with regard to its resistance to the specific sterilization process. As an example, a great deal of work was done with *Bacillus pumilus* E 601 ATCC 27142 to justify its selection for monitoring the radiation sterilization process (Pepper *et al.*, 1956; Chandler, 1959; Borick and Fogarty, 1967). It was shown to be highly resistant to radiation sterilization using both the electron accelerator and cobalt-60 processes, and is now generally accepted in monitoring sterilization by irradiation. Additional work performed by Prince (1971) has resulted in a commercially available spore strip which is presently used to monitor the irradiation process with this microorganism.

Although spore-forming bacteria are widely employed, consideration should also be given to those vegetative types which may be more resistant to a given process. A particular organism may or may not be suitable for monitoring another process. For example, a heat-resistant organism may or may not be used for monitoring the radiation or ethylene oxide sterilization processes. Selection of the organism is dependent upon the factors involved in the sterilization process. Kereluk *et al.* (1970a), in studying the effects of hygroscopic and nonhygroscopic carriers, concluded that the decimal reduction times with ethylene oxide for the vegetative cells of the radiation-resistant organisms, *M. radiodurans* and *S. faecalis*, were comparable to those for spores of *Clostridium sporogenes, B. stearothermophilus* and *B. pumilus* but not those of *B. subtilis* var. *niger.*

Work performed by us showed there was only a slight difference to ethylene oxide resistance between *B. subtilis* var. *niger* and *B. pumilus* E601; these results justify the use of this microorganism in both radiation and ethylene oxide sterilization. The D-values, calculated from the data shown in Table III, indicate the similarity in degree of resistance of the two organisms (8.2 minutes for *B. subtilis* var. *niger* vs. 7.7 minu'es for *B. pumilus*).

It may be appropriate, at this time, to discuss the preparation of inocula employed in biological indicators. This should be done under the supervision of a trained microbiologist who is qualified in the identification of microorganisms and has a thorough knowledge in the maintenance of pure cultures. It is essential that, when sporicidal processes are to be tested the biological indicators contain spores and not the less resistant vegetative cells. Heat-shocking has been a successful method of obtaining a pure spore suspension although there is some feeling that this phenomenon may lower spore resistance. A pure culture of the organism to be used as a biological indicator is grown in its optimal medium. After assurance of its identity and purity, the culture is grown on a solid medium and incubated at its optimum temperature for one week. After growth, the extent of sporulation and identity are determined and the cells harvested and suspended

TABLE III

Reduction in the Spore Population of B. subtilis *var.* niger *and* B. pumilus. *E601 after Exposure to Ethylene Oxide*[a]

Time (minutes)	Percentage survival	Logarithmic equivalents
B. subtilis var. *niger*		
0	100	6.30
15	28	5.75
30	0.6	4.08
45	0.005	2.00
B. pumilus E601		
0	100	6.30
15	17	5.53
30	0.2	3.60
45	0.002	1.60

[a]100 mg/liter at 54°C and 70% RH. Biological indicators used in this study consisted of polyethylene-coated Mylar carriers cut into sections $\frac{3}{4} \times 1\frac{1}{2}$ in., enclosed in glassine envelopes employing a concentration of 1×10^7 spores per carrier.

in water. The suspensions are centrifuged, the supernatant decanted, and the cells resuspended and washed repeatedly. The suspension is filtered aseptically to remove agar chips or other debris. Biological indicators may be prepared from the stock suspension by appropriate dilutions in various concentrations of solvents, e.g., 70–90% isopropyl alcohol.

In order to determine the spore count, one may also heat-shock the stock suspension at 80°C for 15 minutes, followed by rapid cooling in ice water. A viable count is taken of this heat-shocked suspension and the stock suspension is maintained at 4°C. Cultures stored in alcohol at the lower temperature have retained their viability for years although they should naturally be examined periodically.

Other precautions which should be exercised in the preparation of biological indicators are the elimination of residual growth nutrients which could result in unrealistic resistance to the sterilization process. Clumping of cells or protective barriers to the cells should also be avoided. Doyle and Ernst (1967) reported that occluded spores could not be inactivated with ethylene oxide because the crystalline matrix acted as a barrier. Resistance was also greater (900 times and 9 times) for occluded than for unoccluded spores subjected to moist and dry heat at 121°C. Our own findings are in agreement with those of these investigators; a high degree of resistance to ethylene oxide was obtained with a culture of *B. pumilus* when this organism was prepared in an 8.5% concentration of sodium chloride solution. According to Doyle *et al.* (1970), greater resistance to ethylene oxide could be imparted with a mixture of water-soluble resin and plasticizer. It may be seen that, where biological indicators are thus improperly prepared, they will not represent a true indication of the sterility of the product.

Ernst and Doyle (1964, 1968) also investigated various carrier materials used as supporting media for spores, their cleanliness, and the results of severe drying. Extremely high resistance attributable to any given carrier was not observed although the cleanliness of a spore suspension seemed to be an important aspect of the relative resistances of spores to ethylene oxide. Opfell *et al.* (1959) showed that glycerin and/or filter paper in immediate contact with dried spores of *B. globigii* reduced their resistance to ethylene oxide exposure and stated that, in designing evaluation methods to obtain sterility, truly representative inoculation techniques were most important. It is essential, then, that the biological indicator be part of the product or similar to it. Kereluk *et al.* (1970b) presented survival data, including both ethylene oxide-survivor curves and decimal-reduction values, which demonstrated longer kill times for *B. subtilis* spores with increasing thickness of the polyethylene-film enclosure.

B. Types to Be Employed

Biological indicators may be of many types and the selection of the carrier should be such that sterility is meaningfully confirmed. The most significant type is the product itself with direct inoculation of the resistant microorganisms either into or on the product. With drugs, liquids, or powders, the organism can easily be added to the product and distributed throughout by shaking the material. The inoculum so distributed can be withdrawn in portions or *in toto* and added directly to the test tube. If ointments are to be tested, it may be necessary to add the inoculum to the center of the tube with a long needle and syringe. As a general rule, when possible, items identical to the product should be inoculated with the indicator microorganism in an area where achievement of sterility of the test sample would be representative of the entire product. Sutures, as an example, can be inoculated with a syringe, or they can be dipped directly into the inoculum suspension. The amount of solution which will be retained on the product and, consequently, the concentration of the inoculum to be used, must first be determined.

In the case of sterile, disposable devices, it is recommended that the spores be placed in those areas of the product which are most difficult to sterilize. With disposable syringes or disposable gloves, the spores should be placed between the ribs of the rubber plunger or in the deep recesses of the glove fingers, respectively. If the syringes or gloves are too large to fit into a test tube, the inoculated portions may be added to the tube to determine sterility and the results can be applied to the entire product.

It is necessary to prevent the formation of air pockets when testing products with long, narrow orifices, e.g., needles or catheters, because the medium could then not come into contact with the indicator organism, and hence a false indication of sterility would easily result. One way to avoid this entails adding the product slowly to the test medium in a vertical rather than a horizontal position. This allows a steady flow of liquid through the orifice and prevents air pockets from forming.

Although the direct inoculation of the product to be tested is the most meaningful procedure for biological indicators, common carriers such as filter-paper discs, plastic fibers, glass beads, or metal strips may also be employed. These are designated as inoculated carriers, representing biological indicators, by the USP (1970) and NF (1970). The carriers listed may be added directly to the product, or may accompany the product in its prepared condition through the sterilization process. In the latter case, sterility testing can be simplified by merely removing the indicator strip from the product and adding it to the test medium. It is more desirable to use the inoculated product, however, and test it as its own biological indicator. Where this is not feasible, the inoculated carrier added to the product is acceptable. Thus, if a heart machine or artificial kidney is to be sterilized, it is naturally not possible to test the entire unit. Spore strips may be added to those areas which appear to be inaccessible to the sterilization process. Sterility can be determined by removing the spore strip after sterilization and subjecting the microorganisms to thioglycollate and soybean casein digest broths or the optimum medium, and incubation temperature for a minimum of 7 days.

The levels of contamination should be considered both in the inoculated carriers and the simulated products. Spore strips are commercially available with a concentration of 100/ml to over 1×10^6/ml. Since some products are relatively clean as a result of their preparation methods, coupled with the employment of good manufacturing practices, a relatively low inoculum may suffice in the preparation of biological indicators. The microbiologist should be aware that the degree of assurance of sterilization achieved by a process increases with an increase in the number of control organisms per indicator.

It may be necessary to prepare and employ large amounts of inocula for use in biological indicators to meet the demands of production. Batches of biological indicators should be checked regularly to determine that the numbers and types of microorganisms are satisfactory. It is essential that the indicator organism actually employed is, in fact, the one intended for use and that alterations have not occurred as a result of exposure to adverse conditions, particularly during storage.

C. Selection and Use of Media

Just as the biological indicator inoculum should contain no substance that affects the resistance of the indicator, so, too, should the medium selected offer no resistance or inhibition to the microorganism contained in the biological indicator. It should, in fact, promote the growth of the culture. Three basic media are recommended for sterility tests in the USP. However, where biological indicators are employed, the optimum medium for cultivation of the microorganism used at the optimum incubation temperature is recommended. This means that it may be necessary to perform experimental work in order to determine the most effective conditions to promote the growth of the microorganism used in the biological indicator. It may be that fluid thioglycollate or soybean casein digest medium adequately serves the purpose for promoting growth of the indicator employed.

Work performed by us showed that basic media varied among manufacturers and a greater or lesser recovery of cells could be obtained with the same medium from different sources. Standardization of media is now under consideration and consistency from batch to batch would be justified where rapid detection of microorganisms is essential. Member firms of the Health Industries Association were recently requested to participate in a study wherein each laboratory was asked to test spore strips in various media. This was an attempt to standardize the media employed in sterility tests and a committee representing member firms is now actively working on this program.

Use of a general growth-promoting medium is not as crucial with biological indicators as with regular samples. Since resistant microorganisms are involved, it is essential that those which are employed in the test be recovered. The only concern here is that a microbe of greater resistance than that employed may be missed, especially if it is not adaptable to the medium used. This possibility, however, is not considered very likely.

Various types of adventitious biological indicators are now being promoted for sterility tests by manufacturers and it is anticipated that more of these will be introduced in the near future. As already stated, the basic indicators such as spore strips contain viable spores in various concentrations on filter paper or other desired carriers, enclosed in overwraps. Although these may adequately fulfill the needs for assuring sterility of the product, certain precautions must be exercised in their use.

Precontamination levels of the manufactured products and the contamination concentrations of the inoculated carrier should be known, for the microorganism concentration of the carrier should exceed the microbial levels of the product. Since varying degrees of resistance may be shown by the inoculum carriers, the adventitious biological indicator may give a false result of sterility of the actual product, i.e., a failure of the indicator can result when the product was in fact sterile. The chief disadvantage is that the product itself is not being tested in some instances, but rather reliability for sterility is dependent upon the proper addition and removal of the spore indicator.

At various meetings on the use of biological indicators, great concern was expressed regarding the transport of biological indicators without grossly contaminating the manufacturing area with spores from this source. This concern need be valid only where carelessness is prevalent, incompetent personnel are retained, or where proper precautions are not exercised to prevent spreading of spores to the environment. Biological indicators should be maintained in closed airtight containers with proper seals. They can be further enclosed in Kraft paper bags, plastic enclosures or suitable covers, or enclosed containers to prevent their spread. They should be properly stored in closed cabinets in areas where their contact with manufacturing personnel or accidental removal is avoided. They should be distinct in appearance. By this we mean that they should have a separate, distinct color, differing from that of the product being sold. The biological indicator for sutures is a bright red package, different in color from the regular package, with precautionary markings on the label. The aluminum foil contains the identifying number. Manufacturing or quality control personnel involved with biological indicators are properly oriented, know their source, condition, and destination. It is made clear to individuals that this item is solely for testing and is to be returned to the microbiology laboratory. In the many years in which biological indicators were employed at Ethicon, Inc., to our knowledge not a single one was removed accidentally from the plant.

Simulated biological indicators have recently been introduced by manufacturers for sterility tests. These indicators contain media in a separate compartment area and are not in contact with the spore strip. After sterilization, the seal of the compartment or vial is broken and the spores mixed with the media. This would appear to obviate the necessity of a sterility control laboratory. The more sophisticated can employ separate compartments for spores, dehydrated media, sterile water, and an incubator. Although these appear very convenient and their ease of use makes them desirable, here, too, caution should be exercised. The medium, if contaminated, will indicate contamination of the product when, in fact, the product is sterile. When a dehydrated medium is employed, high bacterial counts in the medium will render sterilization difficult as the medium itself may offer protection to the organism. Improper or weak seals can also be present in biological indicators and these are difficult to detect. This, too, can introduce contamination to the indicator which should, of course, be discarded when discovered.

Placement of biological indicators in the sterilizer load is of utmost importance. Since γ rays are extremely penetrating, their placement to monitor this process is not as vital as in heat or ethylene oxide sterilization. Since colder areas can exist in the heat autoclave or stratification can occur with gaseous sterilization, it may be necessary to determine the most critical areas of the sterilizer in placement of the indicators. Brewer and Phillips (1968) feel that the principal factors involved in placing biological indicators in sterilizer loads are: (1) method of placing the indicator in or on the individual items; (2) location and number of indicators to be used in each sterilizer load. Obviously, then, it is essential to place the units in those areas which are most inaccessible to the sterilizing agent. Sterility determined with these samples should certainly assure sterility of the entire load, assuming there is little, if any, variation in the product.

Although some of the disadvantages regarding the use of biological indicators were briefly discussed, the many advantages in their use far outweigh the few shortcomings cited. There is great merit to their use and there is now a wide tendency to employ biological indicators, where possible, rather than testing of regular products for naturally occurring contaminants. The single area where methods have not been devised for their use is in bacteriological filtration and aseptic transfer of the product in a sterile area. In all other sterility determinations, their use is highly recommended. Tables IV and V present some of the factors in sterility testing of various items where biological indicators are employed.

IV. Contamination Control

A. Laminar Flow

One of the most recent engineering advances which has been a tremendous boon to sterility testing is the application of laminar-flow equipment. Parisi and Borick (1968) concluded that laminar flow was not only suitable for sterility testing, but that its use provided a significantly better and microbiologically clean area for carrying out sterility test procedures than conventional sterile rooms, including those with provisions for filtered air.

The laminar-flow concept was initially employed in the electronics and aerospace industries, where low particulate contamination levels were highly desirable. It has recently been adopted for sterility test areas by the pharmaceutical, cosmetic, and medical device industries, and is now being widely employed for the maintenance of clean air during sterility testing.

The laminar-flow room, in contrast to the conventional clean room, has a much greater purge of air efficiency since the unit—wall or ceiling—con-

TABLE IV

Sterility Testing of Items Employing Biological Indicators (Inoculated Product)

Size unit	Biological indicator test	Minimum number of test units	Incubation time	Temperature	Medium	Type of micro-organism
Small (drugs in vials, sutures)	Inoculated item (all)	10	7 Days	Optimum	Optimum	See Table II
Large (bulk items, kits, biomedical components)	Inoculated item (most difficult area)	10	7 Days	Optimum	Optimum	See Table II

TABLE V
Sterility Testing of Items Employing Adventitious or Attached Biological Indicators

Biological indicator (inoculated carrier)	Spore strips, glass beads, metal, etc.
Test sample	Inoculated carrier
Minimum number test units	10 + (10 regular samples[a])
Incubation time	7 to 10 days[b]
Medium[c]	Fluid thioglycollate aqueous soybean casein digest
Temperature	30° C to 35° C, thioglycollate 20° C to 25° C, soybean casein digest

[a]Where regular samples and spore strips or other inoculated carriers are used for sterility tests, a minimum of each sample is recommended.
[b]Dependent on type of product.
[c]Optimum medium to promote growth of selected microorganism may be employed.

tains high-efficiency particulate air filters. The latter are commonly known as HEPA filters and have a 99.97% efficiency rate in the removal of all particles 0.3μ and larger. Since microorganisms fall within this size range, HEPA filters should also be highly effective in filtering out airborne microorganisms (Decker *et al.*, 1965).

Air from laminar flow may be supplied in a vertical direction. Here the units are suspended from the ceiling. The air can also be horizontally derived from work stations which are conveniently mounted on the floor. The units vary in size. A small portable, horizontal laminar-flow unit was used by Parisi and Borick (1969) with highly efficient sterility test results in a large open laboratory. These units are relatively inexpensive and conversion from a conventional sterile room to laminar flow can be easily accomplished. A small portable unit may be purchased for approximately $100 whereas a standard work station may cost over $1000. Large aseptic areas for sterile fill and packaging will, however, require thousands of dollars for installation and equipment.

Numerous investigators (Price, 1938; Borick and Sarra, 1960; Kundsin and Walter, 1962) have shown that a healthy carrier harbors microorganisms on his person. These microorganisms are than shed into the environment, frequently resulting in false positives in sterility tests. Austin (1966), in reviewing "people-generated" contamination, showed that increased body activity will cause a greater emission of particles from the individual into the environment. In planning a new sterility test room, then, knowledge of the contaminant load generated by personnel would greatly facilitate the design of the room and the specifications necessary for supporting equipment.

Cullimore (1970) examined the efficiency of the laminar-flow system in removing microbial cells from the atmosphere and showed that when the prefilter was impregnated with a concentration of 10^9 cells of *Bacillus*, *Pseudomonas*, and *Staphylococcus* only a very few cells succeeded in penetrating the filtration system. These were shown on exposed agar surfaces. It would appear that penetration is not limited to size alone because comparison of the laminar effect on phage with that on pseudomonads showed that, although phage particles are smaller than pseudomonads, there was less penetration by the phage. Fox and Baldwin (1968) measured contamination levels at critical sites in an experimental laminar-flow operating room in which dogs were used as patients. They, too, reported that there was a minimum of a tenfold reduction in the contamination levels upon use of laminar flow.

Coriell *et al.* (1967) studied various conditions in the presence of laminar flow and concluded that if the filter unit is permitted to operate, the laboratory containing the HEPA filter will benefit as a result of reduced contamination. These investigators advocated the use of a small portable unit in the laboratory. It was further shown that reduced contamination prevailed during a period of continued conversation, when an operator sat at the work bench in the presence of laminar flow and read from a book, emitting aerosolized droplets into the environment. Additional work performed by Coriell and McGarrity (1970) showed that a Blake bottle obstruction to the air flow resulted in a downstream cone of turbulent air which drew microbial contamination into the work area of a laminar-flow hood. Consequently, the test area should be clear of obstructions.

In order to minimize possible contamination, both from working personnel and the surrounding environment, and to achieve Class-100 conditions in accordance with Federal Standard 209A (1966), the use of laminar flow is advocated. This means that the particle count of air delivered to the working area by laminar flow is not to exceed 100 particles 0.5 μ in size and larger, per cubic foot (3.5 particles/liter). The air, in addition, should contain no more than one particle 5.0 μ or larger per cubic foot. Guidelines for achieving various clean room classes can be derived from the Federal Standard. For additional information regarding laminar flow and clean rooms for sterility testing, the review by Davies and Lamy (1968), the handbook by Agnew (1968), and the Laminar Flow and HEPA Filter Survey (Anonymous, 1968) should be consulted.

B. Techniques for the Maintenance of Asepsis

Although the use of biological indicators and laminar-flow units, as previously discussed in this chapter, will aid considerably in sterility assurance, various techniques as now recommended in sterility work should also be included. These may be divided into three categories: (1) the personnel; (2) the working area; and (3) the conditions involved in sterility testing.

Since personnel are considered to be the major source of contamination, they must be adequately garbed to prevent carryover of microorganisms during testing of the product. There is a tendency today to cover those performing sterility tests as completely as possible. One-piece suits with long sleeves are preferred, although they may be uncomfortable or objectionable to the ladies on the grounds of design. Sterile caps, masks, and gowns are also worn. The use of sterile masks is questioned by some as it is felt that once in contact with the skin, the masks lose sterility. Also, they have but a limited value in retaining microbes from the respiratory tract as pressure exerted during exhalation, combined with moisture on prolonged use, will permit the escape of aerosols into the working environment. This should not deter their utilization since contamination is certainly minimized with their use.

The techniques of the surgical scrub to maintain asepsis are well recognized. Although it is a readily accepted fact that complete removal of microbes cannot be anticipated, Colbeck (1962) feels that the 2-minute scrub has generally been abandoned and there is a return to the 5- and 10-minute scrub. The use of various antiseptics is considered an aid in reducing skin flora and the effect of some antiseptics was shown by Spaulding (1965). Use of surgical gloves may not give the assurance expected as punctures can occur and these will result in spilling of body fluids into the work area. The use of gloves may present an additional hazard when working with products that are flammable, such as alcohol, for spillage of the material on gloved hands can occur. Testers may obtain severe burns with gloved hands as a result of the delayed reaction to heat. In such instances, it may be necessary to perform sterility tests with well-scrubbed bare hands. Conversation between testers should be avoided as far as possible. Separate shoes or shoe covers should be worn in sterility test areas, and street shoes should never be permitted to enter the sterility test rooms.

Personnel who are in poor health should be excluded from the test area and should be subjected to periodic physical examinations. As stated previously, plate counts are to be maintained during testing to determine which technicians can be relied on for the best performance. A team of two persons for testing, with a third floating technician to service their needs, is recommended. Once in the test area, personnel should remain until completion of the test except in emergencies, and any sterile items required should be passed through the transfer cabinets.

It is essential that the sterility test rooms be maintained immaculately and preferably be serviced by personnel in the department rather than outside maintenance people. If the former are unavailable, servicing should be done with the guidance of a trained supervisor knowledgeable in sterility operations. Rooms should be constructed with a minimum of outlets and no overhangs, if possible. This means that lights should be recessed and flush with the ceiling or walls. Floors, walls, and work stations should be constructed of hard, durable materials which are not affected by harsh disinfectants. Paints used on walls and other surfaces of the work area should contain biocidal agents which will aid in preventing microbial growth.

Floor mats with adhesive materials may have some value in eliminating dirt and debris when placed at the entrance to the sterility or scrub rooms. Since dirt particles harbor microbes, these would be retained on the sticky surface of the mat and not be carried into the test area.

Although there is some controversy regarding the use of UV lights, le Riche *et al.* (1966) felt that their employment is warranted. Two points should be remembered in their utilization. The distance encompassing their bactericidal effectiveness is limited; the lamps should be checked periodically and changed when their efficiency is diminished. They should not be turned on during actual testing to avoid injury to personnel and to avoid possible effects on the test results. It is advisable to connect them to a safety switch, whereby they are turned off automatically when the main lights are turned on. If left on continuously when sterility tests were not in progress, they were found to effect a reduction of the normal count by 50% in Brewer's (1948) laboratory. Their use in the transfer cabinets may further reduce the contamination level.

Testing rooms should be provided with a scrub room or anteroom with easy access to the sterility test area. The test area should be maintained under positive pressure and, if laminar flow is not utilized, air to the test area should be filtered. A small compact area is preferable to a large open laboratory. It is inadvisable to have a sink in the sterility test laboratory since Herman (1968) has shown that this can be a source of contamination.

A recent advance in prevention of contamination of the sterility test rooms is the construction of a unique air shower which is utilized to decontaminate testing personnel prior to their entrance to the test area (Havighorst, 1970). A laminar-flow principle draws microorganisms or other particles from the personnel and filters the air, thus preventing contaminants from entering the test room while on personnel. Controlled filters and blowers may be employed to change the air in the anteroom as well as the test area. More frequent air changes will result in ultraclean enclosures.

Transfer cabinets, with sliding front and back doors, may further aid in reducing contamination levels. This construction prevents prolonged opening of doors when samples are taken to the room for testing or removed for incubation after the test.

Temperature and humidity are important factors in the construction of sterility test laboratories. Since the tests may be of considerably prolonged duration, working comfort of the testers will result in peak efficiency. A coordinated effort is required when two persons are working together and one member opens and closes the sample while the other removes the material for testing. It has been observed that there can be a time lapse among testers with prolonged exposure of the opened items or test tubes to the environment, making them more susceptible to contamination.

Conditions applicable to sterility testing warrant considerable attention. Although various investigators (Borick and Pepper, 1970; Sykes, 1970) have shown that prolonged exposure times to chemosterilizers are necessary to destroy bacterial spores, use of detergent–disinfectants should not be eliminated to clean and treat the rooms. It is suggested that these be changed periodically on the basis of their chemical composition to prevent resistant microorganisms from forming. For example, a quaternary may be alternated with a phenolic or a chlorine-based detergent–disinfectant (Borick *et al.*, 1968) and vice versa. The detergent–disinfectants are not only helpful in removing dirt and debris from hard surfaces, but are effective in destroying vegetative microbial cells. Litsky and Litsky (1968) compared the microbial efficiency of various products used for this purpose and concluded that low bacterial colony counts can be obtained when effective housekeeping techniques are used in conjunction with detergent–disinfectants. It was further recommended that laboratory and in-use testing be performed to evaluate their efficiency. Although detergent–disinfectants are recommended for this purpose, Kronenwett (1969) employed glutaraldehyde solutions on tables and walls and found this chemical to be very effective for controlling contamination. Caution should be exercised when using potent disinfectants of this nature.

Consideration was given to the application of incubation times longer than those presently recommended in USP and NF. Work in this area has shown that this is unnecessary. When incubation was extended to 30 days, although microorganisms were recovered, this could be attributed to extraneous contamination which occurred during the incubation period. Table VI reveals that 26 contaminants were recovered in 37,084 tests of radiation-sterilized items. Where cotton plugs were used instead of metal caps, the incidence of contamination dropped to 4 in 21,777 tests. A lower incidence of contamination was also observed where cotton plugs were employed in ethylene oxide-sterilized materials. The greater overall incidence of contamination with ethylene oxide-sterilized material may be attributed to the use of larger test tubes with loosely fitting caps. The samples in these studies were biological indicators containing *B. pumilus* spores incorporated into the product, but most of the microorganisms recovered were *Staphylococci* and molds.

TABLE VI

Results of Prolonged Thirty-Day Incubation Studies Comparing the Use of Cotton Plugs and Metal Cap Enclosures

Type of closure	Number of tests	Number of contaminants
Sterilized by cobalt-60 (2.5 Mrad)		
Metal caps	37,084	26
Cotton plugs	21,777	4
Sterilized by ethylene oxide (700 mg/liter minimum)		
Metal caps	20,309	92
Cotton plugs	2,276	0

Since most laboratories have converted to metal caps for test-tube enclosures, there is some question as to flaming of the tubes during sterility testing. Dust particles may still adhere to the edges of the tube and, if not eliminated, can subsequently contaminate it, resulting in false positives. There is also concern regarding bending of the flame when testing with laminar flow. Where flaming is desired, it may be necessary to adjust the air flow so that it will not interfere with the flame.

The presence of laminar flow in the incubators would also reduce considerably potential contamination to the tubes subsequent to sterility testing.

Instruments, e.g., forceps and scissors, should be sterilized prior to use and maintained in sterile alcohol or other appropriate solutions. Where they are employed in continuous testing, they should be flamed after each test operation to prevent cross contamination.

Samples for sterility tests should be handled in a special manner to assure that sterility of the product is maintained and that false positives are not recovered either during or after testing. It may be necessary to transport products for tests in overwraps to the test laboratory, or treat the product prior to testing in order to minimize extraneous contaminants. It is the obligation of the microbiologist to be assured that the product being tested for sterility is truly representative of the batches to be utilized commercially.

C. Good Manufacturing Practices

Most organizations involved in producing sterile products have now begun to appreciate the value of good manufacturing practices. It is not our intent to reiterate all of the proposals presented in good manufacturing practices, as these may be obtained from the Federal Register (1971).

Rather, we would prefer to discuss those problems in the manufacturing facility which involve the microbiological aspects of producing a sterile product.

Buildings, facilities, and equipment are all instrumental in obtaining a good, clean product. If these were designed in a way that facilitates their cleanliness and prevents recontamination, the goal of obtaining a relatively clean product, or one that would at least have an acceptably low microbe level, would certainly be more easily achieved. Some products are free of microbes as a result of processing, particularly where high or prolonged heating is essential in their manufacture. However, if the environment in which these items are produced is heavily contaminated, subsequent contamination of the product will result. It is imperative that the surroundings be as clean as possible to prevent this.

Buildings should be inspected periodically and measures taken to prevent the entrance of insects or rodents since these are known to harbor microorganisms and are disease vectors.

All components and materials used in the manufacture of sterile products should be identified and examined to assure that they are of the highest standards and free from infestation. Samples should be taken which are representative of the lot and checked for contamination prior to use. Representative samples of components prone to microbiological contamination should be subjected to microbiological tests prior to use. Microbial levels of the products should be determined as this will aid in setting standards for sterilization of the product and subsequent sterility. Types and numbers of microorganisms found in the product during manufacturing can further act as a guide in the type of biological indicator to be employed to assure product sterility.

Proper storage of the material will further aid the production of clean products. Storage bins with covers and antistatic chemicals will prevent dust collection. Large vacuum systems throughout the plant have been suggested to remove dirt or dust from all packages coming from the outside to the receiving department.

Water used in the manufacture of products should be of good quality and high purity. It, too, should be examined by the laboratory to assure that it is free from coliforms. This is particularly important in those organizations which draw their water supplies from their own wells. The water should be examined in various sections of the manufacturing facility and, where deionized water is utilized, these systems should be tested, as they are known to support bacterial growth.

It was previously stated that personnel involved in sterility testing should be in good health. So, too, should those responsible for manufacture and control of drugs be in good health. Any person who has an illness or open lesion which will adversely affect the safety of the product should be excluded from its manufacture at that time.

All personnel should have sufficient education, training, and experience to enable them to produce the best possible product, and, where necessary, personnel should wear suitable uniforms or garments which will aid in the prevention of potential contamination to the product.

Insofar as laboratory controls are concerned, rules and regulations of the Federal Register, Section 133.11, state that laboratory controls shall include the establishment of scientifically sound and appropriate specifications, standards, and test procedures to assure that components in processed drugs and finished products conform to appropriate standards of identity, strength, quality, and purity. Those drugs which are purported to be sterile should be free from objectionable microorganisms and it will be the responsibility of the microbiologist to perform those tests which will give this assurance.

V. Numerical Evaluation and Types of Tests

Throughout this chapter, we have been discussing the sterility of drugs, cosmetics and devices. The USP and NF discuss sterility testing of liquids, solids, sutures, cotton gauze, and surgical dressings, among other items, and distinguished tests for parenteral vs. nonparenteral devices. Let us consider some of the problems inherent in the latter. According to Webster, a device is anything made from a design; synonyms include an appliance, a contrivance, or an instrument. It is obvious from the definition that a device can be an object of any type or magnitude, and microbiologists whose thought-orientation process is generally in microns, are suddenly faced with the dilemma of sterility testing of objects the size of interplanetary space capsules.

The problems are not insurmountable, but persons performing sterility tests immediately become aware of the fact that the larger the object to be tested, the more difficult it is to maintain aseptic techniques. The microbiologist is confronted with the necessity of introducing suitable methods which will determine the sterility of the product and eliminate false positives through extraneous contamination.

The question constantly arises regarding the numbers of samples required to assure sterility by representative sampling of the product. The USP Table on Procedural Details for Sterility Tests recommends 10 to 60 samples. The greatest numbers of samples are recommended in the area of sterility through filtration. It was felt that this system would offer the greatest potential for contamination and, consequently, larger representative sizes should be employed. Samples chosen in all categories are minimal numbers of test units and are dependent upon many factors. These include the type of sample selected, the physical state of the sample, the sterilization process chosen, and the form of the biological indicator, if selected for testing.

Beloian and Stuart (1968) presented several tables of probability data for lots of varying degrees of assumed contamination when 10 samples were tested. They showed that even if the level of contamination were as great as 10%, i.e., 1 defective sample in 10, each lot would be erroneously passed one time out of every three. A lot defective 0.1% (1 defect per 1000) would be passed satisfactorily under these circumstances in 99 tests out of 100.

Thus, the limits of the test when small sample sizes are used for sterility tests, or when low contamination levels are present, can be appreciated. On the other hand, large increases in sample size may be required to give reasonable assurance of sterility. It was pointed out that a lot contaminated to the extent of 1%, when 500 samples are tested, would be erroneously accepted once in 100 separate tests; or, conversely, a satisfactory test indicates, at a 90% confidence level, that it is sterile; or, at least, not contaminated in more than 1% of the tests.

It should be borne in mind that some products are rejected for sterility when they are, in fact, sterile. This is due to extraneous contamination either in the testing process or during or after incubation. Phillips (1969) suggested that the ultimate in sterility control would be to perform all tests in an absolutely germ-free environment. Obviously, this would be difficult, expensive, and require germ-free conditions.

As previously recommended, the use of laminar-flow cabinets in the sterile rooms significantly reduced the number of false positives during sterility tests (Parisi and Borick, 1968). Their work, shown in Table VII, indicates

TABLE VII

Presence of Contaminants in Sterility Tests and Mock Tests with Laminar-Flow and Conventional Sterile Rooms[a]

Comparison	Number of tests	Number of positives	Percentage of positives	Significance
Sterility tests in laminar flow	6180	39	0.63	$P = < 0.5\%$
Conventional sterile room	8820	142	1.61	Very significant
Mock sterility tests in laminar flow	440	2	0.5	$P = 0.1$
Conventional sterile room	380	6	1.5	Borderline

[a]Reprinted from Parisi and Borick (1968).

that fewer false positives were present in both sterility tests and mock tests when horizontal laminar-flow units were evaluated. Mock tests included all of the physical manipulations of the sterility test without actually incorporating the product into the test tube. (Visitors observing the tests through a glass screen are usually startled by the performance and cannot understand this apparently erratic behavior.) It can be seen from Table VIII that, during sterility testing operations, significantly fewer organisms are present on agar settling plates in horizontal laminar-flow devices than in conventional sterile rooms.

Another consideration regarding sterility tests was incubation beyond presently employed times. Our work has shown that this would involve an undue delay of sterility test results because, when incubation was extended at least to 30 days and biological indicators were employed, the organism used in these tests was not recovered in over 100,000 tests at the termination of the incubation period even though some microorganisms were recovered. Where sublethal doses (0.4–0.5 Mrad) are employed in radiation sterilization using resistant spore-formers, these microorganisms can be recovered after 17 to 18 days. However, when adequate doses necessary to kill the spore are used, recovery of these microorganisms could not be effected in the 30-day incubation time.

The use of biological indicators in sterility testing is advocated as it is felt that not only is their destruction a means of monitoring the sterilization process, but also the lack of recovery of a resistant microorganism to that process gives greater assurance of sterility of the product tested. For this reason, the incubation time for biological indicators was lowered to seven days in USP and NF. This is an inducement to the utilization of biological indicators rather than the performance of conventional sterility tests. It may be anticipated that the reliability of information obtained from sterility tests using biological indicators increases as the occurrence of false positives decreases. The many physical refinements that can be made to the sterility test area, coupled with extreme caution and awareness on the part of the

TABLE VIII

Settling Plate Counts in Horizontal Laminar-Flow Cabinets and in Conventional Sterile Rooms[a]

Comparison	Number of plates exposed	Number of colonies recovered	Significance
Laminar-flow sterile room	299	75	$P = 0.5\%$
Conventional sterile room	765	2361	Very significant
Laminar-flow laboratory	108	97	$P = 0.5\%$
Conventional sterile room	765	2361	Very significant

[a]Reprinted from Parisi and Borick (1968).

testing technicians, can considerably reduce the incidence of false positives.

Physical improvements, as previously discussed, include the laminar-flow work areas, high-efficiency particulate air (HEPA) filtered air supply to the sterile rooms, and a HEPA filter air recirculation system in the incubators and scrub area. The use of metal caps in the sterility tests warrants filtering the air supply to the incubators. This system has a noteworthy effect on the reduction of fungal contaminants which are commonly present in the laboratory and its surrounding environment.

Modern industrial microbiologists, through their own work and frank and open discussions with colleagues, now appreciate the many problems involved in achieving sterilization and in obtaining proof thereof through the sterility test process. This knowledge will surely not only result in better programs to effect sterilization, but also give greater assurance of the reliability of the sterility test method. Benarde (1970) claims that a higher level of mathematical training is being built into the microbiology students' curricula and more biology is being introduced into engineering programs. All of these combined efforts will certainly result in higher quality products with greater assurance regarding their sterility. It is only through the combined efforts of all concerned that these objectives can be met.

VI. Summary

Sterility testing involves the combined use of art and science. In order to achieve sterility, microorganisms must be excluded from the product or environment and a means of determining the effectiveness of the sterilization process must be established. This requires technical competence combined with adept physical manipulations if the desired end result is to be obtained: sterile items.

Sterility can be determined by examination of the regular product with routine microbiological techniques, using membrane filters or biological indicators (BI). Use of the latter was recently advocated by the official United States compendia, and incubation times for sterility tests were reduced if they are employed. Two general types of biological indicators were proposed: those which contain resistant microorganisms added directly to the regular product, and inoculated carriers, which are sold commercially as spore strips or as carriers which accompany the product. The former are preferred over the adventitious biological indicator.

There is a decided advantage in the utilization of BI's because the use of resistant microorganisms gives greater assurance to the sterility process, and extraneous contaminants obtained during sterility testing need not be considered in the interpretation of the test results. For these reasons, there is presently a widespread tendency to employ biological indicators rather than regular samples wherever possible.

Laminar-flow units, either horizontal or vertical, are recommended in the performance of sterility tests. Good manufacturing practices will be of further value in obtaining sterile products. These two factors in conjunction with various recommended sterility techniques will aid substantially in sterility assurance. In order that sterility be accomplished, the following factors must be thoroughly considered: (1) the personnel; (2) the working area and equipment; and (3) the conditions involved in sterility testing.

Since presently recommended sterility sampling gives inadequate assurance of product sterility, an understanding of the statistical limitations of sampling will be extremely helpful. The microbiologist is, thus, better qualified to come to a final decision regarding the sterility of the product.

References

Agnew, B. (1968). "The Laminar Flow Clean Room Handbook," 3rd ed. Agnew Higgins, Garden Grove, California.

Anonymous. (1968). *Hosp. Pharm.* **3**, 3–6.

Artandi, C., and Van Winkle, W. (1959). *Nucleonics* **17**, 86–90.

Austin, P. R. (1966). *Contam. Contr.* **6**, 15–19.

Awe, W. C., Roberts, W., and Braunwald, N. S. (1963). *Surgery* **54**, 322–328.

Beloian, A., and Stuart, L. S. (1968). *In* "Disinfection, Sterilization and Preservation," pp. 114–132. Lea & Febiger, Philadelphia.

Belson, J. J. (1969). *In* "Federal Regulations and Practical Control Microbiology for Disinfectants, Drugs and Cosmetics," S.I.M. Spec. Publ. No. 4, pp. 106–107. Soc. Ind. Microbiol.

Benarde, M. A. (1970). *In* "Disinfection," pp. 5–8. Dekker, New York.

Borick, P. M. (1965). *Biotechnol. Bioeng.* **7**, 435–443.

Borick, P. M. (1968). *Advan. Appl. Microbiol.* **10**, 291–312.

Borick, P. M. (1969). *Pap., 69th Gen. Meet. Amer. Soc. Microbiol., 1969, Miami Beach, Florida.*

Borick, P. M., and Fogarty, M. G. (1967). *Appl. Microbiol.* **15**, 785–789.

Borick, P. M., and Pepper, R. E. (1970). *In* "Disinfection," pp. 85–102. Dekker, New York.

Borick, P. M., and Sarra, J. F. (1960). *Antimicrob. Ag. Annu.* pp. 647–651.

Borick, P. M., Brown, P. M., Dondershine, F. H., and Hollis, R. A. (1968). *Soap Chem. Spec.* **44**, 70–82.

Bowie, J. H. (1961). *In* "Recent Developments in the Sterilization of Surgical Materials" (Dept. Pharm. Sci., Pharm. Soc. Gt. Brit. and Smith & Nephew Res., Ltd., eds.), pp. 109–142. Pharmaceutical Press, London.

Bowman, F. W. (1966). *J. Pharm. Sci.* **55**, 818–821.

Bowman, F. W. (1969). *J. Pharm. Sci.* **58**, 1301–1308.

Bowman, F. W., and Holdowsky, S. (1959). *J. Amer. Pharm. Ass., Sci. Ed.* **48**, 95–96.

Brewer, J. H. (1948). *J. Amer. Pharm. Ass., Sci. Ed.* **37**, 415–416.

Brewer, J. H., and Arnsberger, R. J. (1966). *J. Pharm. Sci.* **55**, 57–59.

Brewer, J. H., and McLaughlin, C. B. (1961). *J. Pharm. Sci.* **50**, 171–712.

Brewer, J. H., and Phillips, G. B. (1968). *Bull. Parenteral Drug Ass.* **22**, 157–169.

Bruch, C. W. (1961). *Annu. Rev. Microbiol.* **15**, 245–262.

Bruch, C. W., and Bruch, M. K. (1970). *In* "Disinfection," pp. 149–201. Dekker, New York.
Buhlmann, X. (1968). *Appl. Microbiol.* **16**, 1919–1923.
Chandler, V. L. (1959). *Nucleonics* **17**, 63–64.
Chapman, D. G. (1969). *In* "Federal Regulations and Practical Control Microbiology for Disinfectants, Drugs and Cosmetics," Spec. Publ. No. 4, pp. 19–23. Soc. Ind. Microbiol.
Christiansen, E. A. (1970). *Proc. U.S.P. Open Conf. Biol. Indicators Sterili. Assurance, 1970, Arlington, Virginia.* Abstract, pp. 1–15.
Colbeck, J. C. (1962). *In* "Control of Infections in Hospitals," Hosp. Monogr. Ser. No. 12, pp. 30–51. Amer. Hosp. Ass.
Cook, A. M. (1961). *In* "Recent Developments in the Sterilization of Surgical Materials" (Dept. Pharm. Sci., Pharm. Soc. Gt. Brit. and Smith & Nephew Res., Ltd., eds.), pp. 185–189. Pharmaceutical Press, London.
Coriell, L. L., and McGarrity, G. J. (1970). *Appl. Microbiol.* **20**, 474–479.
Coriell, L. L., McGarrity, G. J., and Horneff, J. (1967). *Amer. J. Pub. Health* **57**, 1824–1836.
Cullimore, D. R. (1970). *Contam. Contr.* **9**, 16–18.
Davies, W. L., and Lamy, P. P. (1968). *Hosp. Pharm.* **3**, 7–13.
Decker, H. M., Buchanan, L., Hall, L., and Goddard, K. (1965). *U.S., Pub. Health Serv., Publ.* **953**, 1–43.
Doyle, J. E. (1970). *Pap., Annu. Meet. Parenteral Drug Ass., 1970, New York.* pp. 1–9.
Doyle, J. E., and Ernst, R. R. (1967). *Appl. Microbiol.* **15**, 726–730.
Doyle, J. E., Mehrhof, W. H., and Ernst, R. R. (1968). *Appl. Microbiol.* **16**, 1742–1744.
Doyle, J. E., McDaniel, A. W., West, K. L., Whitbourne, J. E., and Ernst, R. R. (1970). Appl. Microbiol. **20**, 793–797.
Drummond, D. W., and Pflug, I. J. (1970). *Appl. Microbiol.* **20**, 805–809.
Engley, F. B., Jr. (1970). *Proc. 70th Gen. Meet. Amer. Soc. Microbiol., 1970, Boston, Massachusetts*, p. 12.
Ernst, R. R., and Doyle, J. E. (1964). *Proc. 64th Annu. Meet. Amer. Soc. Microbiol. 1964, Washington, D.C.*
Ernst, R. R., and Doyle, J. E. (1968). *Biotechnol. Bioeng.* **10**, 1–31.
Ernst, R. R., West, K. L., and Doyle, J. E. (1969). *Bull. Parenteral Drug Ass.* **23**, 29–39.
Federal Register. (1971). "Federal Register," Part 133, Drugs; Current Good Manufacturing Practice in Manufacture, Processing, Packing or Holding, Vol. 36, pp. 601–605.
Federal Standard 209a. (1966). "Clean Room and Work Station Requirements—Controlled Environment." Gen. Serv. Admin., Washington, D.C.
Fox, D. G., and Baldwin, M. (1968). *J.A.H.A.* **42**, 108–112.
Gaughran, E. R. L., and Borick, P. M. (1972). *In* "CRC Handbook of Microbiology." Chem. Rubber Publ. Co., Cleveland, Ohio (in press).
Halleck, F. (1969). *In* "Federal Regulations and Practical Control Microbiology for Disinfectants, Drugs and Cosmetics," S.I.M. Spec. Publ. No. 4, pp. 106–107. Soc. Ind. Microbiol.
Havighorst, C. R. (1970). *Pyramiding* **1**, 5–7.
Herman, L. (1968). *Pap., Meet. Theobald Smith Soc., 1968, New Brunswick, New Jersey*, Vol. 16, p. 1.
Holdowsky, S. (1957). *Antibiot. Chemother. (Washington, D.C.)* **7**, 49–54.
Kallings, L. O., Ringertz, O., and Silverstolpe, L. (1966). *Acta Pharm. Suecica* **3**, 219–229.
Kelsey, J. C. (1969). "Erasmus Wilson Demonstration at the Royal College of Surgeons of England," pp. 214–223.
Kereluk, K., Gammon, R. A., and Lloyd, R. S. (1970a). *Appl. Microbiol.* **19**, 152–156.
Kereluk, K., Gammon, R. A., and Lloyd, R. S. (1970b). *Develop. Ind. Microbiol.* **11**, 296–300.
Kronenwett, F. R. (1969). *In* "Federal Regulations and Practical Control Microbiology for Disinfectants, Drugs and Cosmetics," S.I.M. Spec. Publ. No. 4, pp. 66–73. Soc. Ind. Microbiol.

Kundsin, R. B., and Walter, C. W. (1962). *Anesthesiology* **23**, 507–512.
Lehman, R. A. W., West, R. L., and Leonard, F. (1966). *Arch. Surg.* **93**, 447–450.
le Riche, H. W., Balcon, C. E., and van Belle, G. (1966). "The Control of Infections in Hospitals," pp. 79–165. Thomas, Springfield, Illinois.
Litsky, Y. B., and Litsky, W. (1968). *Hosp. Manage.* **102**, 49–58.
Lloyd, R. S. (1963). *J. Hosp. Res.* **1**, 5–27.
Macek, T. J. (1970). *Proc. Annu. Meet. Parenteral Drug Ass., 1970, New York.*
Mayr, G. (1961). *In* "Recent Developments in the Sterilization of Surgical Materials" (Dept. Pharm. Sci., Pharm. Soc. Gt. Br. and Smith & Nephew Res. Ltd., eds.), pp. 90–97. Pharmaceutical Press, London.
NF (1970). "National Formulary and First Supplement to NF XIII," pp. 874–876, 958–960, and 1057–1062. Amer. Pharm. Ass., Washington, D.C.
Olson, J. C. (1970). Presentation at the 14th Food and Drug Law Institute, Inc. Food and Drug Administration Joint Educational Conf., Washington, D.C.
Opfell, J. B., and Miller, C. E. (1965). *Advan. Appl. Microbiol.* **7**, 81–102.
Opfell, J. B., Hohmann, J. P., and Latham, A. B. (1959). *J. Amer. Pharm. Ass., Sci. Ed.* **48**, 617–619.
Page, R. C., and Borick, P. M. (1967). *Arch. Surg.* **94**, 162.
Parisi, A. N., and Borick, P. M. (1968). *Proc. 7th Annu. Meet. Amer. Ass. Contam. Contr.* Vol. 7, pp. 24–26.
Parisi, A. N., and Borick, P. M. (1969). *Contam. Contr.* **8**, 31–34.
Pepper, R. E., Buffa, N. T., and Chandler, V. L. (1956). *Appl. Microbiol.* **4**, 149–152.
Phillips, C. R. (1961). *In* "Recent Developments in the Sterlization of Surgical Materials" (Dept. Pharm. Sci., Pharm. Soc. Gt. Brit. and Smith & Nephew Res., Ltd., eds.), pp. 59–75. Pharmaceutical Press, London.
Phillips, G. B. (1969). *In* "Federal Regulations and Practical Control Microbiology for Disinfectants, Drugs and Cosmetics," S.I.M. Spec. Publ. No. 4, pp. 74–86. Soc. Ind. Microbiol.
Pittman, M. (1946). *J. Bacteriol.* **51**, 19–32.
Price, P. B. (1938). *J. Infec. Dis.* **63**, 301–318.
Prince, H. N. (1971). Gibraltar Biological Laboratories, Inc., Fairfield, N.J. (personal communication).
Russomanno, R., and Wollish, E. G. (1964). *J. Pharm. Sci.* **53**, 1538–1539.
Shotton, E. (1961). *In* "Recent Developments in the Sterilization of Surgical Materials" (Dept. Pharm. Sci., Pharm. Soc. Gt. Brit. and Smith & Nephew Res., Ltd., eds.), pp. 1–6. Pharmaceutical Press, London.
Sokolski, W. T., and Chidester, C. G. (1964). *J. Pharm. Sci.* **53**, 103–107.
Spaulding, E. H. (1965). *J. Hosp. Res.* **3**, 7–25.
Stierli, H., Reed, L. L.. and Billick, I. H. (1962). *U.S., Pub. Health Serv., Pub. Health Monogr.* **68**, 1–15.
Sykes, G. (1970). *J. Appl. Bacteriol.* **33**, 147–156.
Sykes, G., and Hooper, M. C. (1959). *J. Pharm. Pharmacol.* **11**, 235T–239T.
USP (1970a). "United States Pharmacopeia," 18th rev. ed., pp. 830–835 and 845–857. Mack Publ. Co., Easton, Pennsylvania.
USP (1970b). *Proc. U.S.P. Open Conf. Biol. Indicators Steril. Assurance, 1970, Arlington, Virginia,* Abstract, pp. 2–14.
Tsuji, K., Stapert, E. M., Robertson, J. H., and Wairjaki, P. M. (1970). *Appl. Microbiol.* **20**, 798–801.
Van Winkle, W., Borick, P. M., and Fogarty, M. G. (1967). *Proc. Int. Conf. Steril. Med. Prod.*, IAEA, Vienna, Austria, pp. 169–180.
Wood, R. T. (1971). Pennsylvania State University (personal communication).

QUALITY CONTROL OF ANTIBIOTICS

*Amiel Kirshbaum**

National Center for Antibiotic Analysis,
United States Food and Drug Administration,
Washington, D.C.

*Present address: 11013 Gainsborough Road, Potomac, Maryland 20854.

Although quality control is an important requirement for high-quality production of all drugs, it enjoys its greatest prominence in the production of antibiotics. This is due to the fact that since 1943 antibiotics, unlike any other drugs with the exception of insulin, have been subject to batch-by-batch certification under the Federal Food, Drug and Cosmetic Act as amended (1969), i.e., samples of every batch manufactured for sale in the United States must be sent to the United States Food and Drug Administration (FDA) for testing. In addition the manufacturer must perform all required tests on every batch. Failure to do so for any batch will make it ineligible for certification and distribution.

I. Design and Arrangement of Laboratories

Four general types of laboratories are necessary for the manufacturer producing parenteral antibiotics. These are laboratories for (1) chemical analysis, (2) microbiological assay, (3) testing for microbial contamination, (4) animal testing.

If the manufacturer produces only topical and oral preparations he needs only the first two types, plus simplified versions of the last two types.

A. Chemistry

The design of the chemistry laboratories presents no special problems and should be comparable to that of the usual analytical chemistry laboratories found in drug plants. They should, of course, contain equipment necessary to perform all tests required by the official regulations.

B. Microbiological Assay

The laboratories for microbiological assay should contain stand-up benches (comparable to those found in chemistry laboratories) for sample preparation. In addition, they should contain sit-down benches (about 30 in. in height) for work pertaining to the agar plates. It is imperative that the surfaces of these sit-down benches be perfectly flat and level. The tables should be covered with waterproof, nonbuckling material such as plate glass or heavy formica.

Incubators should be in the same room or area as the plating tables, since carrying of the plates from room to room after addition of cylinders and test solutions increases the possibility that the cylinders will slide and/or the solution will spill.

For turbidimetric assays suitable water baths must be provided. To obtain uniform results, the temperature of the water must be constant, and each bath should be provided with baffles or some other arrangement for circulation so that the temperature of the water is uniform throughout the bath.

It is desirable to have a small cubicle sealed off from other rooms used for microbiological assay, in which microbial suspensions can be prepared, cultures transferred, etc. This room should be comparable to one used for sterility testing. However, it needs only the care normally used for a microbiological testing laboratory and does not need the rigid environmental control required for a sterility testing cubicle.

C. Biological Tests

The location of animal testing laboratories depends upon the general design of the plant. Some plants may have all laboratory animals concentrated in a specific area of the building, while others may have separate animal testing units for each of its separate scientific divisions. There are advantages and disadvantages to each of these arrangements. Naturally, the quality control laboratory has better control over its tests if the animal facilities are in the same general area as its other laboratories. On the other hand, animal fur and dust can be carried into the atmosphere of the other laboratories and adversely affect tests, particularly sterility tests.

For either arrangement, separate holding areas are necessary for each type of test animals, i.e., rabbits, mice, and cats. Each area must have cages, space, watering and feeding facilities that meet specifications of the Federal Laboratory Animal Welfare Act (P. L. 89–544 as amended by H. R. 19846).

Three separate laboratories are necessary for performance of the required animal (biological) tests. The largest is for the pyrogen test; it must be a room closed to trespass by persons other than those performing the test. A smaller room is required for the toxicity tests; it should be provided with a table for inoculating mice and sufficient shelving to hold the cages of the test animals.

A small cubicle will suffice for the histamine or depressor substances test, since only a single animal (cat) is required for all tests performed on any one day.

In addition to these animal facilities, the usual chemistry laboratory must be provided for the preparation of test doses of the antibiotics being tested for pyrogens, toxicity, and/or depressor substances.

D. Sterility Testing

Last but not least, laboratories must be provided for testing for microbial contamination. They should be as far removed as possible from the animal testing laboratories, preferably on a different floor, but if this is not possible they should at least not be contiguous with them and in any event should be sealed off from them. For the performance of the sterility test one or more cubicles is necessary, depending upon the volume of work performed.

The sterility test area should be equipped with high-efficiency particulate-air filter units (HEPA filter) to filter incoming air. It should have positive pressure and air locks at the entrances to rooms. Walls, ceilings, and floors should be nonporous. Ideally it should comply with class 100 conditions as described in Federal Standard No. 209 (1963) entitled "Clean Room and Work Station Requirements, Controlled Environment" and NASA Standards for "Clean Rooms and Work Stations for the Microbially Controlled Environment" (1967) as described in NHB5340–2. Persons other than those performing tests should not have access to the sterility testing laboratories, and plant visitors should not be conducted through this area.

A conventional microbiological testing laboratory should be made available to test for microbial attributes of nonsterile antibiotics and of raw ingredients used in them. This laboratory should be completely separated from and preferably not contiguous with the sterile areas.

E. Laboratory Service Unit

For support and supply of the quality-control (QC) laboratories, a laboratory service unit must be provided, either as a central unit for all laboratories of the entire plant, or as separate units for each laboratory function. In any event it should be well separated from the testing laboratories, and have adequate facilities for preparing and sterilizing microbiological media and for cleaning glassware and other equipment. A chain is no stronger than its weakest link, and a complex test, even if accurately and precisely performed by a well-trained and conscientious scientist, can produce erroneous results if the glassware is unclean.

F. General

In regard to the entire laboratory area, *it is imperative* that adequate utilities be provided. The electrical system should not be overloaded; in addition to safety considerations, voltage fluctuations will adversely affect both readings from spectrophotometric and other instruments and the uniformity of incubator temperatures. Temperatures inside the laboratories must be uniformly maintained throughout the year. Airconditioning is essential for summer work, since high temperatures will adversely effect not only analysts' performance but also microbiological tests and results obtained with laboratory animals. The ventilating systems should prevent the circulation of dust; otherwise antibiotics and other chemicals will be circulated in addition to "house" or "building" dust, and then will adversely affect test results as well as personal health.

The QC laboratories should be located as far as possible from both internal and external traffic. Internal traffic tends to spread contamination which may affect exacting analytical work, and close proximity of the laboratories to highway traffic will make delicate instruments such as analytical balances susceptible to vibrations caused by heavy trucks and speeding motor vehicles.

II. Personnel

The number of personnel employed by the laboratories obviously is related to the variety and volume of work produced by the plant.

However, a complete QC laboratory should have a minimum of one microbiologist, one biologist, and one chemist, each with at least a bachelor's degree in his major subject from an accredited university. Additional personnel should include several technicians, each with at least a high school diploma and some training in the physical and/or biological sciences. Furthermore, there should be a sufficient number of custodial workers to clean and wash glassware and equipment and to feed and care for laboratory animals.

What has been described is the minimum requirement for a small laboratory performing chemical, microbiological, and biological tests. Naturally as the size of the laboratory increases so does the number of personnel, but there should always be a reasonable percentage of professionally qualified employees in relation to the subprofessional and custodial workers.

Some plants have their research laboratories (which may be separate entities from the QC laboratories) develop new methods and improve existing ones. This author believes that this is not the most advantageous approach. The analysts working daily with methods should be in the best position to do the analytical research and development work since their day-to-day familiarity and experience with the QC methods train them to know the best approaches and the most feasible and applicable techniques. A method developed by a scientist of the research laboratory could be sound in theory, but might be so inapplicable to the daily routine and pressures of the QC laboratory as to make it practically worthless.

III. Regulatory Aspects

Antibiotics are the only drugs other than a few forms of insulin for which the official analytical methods appear in the Code of Federal Regulations rather than in the "United States Pharmacopeia" (USP) or the "National Formulary" (NF). Both of these official compendia refer to the Code of Federal Regulations for specifications and analytical methods for those antibiotics for which they have monographs. The Code of Federal Regulations contains not only the analytical methods for all antibiotics for human use approved for distribution in the United States, but also the specifications these drugs are required to meet to be considered safe and pure. These methods and specifications are published, as approved, in daily issues of the *Federal Register*, which is published daily Tuesday through Saturday. Subscriptions to this publication can be obtained by writing to the Superintendent of Documents, United States Government Printing Office, Washington, D.C. (20402). The methods and specifications are recompiled yearly in the *Code of Federal Regulations*. Those pertaining to antibiotics are contained in two of these volumes, namely, Title 21: Chapter I, Parts 130 to 146 e, and Part 147 to end. These may be purchased by writing to the Superintendent of Documents, at the address given above. Hereafter this publication will be referred to as CFR, and it will be cited repeatedly. The specific reference in the CFR will be given alongside a method or specification discussed in this chapter.

It is recommended that those involved in quality control of antibiotics purchase copies of these two volumes of CFR and subscribe to the *Federal*

Register. The latter generally publishes new methods or specifications as proposals, and at the time of publication laboratory directors may evaluate the proposals and object to or otherwise comment on them if they so desire. If such objections have merit, FDA may revise or modify the methods or specifications. Sections 141.1 through 141.550 of CFR give the general details for the basic official analytical methods. Sample preparation methods and any specific modifications of the general methods that are necessary are given in the individual monographs for each antibiotic drug.

It is desirable that QC laboratories use the official methods of the CFR for testing antibiotics. First, if there is a controversy over the results obtained for a specific batch in a private industry laboratory as compared to those of FDA, results obtained with official methods supersede those obtained with nonofficial methods. Second, QC laboratories of private industry are subject to constant inspection by FDA inspectors. If the latter observe significant deviations from official methods, they may take steps to have the private industry laboratory disapproved for certification of its antibiotic drugs. If some instances nonofficial methods may be allowed for "in-house" control, but the private industry laboratory must present data showing that the method produces results comparable to those obtained with the official methods. Nonofficial methods are used with the understanding that the results of the official methods are controlling. Since the latter are generally sound, and become official only after thorough evaluation by both FDA and industry, no worthwhile purpose is served by using nonofficial methods.

IV. Sampling

The number of samples taken for testing and the frequency of collection is obviously dependent upon the size of the batch, and the type of product. For example, fewer samples are required for a syrup that only needs pH and potency tests than for a parenteral drug that also requires tests for pyrogens, histamine, safety, etc. At this point we do not consider the sterility test. The number of samples required for it are specified separately, and it will be discussed later in this chapter when the sterility test is described. Therefore these requirements are over and above those required for sterility.

The CFR specifies the number of samples that must be collected and sent to FDA for testing. The QC laboratory should collect at least three times this number: one set for FDA, one set for testing by the QC laboratory, and one set for reserve. It is suggested that the QC laboratory collect an even greater number for its testing than that required by FDA. The reason for this is that the QC laboratory should do a sufficient number of tests to assure that the batch meets FDA specifications before submitting samples of the batch for certification. Quite obviously, it reflects poorly on the manufacturer to have his product rejected by FDA. Also it does not make good sense to pay the fees required by the certification program for a batch that cannot be sold.

The sampling requirements for submisssion to FDA (excluding those required for sterility) are as follows:

1. For drugs such as dry powders, solutions, ointments and suspensions, take samples at equal intervals, but in no case shall these intervals exceed 5000 containers. [CFR 146.2 (c) (8) (i).]

2. For drugs which as tablets or other such unit-dosage forms, take single tablets at equal intervals, but in no case shall these intervals exceed 5000 tablets. [CFR 146.2 (c) (8) (ii).]

3. For drugs packaged for repacking or for use in the manufacture of another drug, the samples must be representative of the batch. Such samples may be taken from a composite composed of portions taken from a representative number of bulk containers, the composite consisting of no more than 10 times the amount required for conducting the required tests and assays. [CFR 146.2 (c) (8) (iii).]

The aforementioned references give general directions for sampling. Further information is found in the specific monograph of the CFR for each drug. For example, if a batch consisted of only 5000 containers, quite obviously one sample would not be sufficient for all required tests. Therefore a minimum number of samples is specified. These of course must be taken at equal intervals during tableting or filling.

Caution must be exercised in the taking of samples to assure that the antibiotic is not altered in the physical act of sampling. This involves precautions to assure that the antibiotic is not exposed to the air, that the worker does not affect it with his hands, and that it is not affected by the utensils with which it is taken or by the container into which it is placed, if it is material in other than a final container. If such care is not taken, the following are some conditions that might affect the sample:

1. A dry material can pick up moisture from the atmosphere and/or from an improperly dried container into which it is placed.

2. A sterile material can become contaminated with airborne microorganisms, from the worker, or from an unsterile container into which it is placed.

3. A pyrogen-free material can pick up pyrogens from an improperly cleaned and/or inadequately heat-treated container into which it is placed.

4. A nonpenicillin material can become contaminated with penicillin in the same manner in which a sterile material can become contaminated with microorganisms as described in (2).

Perhaps more important than any of the above considerations is the fact that a careless worker can contaminate the batch itself if he fails to observe proper technique in removing the sample.

Therefore quality control demands that, in sampling, the sample be taken in a relatively dry atmosphere, relatively free of dust, and free of both chemical and microbial airborne contamination, and that exposure last only long enough for transferring the material from the batch to the sample container. In addition, any utensils used for the sample transfer and the containers into which it is placed should be chemically clean, sterile, and pyrogen-free. Also clothing and hands of the worker should be as free of contamination as is possible to attain.

V. Replicate Testing

The number of samples required to be collected for a batch should not be confused with the number of samples required for each test. If a batch is small and only five containers are required by the CFR, all of the containers will probably be utilized to perform the required tests. However, if a batch is large, e.g., 1,000,000 containers, and 200 containers are collected, it should not be necessary to test all of them.

This chapter will not go into statistical analysis. It is recommended that a statistician evaluate the precision and accuracy of the tests as performed by the specific QC laboratory and that he apply methods for rejection of results that do not fit and determine the number of replicate tests necessary to obtain values with a high degree of confidence, using statistical analysis such as that outlined in "United States Pharmacopeia" (USP, 1970a).

However, special attention should be given to the assay for potency of the raw antibiotic powder, described in CFR 146.2 (c) (8) (iii) as a drug "packaged for use in the manufacture of another drug." Since the potency value in terms of units of micrograms per milligram obtained for this material is used in calculating the number of grams or kilograms required for formulating the final dosage form, a significant error in assay will cause the potency value of the final dosage form to be in error before it is even produced.

It is recommended that at least two separate weighings of such raw ingredient powder be assayed on each of three different days (six different assays using six different weighings). If all the individual results are not within the normal distribution of the group or show too much variance, additional assays should be done until a mean potency is obtained with confidence limits of $\pm 2.5\%$ (or better) at $P = 0.05$.

VI. Potency Assays

A. General

While the number of different types of required tests varies from one antibiotic and one dosage form to another, the one test that is always required is the assay for potency. Potency is not an absolute value. It is actually relative potency, i.e., relative to a reference standard. FDA maintains a master and a working standard for every antibiotic for human use authorized for sale in the United States. The definitions of these reference standards are found in CFR 145.3 and the definitions of the terms "unit" and "microgram" as applied to them are found in CFR 145.4. FDA will supply portions of the working standards free of charge to any manufacturer producing antibiotic drugs for sale in the United States. However, they will supply only about 240 mg once every 6 months. FDA recommends that the laboratory establish a "house standard" for its daily work and use the official standard only for periodic checking of the house standard.

If a house standard is established, its potency should be assigned only after a sufficient number of assays against the official standard to give a value with a high degree of confidence. It is recommended that at least two assays be performed on each of three or more different days using a new portion for each assay for a total of at least six assays. For the design of these assays see Section VI,D.

The reference standards should be carefully stored and handled. It is not desirable to have only one container stored in a refrigerator or deep-freezer. If all the material were in one container it would be subject to constant warming and re-refrigeration of the antibiotic powder as portions were withdrawn every day or so. This could very likely result in a premature loss of potency. It is desirable to subdivide the standard into a number of smaller containers, each of which contains no more than a week's supply. These containers should then be stored in a deep-freezer, and only one at a time removed as needed. The latter may usually be kept at room temperature if used within a week or less. Also, whenever a portion of the standard is removed for use in an assay, it is essential that the analyst do it in such a manner that it will not pick up moisture, nor be contaminated in any way.

Standards may be purchased for a nominal fee from the USP or NF. The potencies of these standards have been established in terms of the official FDA standards. It is recommended that those requiring such materials write to the following addresses, requesting lists of available standards: USP Reference Standards, 12601 Twinbrook Parkway, Rockville, Maryland (20852); The National Formulary, 2215 Constitution Avenue, N.W., Washington, D.C. (20037).

The test organisms required for microbiological assays are listed in CFR 141.104. Cultures of these may be purchased by writing to: American Type Culture Collection, 12301 Parklawn Drive, Rockville, Maryland (20852).

B. Sample Preparation

Regardless of which type of assay is used, the first step in its performance is sample preparation. Since this involves many variations, this step is described in the specific monographs for the various antibiotics and dosage forms. In many instances it is the step most subject to error, and therefore erroneous assay results can be traced to faults in sample preparation. This fact is frequently overlooked by statisticians, who measure the error of the assay in terms of its biological variation and make the assumption that insignificant error is involved in the preliminary steps.

The first step in sample preparation is measurement of an aliquot or representative portion of the sample. As simple as this sounds, it is a step often subject to error and is one of the main reasons for discrepancies between results obtained by the private laboratory and those obtained by FDA. This is due to the fact that FDA prepares and removes the sample in the same manner as is directed on the label and as it is used clinically. For example, if the sample is a vial of sterile oxytetracycline hydrochloride intended for injection, it is first reconstituted with the volume of diluent directed on the label, the diluent being added with a needle and hypodermic syringe. Next, an accurately measured representative portion is removed with a needle and syringe as directed on the label. This portion is then further diluted for assay [CFR 148m.11(b)(i)].

Another example is that of a one-dose bottle of tetracycline syrup. The container may be labeled to say that it contains "one dose of tetracycline, 125 mg." Since the manufacturer is claiming that the bottle contains a full dose, the entire contents are poured out into a receptacle and prepared for assay as described in the monograph for tetracycline syrup.

In assaying each of the samples described in these two examples, the private laboratory analyst might get divergent results from those of FDA if he does not remove the material as described. For example, if he were merely to wash out the contents of the oxytetracycline HCl vial, he might get an assay of 97% of label claim and feel that the sample passed the official requirement since it exceeded the minimum requirement of 90%. However, FDA's assay might only be 87% for this sample, and it would be rejected. In this example the assay of the private laboratory might be essentially the same as FDA's on a microgram per milligram basis, but significantly different from that of FDA because it did not follow the proper protocol.

The sample must also be measured and reported as indicated on the label. For example if it is labeled in terms of "units per milliliter," it should not be assayed in terms of "units per gram."

Tablets and capsules should be assayed and reported in terms of "units or micrograms per tablet or capsule." Some laboratories have been known to grind a certain number of these dosage forms, then assay and report their results in terms of units or micrograms per milligram of powder. This obviously could result in discrepancies from the results obtained by FDA.

In removing a portion of the sample for assay, the analyst should make sure that he is removing a representative portion. This is particularly essential for a suspension. He must make sure that it is properly shaken before removing the portion. At the same time it should not be shaken so hard that it has air bubbles in it. Also, in removing the portion, the analyst must make sure that the measuring device he is using will deliver the required amount after he has removed it. For example, if he is assaying a thick syrup, he may not deliver a required 1-ml volume if he removes the portion with a narrow-bore pipette. In this instance, a hypodermic syringe fitted with a 13-gage needle might be the best measuring device to use. A pipette calibrated "to contain" a certain volume could be used provided the contents are washed out. The analyst should be course predetermine that he is delivering the required volume of the type of sample being assayed.

After the aliquot or representative portion of the sample is removed, it is prepared for assay as described in the specific monograph. Although there are a variety of methods, most of them fall into one of three general categories:

1. Merely dissolving or suspending the sample in a liquid;

2. Placing the sample (in this case, usually an ointment) in an organic solvent such as ether, and then extracting with an aqueous phase;

3. Placing the material in a blending jar with a diluent, then blending for several minutes with a high-speed blender. After this step a part of the stock solution is removed and further diluted as described in the specific monograph.

C. Chemical Assays

As a general rule FDA does not recommend alternative test methods. However, in some instances chemical methods for potency are so valuable that they are listed in the CFR as alternatives to microbiological assays. The main chemical methods listed are: the iodometric assay (CFR 141.506); the hydroxylamine colorimetric assay (CFR 141.507); vapor phase chromotography (CFR 141.571); ultraviolet spectrophotometric assay; and colorimetric assay (references for the last two are under specific monographs).

Those antibiotics that may be readily assayed by chemical methods are:

1. Iodometric: most penicillin dosage forms (except ointments), cephalothin and cephaloridine;

2. Hydroxylamine colorimetric: all penicillin and cephalosporin powders (except carbenicillin). Note: these antibiotics may also be assayed by the iodometric method, but are listed here because the hydroxylamine method may be readily automated. This will be discussed later in the Subsection E under Automation;

3. Vapor phase chromatography: lincomycin and clindamycin (this is the definitive method for assigning clindamycin potency);

4. Ultraviolet: chloramphenicol succinate and palmitate, dactinomycin, and griseofulvin;

5. Colorimetric: cycloserine and troleandomycin.

D. Microbiological Assays

Two types of microbiological assays are generally used for the assay of antibiotics: the turbidimetric assay and the diffusion plate assay.

The official methods described in the CFR are one-dose assays. By this approach a standard response line is prepared, generally composed of five equally spaced doses of the reference standard. The unknown is diluted to only one concentration, usually the same as the midpoint or reference concentration of the standard response line. From the standpoint of statistical design, an assay method that involves two or more separate doses of the unknown is preferable to a one-dose method. However, when it has been predetermined that the response of a test organism to different concentrations of a particular antibiotic is comparable to that of the standard, a single dose will give an accurate assay. If this is done, the method is satisfactory for QC assay of antibiotics. This does not however, obviate the necessity for running a sufficient number of replicate assays. In establishing the potency of a house standard, a three-dose factorial design is recommended. Kirshbaum *et al.* (1956) have described such a design for a plate assay. A factorial design for a turbidimetric assay can be found in USP (1970b).

The general procedure for the turbidimetric assay is described in CFR 141.111. This consists essentially of adding 1 ml of each standard response line concentration and of the proper dilution of the unknown to test tubes. Next 9 ml of broth inoculated with the recommended test organism is added to each. The tubes are then incubated in a 37° C water bath for 3 to 4 hours. After incubation, the turbidity is measured in a spectrophotometer. From these readings a standard response line is plotted, and the potency of the unknown is calculated from the standard curve.

The general procedure for the agar diffusion plate assay is described in CFR 141.110. The basic method consists of preparing standard response line concentrations and dilutions of the unknown in the same manner as described for turbidimetric assays. The final dilutions are added to stainless steel cylinders placed on the surface of agar inoculated with a test organism in a petri dish. After overnight incubation of the plates, the analyst measures the diameters of zone of inhibition produced by diffusion of the antibiotic and subsequent inhibition of growth of the test organism. A standard response line is plotted, and the difference between zones of inhibition produced by the unknown compared to those produced by the reference concentration of the standard is read from the standard response line. From the concentration read on the response line the analyst can calculate the potency of the unknown.

Many antibiotic powders and dosage forms may be assayed by either chemical, turbidimetric, or plate assays. The selection of the method of choice will be discussed later. However, the latter method is more versatile than the others, and in addition to its applicability to powders and dosage forms, it is used for the assay of antibiotic susceptibility discs, for the determination of penicillin contamination in nonpenicillin drugs, and for the detection of aflatoxins in antibiotics.

Antibiotic susceptibility discs are drugs as defined by the Supreme Court of the United States (1969). The methods for their assay are described in CFR 147.1–147.2. These methods differ from those used for the assay of other antibiotic drugs in that no extractions and dilutions of the drugs are involved; the unknown disc is placed directly on the inoculated agar surface. The standard response line concentrations are placed on discs rather than in cylinders. The reason for this approach is to test the performance of the disc in a manner comparable to the way it will be used in the clinical laboratory.

The agar diffusion plate assay is also used for the detection of contaminants such as aflatoxins in antibiotics and penicillin in nonpenicillin antibiotics. Aflatoxins are highly toxic metabolites produced by *Aspergillus flavus*. Peanut meal or other grains used in the fermentation production of antibiotics might contain the mold. Therefore the QC laboratory should monitor these raw ingredients as well as the antibiotics themselves for the presence of aflatoxins. The methods of choice for such tests are chemical procedures and will be discussed later in Section IX. However, a diffusion plate assay reported by Clements (1968) is available to supplement the chemical method. The test organism is *Bacillus megaterium* which is sensitive to 1 μg of aflatoxin B per milliliter.

Penicillin might appear as a contaminant in other antibiotics. The tolerances established by FDA for such contamination appear in CFR 133,11(h).

They are: 0.05 unit of penicillin per maximum single dose of an injectable drug and 0.5 unit per maximum single dose of an oral drug. Consequently the QC laboratory should monitor nonpenicillin antibiotics to ensure that they are free from these kinds of penicillin contamination. While FDA has not published official methods, they have published quasiofficial ones (Anonymous, 1965) which may be obtained upon request to FDA. These methods use *Sarcina lutea* as the test organism. Some antibiotics which have little inhibitory effect on this organism may be tested directly simply by dissolving them in the appropriate buffer. However, extraction procedures are required for such antibiotics as erythromycin and neomycin so that any possible penicillin contamination may be separated from these antibiotics, since their activity would interfere with the assay for penicillin.

In performing the assay for penicillin contamination, the QC laboratory quite obviously must exercise rigid environmental control, so that it does not itself contaminate the sample with penicillin. This involves performing the tests in a laboratory in which penicillin is not handled, and ensuring that all glassware and equipment are free of penicillin and that analysts (prior to the assay) do not handle penicillin or even enter an area in which it is present.

E. Automation

Consonant with modern trends, automation has been applied to potency assays, and further efforts are continuing in that direction. While the individual QC laboratory should feel free to develop automated procedures it should be borne in mind that the official methods published in the CFR are the methods of choice and are those which dominate in any legal controversy. Therefore, it is most desirable to direct any efforts for developing automation to repetitive steps of the official method which do not affect the basic assay. Kuzel and Kavenagh (1972) and Rippere and Arret (1972) have reported methods which automate repetitive steps of turbidimetric assays without affecting their official status. Such automation takes the test tubes after incubation, removes the broth culture from them and transfers the latter to a spectrophotometer. This instrument then automatically reads the turbidity and prints out the results. If a computer is available it can be programmed to make all the necessary calculations of sample potency.

FDA in collaboration with an engineering firm has designed an electronic instrument which will read and measure zones of inhibition in agar diffusion plate assays. The instrument has the capability of rejecting zones that are either out-of-round, or fall outside the normal distribution of other zones for a set of readings. The instrument embodies a small dedicated computer which can be programmed to calculate individual potency values and obtain the average potency for a batch.

Automation such as that described in the preceding paragraphs not only has the advantage of increasing work capacity, but actually improves the accuracy of the assay, since automatic readers can not only measure responses more accurately than the human eye but they eliminate human bias as well.

The hydroxylamine colorimetric assay previously described has been automated by using the Technicon AutoAnalyzer. Lane and Weiss (1966) reported favorable comparison of this system with the penicillin assay by iodometric and microbiological procedures. The use of this automation does not affect the official status of the hydroxylamine colorimetric assay.

F. Choice of Method

As mentioned earlier, the policy of FDA is to refrain from publishing alternative methods. However, some monographs do include alternative methods for assay. For products covered by these monographs several factors must be considered in selecting the method to be used in a particular laboratory.

Chemical methods are generally the easiest to perform, the least time-consuming, the most economical, and the most precise. From a consideration of these factors, it is seen that they are the best methods to use in a busy QC laboratory. However, in cases of controversy, results obtained by the official microbiological assay take precedence over those obtained by the chemical assay. Therefore the laboratory using the latter must periodically determine that it is getting results that compare favorably to those obtained by microbiological assay.

The turbidimetric assay is less time-consuming than the plate diffusion assay in that results can be obtained after 3–4 hours of incubation, rather than overnight. In other words, an assay result can be obtained the same day the assay is initiated rather than waiting until the next day. This method is also more economical than the agar diffusion plate assay, requiring less personnel and equipment for its performance. The fee for the turbidimetric assay as charged by FDA is based upon a cost study and is only half that assessed for the plate assay (CFR 146.8).

While materials such as the purified antibiotic powder or high-potency preparations such as tetracycline syrups can be readily tested by turbidimetric assay, the latter is subject to interference in testing preparations containing more than one active antibiotic ingredient or in assaying formulations producing cloudy final dilutions such as when ointments are assayed. Consequently, diffusion-plate assays are preferable for assaying such materials.

In some instances the time-saving advantage of the turbidimetric assay over the diffusion plate assay may prove to be a disadvantage, because in order to get the test material into the water bath with sufficient time left in the work day for incubation, spectrophotometric readings, and calculation of results, the laboratory must complete the initial steps of the assay, i.e., sample preparation, addition of inoculated broth, etc., within the first 2 or 3 hours of the work day. Conversely, since the diffusion plate assay is an overnight test, the analyst is not under pressure to complete the initial phases of the assay within the first couple of hours of the work day. He can spread his work more uniformly throughout the day, and can then place the plates in the incubator at the close of his work day.

Consequently, whenever, the QC laboratory has a choice in the assay method to be used, it must weigh all the factors mentioned in these preceding paragraphs to determine which methods best suit its individual needs. However, all other factors being equal, the following order of priority is recommended:

1. Chemical method—when approved by CFR, with periodic comparison to the microbiological method.
2. Turbidimetric method—for preparations containing only a single antibiotic ingredient and which can be prepared for assay in a relatively short time.
3. Diffusion plate method—for all other preparations.

VII. Biological Tests

The biological (or animal tests) required by the Antibiotic Regulations are described in CFR 141.3–141.7, inclusive. These regulations describe three different tests: a pyrogen test (CFR 141.4); a safety test (CFR 141.5); and a histamine test (depressor substances) (CFR 141.7).

A. Pyrogen Test

For performance of the pyrogen test, all glassware, syringes, and needles used must be rendered free from pyrogens by heating at 250°C for not less than 30 minutes or by any other suitable method. Test solutions and diluents must be heated or autoclaved sufficiently to make them pyrogen-free.

The test in its simplest form involves the injection of the test solution into the ear vein of each of three rabbits. The temperature of each is taken rectally before injection and at hourly intervals for 3 hours thereafter. If no rabbit shows an individual rise in temperature of 0.6° C or more above its respective preinjection control temperature, and if the sum of the three temperature rises does not exceed 1.4°C, the sample passes. However, if these conditions are not met, the test is repeated with five other rabbits. If not more than three of the eight rabbits show individual rises of 0.6° C or more, and if the sum of the eight temperature rises does not exceed 3.7°C, the sample then meets the requirements for the absence of pyrogens.

The pyrogen test must be carefully controlled in order to obtain reliable results. As mentioned earlier, glassware and diluents must be properly heated to render them pyrogen-free. Rabbits used for the test must have maintained their weight on an antibiotic-free diet for at least 1 week prior to the test. They must be housed individually in an area of uniform temperature (±3°C) and free from disturbances likely to excite them. Animals should not be used more frequently than once every 48 hours or within 2 weeks after they have been given a test sample that was pyrogenic. Proper controls must be run as specified in CFR 141.4.

The official methods do not mention a positive control. Some investigators maintain that a positive control is not desirable. Since a pyrogen contaminant is not a uniform entity, they maintain that the use of a pyrogen reference standard could produce a rabbit colony specifically sensitive to that particular entity. This author feels that it is desirable to test the sensitivity of the rabbit colony with a uniform substance capable to producing a known pyrogenic response. Castor *et al.* (1972) have reported the results of a collaborative study of a pyrogenic material in which twelve different laboratories participated, including, in addition to nine domestic laboratories, one each in Belgium, Canada, and Australia. Although responses in rabbits varied considerably, it could be concluded from the study that 0.001 mg/kg would produce a minimal pyrogenic response as defined by the USP.

For measuring temperatures in simplest form an accurate clinical thermometer can be used. However, a number of different types of thermocouples, thermisters, and automatic electronic measuring devices are commercially available.

It is interesting to note that of all official tests required for antibiotic QC, the pyrogens test is one of the most expensive. The fees charged in the antibiotic certification program, CFR 146.8, based upon cost-survey studies are $62.00 for a three-rabbit pyrogen test, and $162.00 for an eight-rabbit test. This may be compared to only $7.00 for a turbidimetric assay.

B. Safety Test

The safety test is described in CFR 141.5. In simplest form, this involves injection of the test does into each of five mice. The mice are then housed in a suitable container, given adequate food and water, and observed for 48 hours. If no animal dies within this period the sample passes. If one or more animals die, the test is repeated one or more times, using five or more previously unused mice for each test. If repeat tests are required, the sample passes the safety test if the total number of dead mice is no greater than 10% of the total number of animals tested, including the original test.

It should be borne in mind that this is a safety test and not a true test to demonstrate the lack of toxicity of the drug as used clinically. The latter must be proved by complete and adequate studies reported in the New Drug Application before it is approved by FDA. The safety test is one designed to show that each batch submitted for certification is not contaminated with adventitious toxic substances. The latter could be anything from arsenic that had inadvertently gotten into that particular batch to some toxic breakdown product that appeared in the particular batch for some inexplicable or unpredicted reason.

Since the contaminant is unknown and could therefore be anything, its stability in solution *a priori* is unknown. In view of the fact that highly toxic material could be quite unstable in solution, test solutions should be tested shortly after preparation. Otherwise a highly toxic but unstable contaminant could decay if the test solution were held for a long period, and the safety test would then give a satisfactory result although the drug would be highly toxic if administered to a patient shortly after its reconstitution.

Two antibiotics that have been approved for certification require more extensive tests for toxicity: the antitumor drugs dactinomycin and mithramycin. They are subjected to LD_{50} tests which are published in the CFR: dactinomycin, 148u.1 (b)(4), and mithramycin, 148v.2 (b)(4). These two antibiotics are unique in that, as antitumor drugs, their effectiveness depends upon a sufficient amount of cytotoxic activity to destroy neoplasms, yet they must not be so toxic as to destroy healthy tissue. Therefore, the specifications require that the LD_{50} must exceed a certain minimum but must not exceed an upper limit, e.g., the LD_{50} must not be less than 0.65 and not more than 1.23 mg of dactinomycin per kg of body weight [148u.1(a)(1)(iv)].

Since both dactinomycin and mithramycin are toxic and corrosive, they must be handled in the laboratory with special care. Transfer all such powders in a special hood while wearing rubber gloves. Avoid inhaling fine particles of the powder. Do not pipette by mouth. If any of the substance contacts the skin, wash copiously with soap and water. Dispose of all waste material by dilution with large volumes of trisodium phosphate solution.

C. The Test for Histamine-like Substances (Depressor Substances)

The histamine test is described in CFR 141.7. In simplest form it consists of anesthetizing a cat, surgically exposing the common carotid artery, then inserting a cannula connected to a manometer arranged for making a continuous record of blood pressure. The femoral vein of the leg is exposed and injections of a histamine standard are given until the drop given by equivalent doses of histamine is relatively uniform. The decrease in blood pressure given by 0.1 μg/kg of histamine standard is subsequently employed as the standard in testing samples. The test solution of the sample is then injected, alternating with a dose of the standard equivalent to 0.1 μg of histamine/kg. The sample is satisfactory if the decrease in blood pressure obtained with the sample is not greater than the decrease obtained with 0.1 μg of histamine standard/kg of body weight.

VIII. Tests for Microbial Contamination

A. Sterility Tests

1. Environmental Control

All antibiotics labeled as sterile must be tested to assure that they are free from microbial contamination. The general sterility test methods are described in CFR 141.2. These state that "the test must be performed . . . in an area as free from contamination as it is possible to achieve." In Section I,D of this chapter some comments were made on the design of the sterility testing area. Surfaces of such rooms should be washed daily with an effective germicide. In addition the rooms should be sprayed daily with a disinfectant such as 5% phenol or 2% glutaraldehyde.

This cleaning and maintenance should be done after the completion of each day's work so that the rooms remain unoccupied for some time, preferably overnight, before the next sterility testing operation is started.

Personnel who perform the sterility tests should wear sterile caps, gowns, masks, shoes, and gloves. In the 1960s the pharmaceutical industry began using laminar-flow hoods to provide clean, sterile dust-free areas for manufacturing and for sterility testing. Laminar airflow is defined as airflow in which the entire body of air within a confined area moves with uniform velocity along parallel flow lines. In operation a laminar flow of ultraclean filtered air rinses airborne particles from the working area. These hoods provide a sterile atmosphere in which sterility tests can be performed, and therefore are essentially a "must" for the performance of the tests. Bowman (1968) has reported the advantages of using such equipment.

The QC laboratory should make some checks to determine the effectiveness of the measures taken for environmental control. The most common approach is to expose plates containing a rich nutrient agar medium in the sterile cubicles while sterility tests are being performed. When the day's work is completed these plates should be incubated and observed later to determine the number of colonies that develop. An appraisal of the effectiveness of the environmental control measures should be based on the record of such plate counts made at regular intervals over a period of several weeks.

2. Sample Size

Unlike all other QC tests for antibiotics, the *Antibiotic Regulations* require a specific fixed sample size, namely, 20 samples for a sterility test. Also unlike all other tests, a sampling is required from each separate filling operation rather than one sampling from the entire batch. CFR 141.1 defines a filling operation as "that period of time not longer than 24 consecutive hours during which a homogeneous quantity of a drug is being filled continuously into market size containers and during which no changes are made in the equipment used for filling." In the case of a bulk powder packaged for repacking or for use in an ingredient in the manufacture of another drug, CFR 141.1 states that the sample required for sterility testing may be packaged in one container in lieu of 20 containers, or in 2 containers in lieu of 40 containers, under certain specified conditions.

3. Test Methods

The actual sterility test methods are described in CFR 141.2. Two different methods are used—the membrane filtration test, CFR 141.2 (e)(1), and the direct method, CFR 141.2 (e)(2). For each method, the portion of sample taken from each of 20 immediate containers for the test is 300 mg of solids or 1 ml by volume (of liquids) or the entire contents if the container contains less than these amounts, except that if it is a liquid drug containing penicillin in a concentration greater than 300,000 units/ml, the volume that contains 300,000 units is taken.

The membrane filtration test in its simplest form involves placing the sample taken as described above in a sterile 500-ml Erlenmeyer flask containing 200 ml of diluting fluid. After the antibiotic has dissolved, the solution is filtered through a bacteria-retentive membrane filter (porosity 0.45 μ). Then three 100-ml portions of diluting fluid are filtered through the membrane to remove residual antibiotic. By means of a sterile circular blade, paper punch, or other suitable sterile device, a portion approximately 17.5 mm in diameter is cut from the center of the filtering area. This cut area is then transferred to a sterile test tube containing 90 ± 10 ml of sterile thioglycollate broth. Using sterile forceps, the remaining outer portion of the membrane is transferred to a second tube containing 90 ± 10 ml of sterile soybean-casein digest medium (SBCD). The tube of thioglycollate broth is incubated at 30–32°C and the tube of SBCD is incubated at 22–25°C for 7 days each.

For the laboratory performing numerous tests, manifolds are commercially available which will hold as many as 6 filter funnels, allowing six membrane filtration tests to be performed concurrently (Fig. 1).

For the direct method, the sample taken from each of 20 immediate containers is transferred into individual sterile test tubes containing 90 ± 10 ml of thioglycollate broth and from each of the same 20 immediate containers a second equivalent portion is transferred to individual sterile test tubes containing 90 ± 10 ml of sterile SBCD. The 20 tubes of each type of broth are incubated in the same manner as described for the single tubes prepared for the membrane filtration test.

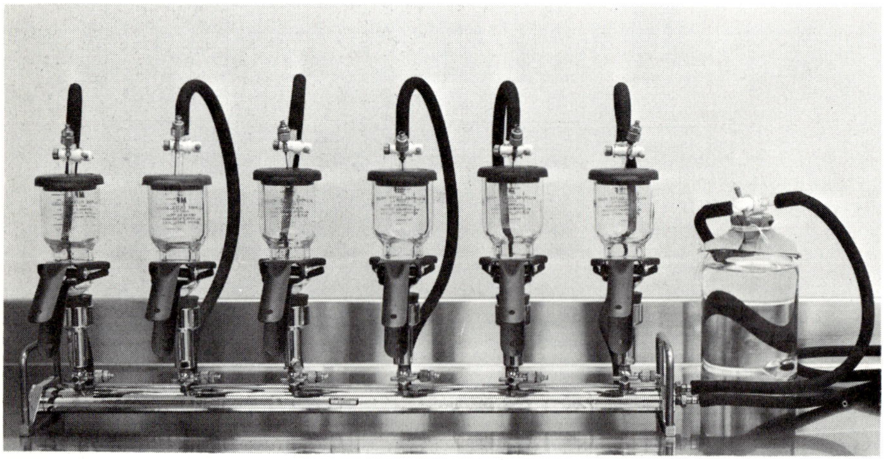

Fig. 1. *Commercial manifold for the membrane filtration test. Courtesy of Mrs. Frances W. Bowman, National Center for Antibiotic Analysis, United States Food & Drug Administration, Washington, D.C.*

4. Evaluation of Results

The batch or the part of the batch represented by a particular filling operation meets the requirements of the test if after incubation no sample tube shows growth. If growth is observed in any sample tube, a second test is run in the appropriate medium, except 40 instead of 20 containers are tested. The batch meets the requirements if no tube on the second test shows growth.

The paragraphs on evaluation of results in CFR 141.2 (f)(1) and (2) each contain this sentence in conclusion: "In any event, further tests may be justified if there is sufficient reason to believe that the results obtained in the first and second tests may not be valid." This statement transcends direct objective criteria and invokes judgmental inference. The QC analyst must apply his expertise to determine if further tests are necessary. While it is difficult to give examples of such inference, the following are examples of results that might warrant further testing:

1. If four out of five filling operations of the same batch gave positive results, it would seem likely that the fifth filling operation might also be contaminated. Therefore it would be desirable to retest the fifth filling operation even though the original test on it was negative.

2. If on the same day three analysts had each performed approximately five sterility tests (a total of 300 containers) and all results were negative, while a fourth analyst on the same day had performed an additional five sterility tests of comparable samples and all five produced positive results, it would seem likely that the results obtained by the fourth analyst were subject to question, and his work should be repeated. The two examples given here are extreme, but they do point out that in some instances, the QC analyst must apply inferential analysis and can not always blindly follow quantitative directions to arrive at a "positive" or "negative" conclusion.

5. Choice of Method

The membrane filtration method is superior to the direct method for many reasons and should therefore be used whenever possible. First of all, it separates the antibiotic from any possible microbial contamination and therefore removes the possibility that antibiotic activity will destroy latent contamination and therefore mask its presence. For example, if neomycin sulfate were tested for sterility by the direct method, 300 mg would be added to approximately 100 ml of broth. This antibiotic has a potency of approximately 700 μg/mg. Therefore each milliliter of broth would contain $300 \times 700/100$ or 2100 μg of neomycin base! Few microorganisms could survive this concentration of neomycin. Therefore, it would be nearly impossible to obtain a positive result.

The membrane filtration test is also less expensive than the direct method because a total of only two tubes of broth is required for the test compared to 40 tubes for a single direct method test. Quite obviously less incubation space is required.

As a result of the many advantages, if it is at all possible to solubilize and filter an antibiotic the membrane filtration test should be used. CFR 141.2 (c) lists four different diluting fluids to enable solubilization of most antibiotics.

The USP (1970c) introduced the use of biological indicators as an approach to sterility testing. However, these cannot be considered for the sterility testing of antibiotics since they are almost always sterilized by filtration and sterile crystallization or freeze-drying rather than by steam sterilization; therefore they are not sterilized in the final container. Bowman (1969) has written an excellent survey article on the sterility testing of pharmaceuticals which is recommended for further reading on this subject.

B. Nonsterile Drugs

Until a few years ago, there was little if any microbiological QC in relation to nonsterile drugs. Kallings and Everfeldt (1965) in Sweden published the results of their studies of the microbial content of nonsterile drugs which showed that many commercial nonsterile medicinals were heavily contaminated with microorganisms, including pathogens. This report evoked concern and interest in the problem throughout the world. The USP (1970d) for the first time published tests for determining microbial contamination of nonsterile drugs. The introductory paragraph states that the chapter provides such tests "in pharmaceutical articles of all kinds, from raw materials to the finished dosage form." On page 800 of USP XVIII there is a statement which reads: "Pharmacopeial articles" should be monitored for "microbial attributes . . . with greatest emphasis being placed on raw materials of animal or botanical origin, especially those that support microbial growth and are not rendered sterile during subsequent processing."

Although the *Antibiotic Regulations* have no specifications for microbial attributes of nonsterile antibiotics, the latter are required under Section 501(a) of the Food and Drug and Cosmetic Act to be free from harmful microorganisms.

Furthermore the relatively new Good Manufacturing Practices (GMP) regulations published in the *Federal Register* (1971) require the inclusion of laboratory controls for "freedom from objectionable microorganisms for those drugs which should be so by virtue of their intended use."

Therefore the QC laboratory should monitor both the raw materials used in the manufacture of antibiotic drugs and the finished dosage forms for the presence of excessive numbers or harmful types of microorganisms. Since control of nonsterile drugs including raw ingredients is covered elsewhere raw ingredients will not be discussed in this article. In regard to nonsterile antibiotics, Bowman *et al.* (1972) examined 261 market samples of antibiotics from 38 different manufacturers and found them to be in excellent condition with regard to freedom from unsatisfactory microbial contamination. No contamination was detected in 75% of the drugs examined. The remaining 25% had counts of less than 50 organisms per item tested, e.g., tablet, capsule, gram of ointment, or milliliter of liquid preparation, and none were found contaminated with the four "harmful" indicator organisms specified in USP XVIII. As a result of this study FDA has deemed it unnecessary, at the present time, to require batch-by-batch testing of nonsterile antibiotics for microbial limits. However, they will be spot-checked. The industrial laboratory should perform such tests as it deems necessary to assure that its nonsterile drugs remain in the excellent condition found by Bowman in her survey. The USP XVIII microbial attributes tests are not suitable for testing antibiotics without some modification. This is primarily due to the fact that the inherent antimicrobial activity of antibiotics would tend to prevent the growth of possible microbial contaminants during the tests. Therefore while the USP methods specify a 10-ml or 10-gm sample, Bowman reduced this to a 1-ml or 1-gm sample. She then divided antibiotics into three categories: (1) insoluble antibiotics, (2) soluble antibiotics, (3) petrolatum-based antibiotics.

She proceeded with her tests as follows: The sample of insoluble antibiotic was placed in 9 ml of sterile peptone water; then a series of tenfold serial dilutions were prepared by transferring 1 ml of the above to 9 ml of sterile peptone water, and 1 ml of each dilution was added to 40 ml of liquified SBCD agar in separate petri dishes. The plates were then incubated for 48–72 hours at 35–37°C. After incubation, colony counts were made.

For soluble antibiotics the sample was dissolved in 200 ml of sterile peptone water and the solution was filtered through a 0.45 μ porosity membrane filter, which was washed three times with 100 ml of sterile peptone water. The membrane was then placed on the surface of 20 ml of solidified SBCD agar in a petri dish which was incubated as described in the preceding paragraph. After incubation, counts were made.

Bowman tested petrolatum-based antibiotic products by taking a 1-gm sample and proceeding as described on page 848 of USP XVIII.

Any microorganisms isolated in the above tests were examined by USP XVIII methods to determine if they were any of the indicator organisms specified in USP XVIII as harmful pathogens.

IX. Chemical Tests

A. General

The variety of chemical tests that must be performed by the antibiotic QC laboratory is considerable. Furthermore the specifications for passing vary from product to product, unlike such tests as sterility, which has only a pass or fail result, or a pyrogens test, which has the same specifications for all products. For example, the moisture limit for oxytetracycline hydrochloride is 2.0%, CFR 148n.2 (a)(1)(vi), while for oxytetracycline it is 9.0%, 148 n.1 (a)(1)(vi). Therefore the QC chemist must have appropriate card files, charts, or other records to keep him informed as to the types of tests and passing specifications for each product examined.

Basic procedures for chemical tests are described in CFR sections 141.501 through 141.570. However, a better perspective of the variety can be obtained by examining the fee schedule in CFR 146.8, which lists 31 different chemical tests.

The QC chemical laboratory should be well-equipped with the usual glassware, burettes, pH meters, analytical balances, etc., that are necessary in an analytical chemistry laboratory. In addition, the laboratory should have the instruments or equipment listed below as essential, and should consider having those listed as desirable:

Essential
- Ultraviolet, visible, and infrared spectrophotometers
- Centrifuges
- Ovens
- Tablet disintegration apparatus (CFR 141.540)
- Polarizing microscope
- Gas–liquid chromatography
- Polarimeter
- Muffle furnace
- Sample transfer box (dry box)
- Equipment for paper, column, and thin-layer chromatography

Desirable
- Atomic absorption spectrophotometer
- Spectrofluorometer
- Lyophilizer (freeze-dryer)
- Potentiograph

QC chemical tests can be divided into five different categories, i.e., potency, purity, identity, stability, and other. Those for potency have been discussed in Section VI,C. of this article. It is difficult, however, to attempt to categorize all the tests, since many of them fall into two or more categories.

Among tests that are related to stability of the drug are those for pH and moisture or loss on drying. These tests are done on all antibiotics to which applicable.

Tests for purity include tests for contaminants, including those for metal particles in ophthalmic ointments, and for arquad (monoalkyl trimethyl-ammonium salt) content. The latter may appear in the antibiotic as a carry-over from the manufacturing process. As mentioned in Section VI, D of this article, aflatoxin might appear in the antibiotic as a contaminant from mold growth. While the test for this toxin is not a required test for batch-to-batch certification, the QC laboratory should monitor its antibiotics for its possible presence. Blakely (1969) has reported a chemical method using thin-layer chromatography that has a sensitivity of about 2 μg of aflatoxin per kg of antibiotic and is therefore more sensitive than the microbiological assay. The chemical test is therefore the method of choice.

The test should be performed on ingredients such as peanut meal used in the fermentation process and the antibiotic powder used to manufacture the dosage forms rather than on the forms themselves, since if aflatoxins are involved at all they would have been introduced among the raw ingredients or produced during the fermentation process. Also their concentration would be greater in the raw materials and therefore easier to detect than after dilution in the preparation of dosage forms.

Among other chemical tests that the QC laboratory must be equipped and trained to perform (the number and variety depending upon the antibiotic and the dosage form) are: nonaqueous titration; paper, thin-layer, and gas–liquid chromatographic tests; residue on ignition; heavy metals; epi-anhydro and anhydrotetracycline in tetracyclines; gentamicin C fractions in gentamicin; penicillin G content; color identity ultraviolet absorptivity; infrared identity; total chlorine; free chloride; specific rotation; sulfate content; crystallinity; disintegration time for tablets; and specific surface area.

B. Supportive Tests

In addition to the large number and variety of official and quasiofficial chemical tests that have been described, a great variety of supportive tests or observations should be made by the QC laboratory. Most of these are the responsibility of all analysts of the QC laboratory, whether they are chemists, microbiologists, or biologists. However, for the sake of delineation they are described here under chemical tests.

The policy of FDA is that a container should deliver the amount of drug claimed on the label. For example if a vial of procaine penicillin in oil is labeled "10 ml, 300,000 units/ml" it must deliver 10 separate 1-ml aliquots, and it must deliver them as they would be used by the physician. Therefore the withdrawable contents of this vial should be tested by withdrawing 1 ml at a time with separate and clean hypodermic needle and syringe of appropriate size. The vial would not meet FDA standards if 10 ml could be withdrawn at one time with a large syringe and needle but if the 10 separate 1-ml aliquots could not be obtained.

If a bottle of syrup is labeled 60 ml, or 12 separate 5-ml doses, it must be tested by pouring the contents into a calibrated device such as a graduate, and, to be satisfactory, 60 ml must be measured in the graduate.

The test for withdrawable contents is not one required for batch-to-batch certification, but the QC laboratory should monitor its antibiotics to make sure they deliver the amounts indicated on the label.

The QC analyst should be constantly alert during the performance of required tests to make any observations that would detect an unsatisfactory product, due either to departures from normal in the product itself or to mechanical defects of the container. Among these are appearance: an unusual color, texture, consistency, or odor should be further explored and investigated.

Caking of a suspension should be noted. Normal settling which requires a minimum of shaking to resuspend is satisfactory. However, if the analyst has to shake the suspension vigorously for a prolonged period, or place it on a mechanical shaker to suspend it, the product is not likely to be satisfactory. A similar judgment can be made on syringeability. If a preparation is one that is administered with a needle and syringe, and is therefore withdrawn in this manner for analysis, it should be easily syringeable. If the analyst finds that it is extremely difficult to force the material from the syringe, the product cannot be considered satisfactory.

Although modern production methods produce relatively clean antibiotic products, in some instances visible foreign matter, such as glass, hairs, rubber particles, etc., may appear in the product. Observation of such foreign matter should be immediately followed up to determine if it was present in only one container, that had become contaminated by chance, or if it is present in other containers of the batch.

Mechanical defects that might be observed are improper closures, leaking ointment tubes, defective cartridge needles, and chipped glass. The analyst should also observe the labels on the containers he tests and report any faulty labeling, particularly mislabeling. While it might be argued that some of the supportive tests described herein are the responsibility of in-line inspectors, some containers with defects such as those described do slip by, and a chemist who observes and ignores an incorrect label on a container he is testing cannot be said to be performing proper QC work.

X. Controls and Quality Assurance

A. General

The designation "quality assurance" is often used interchangeably with "quality control," but in this article we will use it to define the controls used to assure that quality control tests are meaningful and valid. A test painstakingly performed with an inaccurate measuring device is invalid and useless ("a chain is no stronger than its weakest link"). It follows therefore that the QC laboratory must have a program to assure itself of a consistently high quality of analytical performance. The program must provide a measure of the precision and accuracy of methods of analysis and a permanent record of instrument and equipment performance.

Analytical balances should be checked at least monthly checking their calibration against weights traceable to National Bureau of Standards calibration.

Distilled water from stills should be checked at least monthly by checking the electrical conductivity and determining the specific resistance.

Whenever pH meters are used, their accuracy and calibration should be checked using buffers that have been checked against NBS standards.

Spectrophotometers should be checked at least weekly, with regard to their photometric accuracy and reproducibility, resolution, and wavelength calibration.

Thermometers should be checked when purchased and at least monthly thereafter by checking their calibration against thermometers of NBS calibration or calibrated against a precision melting point standard.

Water baths used for turbidimetric assays should be checked daily by checking the temperature with a calibrated thermometer and checking the circulation using the manufacturer's instruction.

Temperature of both incubators and refrigerators should be checked daily using a calibrated thermometer and checking the temperature in various areas to assure that it is uniform throughout.

Automatic pipetting machines used for dispensing measured quantities of melted agar and broth in microbiological assays should be checked whenever used to ensure that the volumes delivered are accurate and uniform.

Media for microbiological assays should never be used the same day of preparation. Representative flasks from different batches of media should be incubated at appropriate temperatures for 24–48 hours and sterility assured before such media are used for analytical testing.

B. Controls on Analytical Tests

1. General

A laboratory testing a large volume and variety of samples has built-in controls. For example, if the laboratory is performing the microbiological assay of ten different batches of tetracycline capsules, and one batch assays 80% of label while all other batches assay 100 to 105% of label, the nine latter batches serve as controls to indicate that the basic assay itself is apparently satisfactory. However, if only the first batch were assayed, and there were no other controls, the QC analyst would have no assurance that the low potency might not be due to a misdilution or some other laboratory error.

It is impossible to list or describe all controls that the antibiotic QC laboratory should maintain. However, a few of the most pertinent will be described.

2. Microbiological Assay

1. Freshly prepared reference standard stock solutions should be assayed against the previous stock solution.

2. Standard stock solutions should be prepared to contain varying percentages of usual concentrations, e.g., if the method requires a stock solution of 1000 μg/ml, additional solutions should be prepared to contain 800 μg/ml and 1200 μg/ml. The supervisor should distribute portions of all three stock solutions labeled 1000 μg/ml to the analysts. The subsequent assay results will disclose the ability of the assay to detect varying concentrations and/or the reliability of the analyst.

For assays for penicillin contamination, both positive and negative controls should be assayed, i.e., diluents such as buffers and water should be assayed to assure they are negative; a minimal concentration of the penicillin reference standard should be assayed to assure the method will detect low concentrations of penicillin.

3. Biological Tests

a. Pyrogen Test

1. A test should be performed using a solution such as pyrogen-free saline as a negative control.

2. A test should be performed using a sample known to be pyrogenic material as a positive control. See Section VII, A of this article.

b. Safety Test

1. A test should be performed using an innocuous material such as physiological saline as a negative control.

2. A test should be performed using an LD_{50} concentration of a chemical such as sodium citrate or any other suitable compound as a positive control.

c. Histamine Test

1. A test should be performed using an inactive material such as physiological saline as a negative control.
2. A test should be performed using an antibiotic solution plus a concentration of the histamine standard as a positive control.

4. Sterility Tests

1. Plates should be exposed as described in Section VII, A of this article as a check on the environment.
2. In addition an air sampler such as a Reynier Slit Sampler should be used for sampling the air under laminar-flow hoods and in other locations of the sterile area. The Reynier Sampler uses a 150-mm diameter petri plate with approximately 50 ml of their blood agar or nutrient agar for recovering microorganisms. The plates should be incubated at 30–32° C, and the results recorded in a notebook to establish records of microbiological content of the environment from day to day.
3. As an additional control on the efficacy of laminar-flow hoods, sterile membranes in a manifold or additional filtration units connected to a vacuum source should be exposed to the laminar airflow for approximately 30 minutes. The membranes should then be transferred aseptically to tubes containing thioglycollate broth and SBCD broth, respectively, which should be incubated at appropriate temperatures for 7 days and then examined for microbial growth.
4. A portion from a representative sample of each sterilizer load of diluting fluids should be filtered through a membrane filter using the forceps, funnels, cutters, and manifolds used for the day's work. The membrane filter should then be incubated as described for an official test and the tubes examined for growth. This serves as a control, not only for the diluting fluid, but also for the entire system used for membrane filtration tests.
5. As a control on media, biological indicators using *Bacillus stereothermophilus* spores impregnated on paper strips or enclosed in ampuls should be included in each sterilizer load. Previous experiments should have been conducted to demonstrate the number of spores required. Broth tubes containing these biological indicators should then be incubated for seven days at 55° C. The entire sterilizer load should be rejected if any control tubes shows growth after incubation.
6. As a positive control, i.e., to demonstrate that there is nothing in the testing system that will inhibit growth, an analyst should inoculate one or more flasks of diluting fluid with a low inoculum of a test organism such as *Bacillus subtilus* and then use this diluting fluid for performing both

membrane filtration and direct method tests. After incubation, growth should be observed in the tubes. It must be stressed that the performance of this control test should be in an area other than the sterile area, since microorganisms should not be introduced into the latter.

7. Bacterial membranes should be subjected to a microbiological quality control evaluation as described by Bowman *et al.* (1967).

5. *Chemical Tests*

As in the other laboratories, specially prepared test solutions should be used for checking the accuracy of the various tests. Following are some of the most pertinent:

a. Karl Fischer Moisture Test. Test one or more hydrated compounds and compare the theoretical water content to the result obtained.

b. Crystallinity. Test an amorphous material as a negative control and a crystalline material as a positive control.

c. Tetracycline Absorptivity. Since the absorptivity levels of tetracycline phosphate, tetracycline hydrochloride, and tetracycline base are significantly different from one another, unlabeled samples of each should be given to the analyst as a check on both the test system and his analysis.

d. Disintegration Test. Use samples of enteric-coated tablets as negative controls, since they should not disintegrate in gastric juice, and use samples of soluble tablets as positive controls.

e. Infrared and Ultraviolet Identity. The laboratory should maintain spectra of each antibiotic reference standard—these permanent records, available for comparison to daily tests serve as controls.

f. Specific Rotation. USP dextrose and another USP-grade compound should be checked periodically.

g. Melting Point. USP melting point standards should be checked periodically.

h. Heavy Metals. A lead solution of known concentration should be checked periodically.

i. General.

The *Antibiotic Regulations* do not specify controls as a general rule. Therefore the tests described in this section serve as guides rather than absolute directives. Any test that will properly demonstrate precision, accuracy, and analyst reliability will suffice. For example, samples that have been previously analyzed and for which repetitive tests have demonstrated accurage analysis might be retained and periodically retested as a check on the laboratory's reproducibility. However, such samples should be stable. For example, potency of procaine penicillin in oil is relatively stable, and an accurately assayed vial of this material can be retained as a control. Conversely, crystalline potassium penicillin G that has been reconstituted in water is relatively unstable, and would not serve as a reliable control for continued use.

One can positively state that antibiotics reaching the consumer in the United States are of the highest quality. This is due and will continue to be due to the type of quality control and assurance described in this article.

References

Anonymous (1965). "Procedures for Detecting Penicillin Contamination in Drugs." Division of Antibiotics and Insulin Certification, U.S. Food and Drug Administration, Washington, D.C.

Blakely, J. (1969). Private communication.

Bowman, F. W. (1968). *Bull. Parenteral Drug Ass.* **22**, 57.

Bowman, F. W. (1969). *J. Pharm. Sci.* **58**, 1301.

Bowman, F. W., Calhoun, M. P., and White, M. (1967). *J. Pharm. Sci.* **56**, 222.

Bowman, F. W., White, M., and Lyles, R. L. (1972). *J. Pharm. Sci.* (in press).

Castor, G. B., Kantor, N., Knoll, E., Blakely, J., Nielsen, J. K., Randolph, J. D., and Kirshbaum, A. (1971). *J. Pharm. Sci.* **60**, 1578.

Clements, N. L. (1968). *J. Ass. Offic. Anal. Chem.* **53**, 219.

Federal Food, Drug and Cosmetic Act as Amended (1969). Sect. 507. Superintendent of Documents, U.S. Govt. Printing Office, Washington, D.C.

Federal Register (1971). 133.11 (e)(1), p. 605.

Federal Standard No. 209A (1963). "Clean Room and Work Station Requirements, Controlled Environment." General Services Administration, Business Service Center, Washington, D.C.

Kallings, L., and Everfeldt, F. (1965). Final Report of the 1964 Inquiry by the Royal Swedish Medical Board into Microbial Contamination of Medical Preparations, Stockholm, Sweden.

Kirshbaum, A., Arret, B., and Kramer, J. (1956). *Antibiot. Chemother. (Washington, D.C.)* **6**, 660.

Kuzel, N. R., and Kavenagh, F. W. (1972). *J. Pharm. Sci.* (in press).

Lane, J., and Weiss, P. (1966). *Automat. Anal. Chem., Technicon Symposia, 1965* Vol. I, p. 224.

NASA Standards NHB 5340.2 for Clean Rooms and Work Stations for the Microbially Controlled Environment (1967). Superintendent of Documents, U.S. Govt. Printing Office, Washington, D.C.

Rippere, R. A., and Arret, B. (1972). "An Automated Turbidimetric Microbiological Readout System" (in press).

Supreme Court of the United States (1969). United States v. Bacto-Undisks, No. 343, October Term, 1968.

USP (1970a). "United States Pharmacopeia," 18th rev. ed., pp. 867–882. Mack Publ. Co., Easton, Pennsylvania.
USP (1970b). "United States Pharmacopeia," 18th rev. ed., p. 864. Mack Publ. Co., Easton, Pennsylvania.
USP (1970c). "United States Pharmacopeia," 18th rev. ed., p. 832. Mack Publ. Co., Easton, Pennsylvania.
USP (1970d). "United States Pharmacopeia," 18th rev. ed., p. 800 and pp. 846–851. Mack Publ. Co., Easton, Pennsylvania.

DESIGN OF FACILITIES

G. Briggs Phillips and Robert S. Runkle

Becton, Dickinson Research Center,
Raleigh, North Carolina

I. Introduction

The quality of the many thousands of products produced by the drug industry depends in no small part on the adequacy of facilities in which they are manufactured, packaged, and stored. Industrial firms engaged in these activities have long been leaders in the design of facilities and adequate techniques for product quality control. As examples, drug firms were among the

*Present address: Research Triangle Park, North Carolina 27709

first to employ modern day air-handling and air-filtration systems, glove and transfer cabinets, and germicidal ultraviolet radiation. In recent years, the needs of the aerospace program for environmental control methods, monitoring techniques, and improved design criteria have stimulated further advancement of the state-of-the-art of facility design for improved quality control. The drug industry, as well as many other industries, has benefited from this new knowledge by utilizing it in the design and construction of new facilities.

This article on design of facilities is not intended to be a complete treatise on the subject but to present selected information on facility design and planning and to provide selected design criteria of the type most appropriate to the production of high-quality products. Emphasis is placed on the need for monitoring the environmental control aspects of facilities and the interrelationships that exist between the facility and the people working in it. Finally, the bibliography presented should provide a useful reference source for those desiring to acquire additional information on particular subjects.

To the extent that it can be expected that environmental control measures needed in the drug industry will become more exacting in the future, even more careful consideration of facility design parameters is indicated. It is evident that new techniques for environmental control will be developed and that these will be put to use as needed in the drug industry. It follows, therefore, that any investment in new facilities should be made only after careful analysis of the subject matter of this chapter.

II. Facility Design, Planning, and Selection

Whether the contemplated project is the design of a new facility or the remodeling of an old one, the first step should be the selection of a planning team to furnish a description of all activities expected to take place in the proposed facility (National Institute of Health, 1962). Because the number of personnel, equipment, space allocations, design specifications, environmental control criteria, and other requirements will be based on this description, care should be given to the appointment of competent people to describe each function. The team should then use these functional descriptions as a basis for formulating basic policy decisions concerning control techniques, methods, and procedures and for the drafting of the program of requirements.

A program of requirements is a detailed analysis of all current and projected needs of a facility. There are various guides (National Institute of Health, 1968a) to the preparation of a Program of Requirements but, essentially, it is a description of the functions to be housed in the facility, the space required, and the cost estimate. Functions refer to managerial, research, production, and support activities. The type and extent of these functions, considered in conjunction with federal, state, and local regulations, determine the site requirements, the design criteria, and the environmental control criteria for internal and external environments. The architectural engineering firm needs all the data available for the preparation of the building program.

Some points to be considered in the selection of a site are the soil conditions and the seismic state of the area, the reliability of the water and electricity sources, the effect of the prevailing air and water pollutants on plant processes, and the effect of plant operations on the ecology of the community. Auxiliary sources of water and electricity sufficient to assure safety of personnel, community, equipment, processes, and products should be planned in case of failure of community supplies (Walter Kidde Constructors, Inc., 1965).

Since flexibility and economy of space and costs are essential to change and efficiency in biological production and research, careful attention should be given to the design of a facility planning module. This is defined as the smallest repetitive unit of space needed for a unit of production, an independent operation or control function (Snow, 1963). Architects and planners who have these basic units to work with can create and rearrange floor layouts with ease during the design stage (Walter Kidde Constructors, Inc., 1965; Runkle and Phillips, 1969). If the module plan is not used, later changes may be difficult and costly.

The program requirements and policies of the organization determine the optimal dimensions of the module and the materials used in its construction (Snow, 1963). A typical example for a laboratory unit is that of the rectangular module incorporating a double work depth designed for biomedical use (Fig. 1). This configuration is applicable in those situations in which laboratory furnishings can be aligned with the walls leaving the center length free for work activities.

The width of the net area (usable space) is limited to the depth of the equipment in the module and the passing and working aisle. Some standards for aisle depth are listed in Table I. Length of usable space is obtained by measuring the wall space needed for benches, sinks, hoods, and other items necessary for the operations to be conducted. In Fig. 1 these dimensions are referred to as design bench length and work depth.

The sharing of a common aisle makes the double work depth unit more economical than the single work unit or one in which bench space is allotted to the center area. The gross area of the module includes the net area plus unusable space taken up by wall thicknesses, connecting doors, windows, columns, pipe chases, utility curbs, and similar encroachments. In general, a favorable net-to-gross ratio is maintained by increasing modular length rather than modular width. An increase in modular length results in the

TABLE I

Aisle Widths, Based on Anthropometric Data for Average and Large Men[a]

Activities in aisle opposite each other	Dimensions[b]	
	Average men	Large men
One working (sitting or standing) and one passing	43.2 in.—adequate for normal-sized people only	48.1 in.—adequate for all subjects
One working and one rising from sitting to standing position (18 in. allowed for chair)	57.4 in.—not quite adequate	63.2 in.—considered adequate
One working and one bending (36 in. allowed for average bending)	43.2 in.—adequate for normal-sized people only	48.1 in.—adequate for all subjects
Two working and one passing	61.9 in.—60 in. inadequate	69.2 in.—66 in. considered adequate

[a]Based on table in Runkle and Phillips (1969).
[b]3 in. allowed between people while stationary and on either side of those passing.

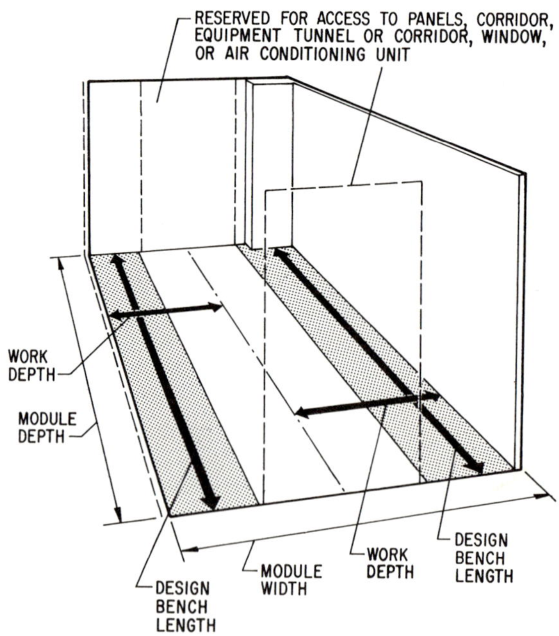

Fig. 1. *Space elements of building module.*

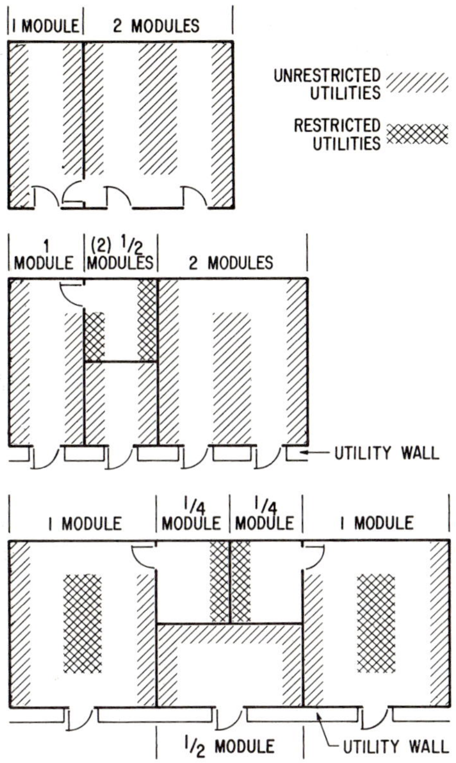

Fig. 2. *Variations of planning modules.*

addition of less unusable footage than an increase in modular width. Setting the module perpendicular to the corridor keeps corridor length to a minimum and reduces servicing and maintenance expenses.

Single modules can be subdivided into special purpose areas or combined to form suites; suites can be converted to single modules. Some possible arrangements are shown in Fig. 2 (Runkle and Phillips, 1969). The degree of flexibility attainable will depend on a distribution of service and support installations within the module that will allow addition of partitions and door connections without major reconstruction or unnecessary relocation of utilities.

Mobile laboratory units, self-sufficient except for water and electricity sources, have been described in several recent publications (Griffith, 1964; Matson and Baldwin, 1969). In both instances, semitrailers for infectious disease research were designed and tested. These units included air balance and filtration systems, primary and secondary barrier systems for internal environmental control, and decontamination systems for maintaining external environmental integrity. Additional prototypes of relocatable laboratory modules, based upon prefabrication techniques, are currently under evaluation at the National Cancer Institute.

The mobility of a laboratory or control facility is an unusual specification for the drug industry but it is interesting to note that such units are feasible and may be useful as temporary production units or laboratories for the drug firms during expansion.

The pharmaceutical industry is continuously concerned with the control of contamination: contamination of experimental animals, products, and cultures by extraneous microorganisms, other products, organic and inorganic particles, liquids, and gases; contamination of personnel and by personnel; contamination of people, animals, plants, air, water, soil, etc. outside the facility (J. H. Brewer and Phillips, 1971). There should be sufficient flexibility in the design of the facility to provide the needed control and yet to allow for changes in staff, in production or research activities and materials, and in legal rulings without undue disruption and expense. For example, a change in the method of animal inoculation from the use of a noninfectious microorganism to a highly infectious agent could result in large expenditures and regrettable loss in time if the distribution of utilities and ventilation and air-conditioning systems have not been judiciously planned.

The layout of the functional zones within a facility is a significant factor in the establishment and maintenance of environmentol control (Phillips and Runkle, 1967). A plant, for example can be divided into five major functional zones: the clean zone, and production/laboratory zone, the animal zone, the engineering support zone, and the production/laboratory support zone. The isolation of various sections or areas by functions can simplify environmental control by means of structural containment and regulation of traffic, material transport, and airflow. Figure 3 illustrates these five zones.

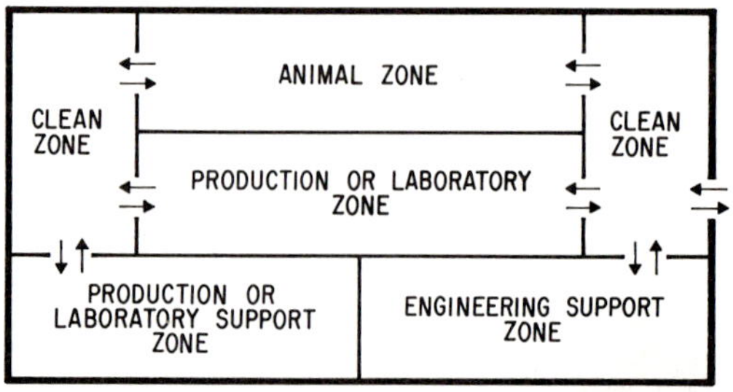

Fig. 3. *Functional zones of hypothetical production facility or laboratory.*

The clean zone houses the entrance area, administrative offices, libraries, cafeterias, shipping, receiving and clean storage areas, transitional rooms, and other activities that do not require a protected environment. Transitional rooms provide change rooms containing showers, toilets, and storage space for clothing. Germicidal ultraviolet (UV) and other barriers can be used to control the transfer of contamination from one zone to another. Ethylene oxide gas chambers, UV air locks, and other double-access devices may be installed for passing materials and equipment between zones. Viewing panels and speaking diaphragms can be incorporated in doors and walls for communication between protected and nonprotected zones. Transitional spaces, such as air locks, can be placed wherever a transference of materials or people occurs between protected and nonprotected areas and between areas where cross-contamination is possible.

The production and laboratory zone is a protected area and may contain offices, toilet facilities, cold rooms, incubation rooms, instrument rooms, controlled and/or isolated production spaces, in addition to laboratories and transitional rooms. Intelligent selection and use of primary barriers for containment of materials at their point of use cannot be overemphasized: The less the dispersion of contaminants from their point of origin, the less will be the complexity of the secondary barriers required and the greater the safety for products and personnel. Primary barriers are devices designed to prevent, absolutely or partially, the spread and materials to or from the atmosphere immediately surrounding a procedure or unit of work. Some examples of these primary barriers are closed-vial filling machines, closed-tablet machines, ventilated animal cages, laminar downflow cabinets or laminar-flow production areas. Secondary barriers prevent the spread of contaminants into or out of large units of the facility (zones). Air filters, UV air locks, and differential air pressures and other such building features are commonly used secondary barriers.

The production and laboratory support zone may be located in either a protected or nonprotected area depending on the type of work being performed. If the greatest protection attainable is desired for a product or procedure or if highly infectious microorganisms are being handled, then the support zone should be separated and placed in an unprotected area. Otherwise, it may be more practical to include the support activities in the protected area. Rooms for washing and sterilizing glassware and other equipment, storage, preparation of raw materials, culture media, and similar uses are often housed in an unprotected zone.

The animal zone may consist of rooms for animal inoculation, autopsy, incineration, infected-animal holding, washing and sterilizing of equipment, breeding, and exercise. Again, the separation of these functions into protected and nonprotected areas will depend on the procedures being conducted. In some instances, the most practical arrangement may be the provision of a separate building for animals; this sometimes is required by a regulation. Maintenance requirements for animals with unusual needs, large animals, a wide range in species, or simply large numbers of animals, may be more efficiently fulfilled in a central location apart from the main facility. Details concerning various aspects of animal facility design have recently been published (Graham and Feenstra, 1957; Crossman and Elsea, 1961; Faust, 1962; Hill, 1962; N. R. Brewer, 1964; Fox, 1964; Kraft *et al.*, 1964; Runkle, 1964; Jonas, 1965; Institute and Laboratory Animal Resources, 1965).

The engineering support zone houses the pipes, ducts, pumps, blowers, and filters, the liquid waste system, and most of the air-handling systems. The reliability of engineering support activities is vital to the operation of the facility. Redundant equipment may be necessary for use in case of failure of components indispensable to the effectiveness of contamination barriers. This zone may account for over half the cost and space allotted to the entire facility. A cardinal point in favor of the "zone" concept for the design of facilities for the drug industry is that it provides for the most efficient expenditure of construction money. The concept allows the identification of the most critical and most expensive areas of the facility and the separation of less critical functions into zones for which the net construction cost per square foot will be less.

After the presentation of the program of requirements to the selected architectural engineering firm, the planning team should not be disbanded; if they continue to participate in the planning, design, review, inspection, and activation stages, costly changes may be precluded and the transition from the old facility to the new can be made more efficiently. The selection of this planning team and the identification of one individual from it and the architectural engineering firm as focal points for all communication can contribute appreciably to the success of the project (Crossman and Elsea, 1961). A summary of the planning functions required for the facility director, the planning team, and the architectural engineering firm is presented in Fig. 4.

III. Selected Design Criteria

Environmental control implies the harnessing of hazardous materials to the extent that their absence or presence at specific locations can be regulated. While perfect control may never be attainable, the degree to which control is to be achieved can be estimated accurately. Initially, then, all risks and problems associated with quality control in the drug industry must be

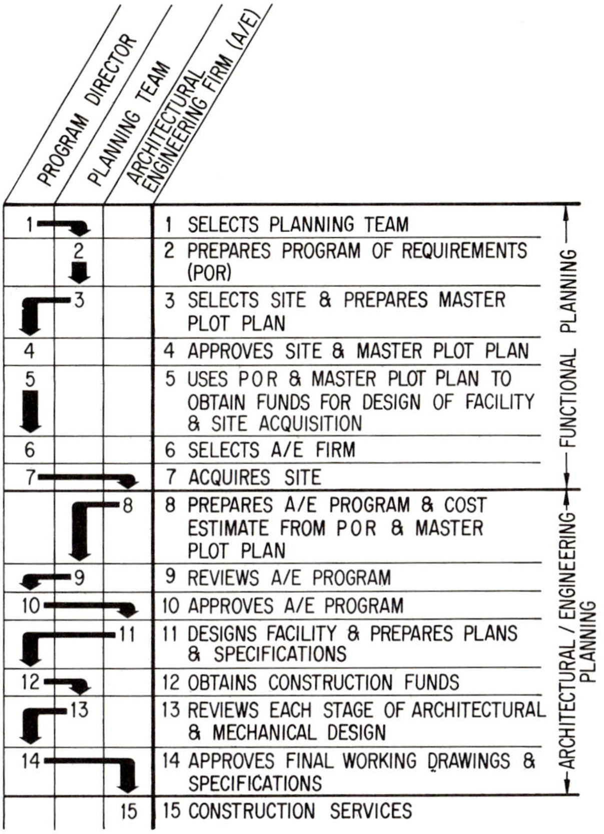

Fig. 4. *Outline of planning responsibilities.*

identified and defined as precisely as possible. Literature searches, visits to other facilities, and exercise of the imagination should enable the planning team to choose an appropriate combination of barrier techniques. These "techniques" should be designed to maintain an acceptable level of environmental control under ordinary circumstances and to forestall widespread contamination when breakdowns and accidents occur. Air filtration, direction of airflow, water and sewage treatment, UV irradiation, and laminar-flow techniques are typical barrier systems widely used in securing control.

Barrier systems are set up to prevent or limit the migration of contaminants from one area to another. Primary barriers are those designed to retain or exclude contaminants from the immediate production area or critical space within the quality-control laboratory. Secondary barriers are intended to prevent the spread of contaminants to or from the space and surfaces immediately surrounding the primary barriers. As stated in the previous section on facility design, the more effective the primary barrier systems are, the less elaborate the secondary barrier systems, and thus the building, need be. Treatment of supplies through sterilizers, air through filtration or incineration, or liquid waste with heat or chemicals will always be less costly when the waste matter originates from a smaller primary barrier enclosure (Phillips and Runkle, 1967). Primary barriers frequently are designed to provide gastight enclosures with controlled entrance and from which there can be no escape of contaminants. The systems vary in size and complexity according to the requirements of the operations being performed. In some instances, entire rooms for assembling medical products serve as primary barriers, as shown in Fig. 5. Other applications of primary barriers have been for production of germ-free animals, isolation of patients, or gastight biological safety cabinet systems incorporating a complex array of primary and secondary barrier features as illustrated in Fig. 6. Materials may be moved in and out of barriers through air locks, double-door autoclaves, dunk baths and other means that prevent exchange of contaminants. Closed ventilated animal cages, safety blendor bowls, and closed centrifuge cups are examples of less complex absolute barriers.

Fig. 5. *Large laminar airflow for manufacture of medical devices. Photo courtesy of Becton, Dickinson and Co.*

Fig. 6. *Total containment system for animal testing. Photo courtesy of U.S. Army.*

Partial barriers may be used wherever absolute isolation is not obligatory. However, precautions must be taken to prevent excessive escape or entrance of contaminants when ventilation systems fail. Also, personnel must be trained to work without creating excessive disturbance of air patterns. Laminar-flow benches, fume hoods, and negative pressure safety cabinets can all serve as partial barriers. The open panel laminar flow cabinet shown in Fig. 7 offers protection for both product and personnel by the control of internal and external air flow patterns. Figure 8 illustrates the use of a down-flow laminar unit over an aseptic packaging operation.

Secondary barriers include all structures and equipment surrounding primary barriers that aid in preventing the spread of contaminants escaping from primary barriers. Materials used in the construction of floors, ceilings, walls, ducts, and furnishings should be impervious and resistant to any decontaminating agents employed. There should be no surface crevices to harbor hazardous materials. Watertight seals should be made to floor, wall, and ceiling surfaces wherever fixed equipment is installed. Many pharmaceutical firms use standards proposed by the Federal Standard No. 209A (1966) and the NASA Standards NHB 5340.2 (1967) for air cleanliness standards (see Table II).

These standards can be applied for the establishment of air cleanliness criteria in production and quality-control areas. Supply air for animal and

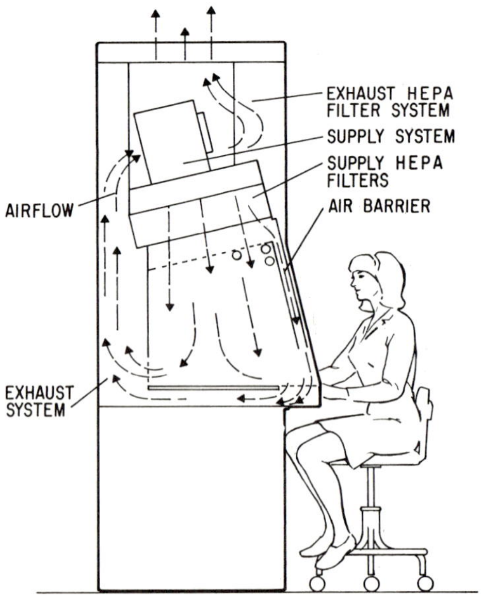

Fig. 7. *A laminar-airflow biological cabinet.*

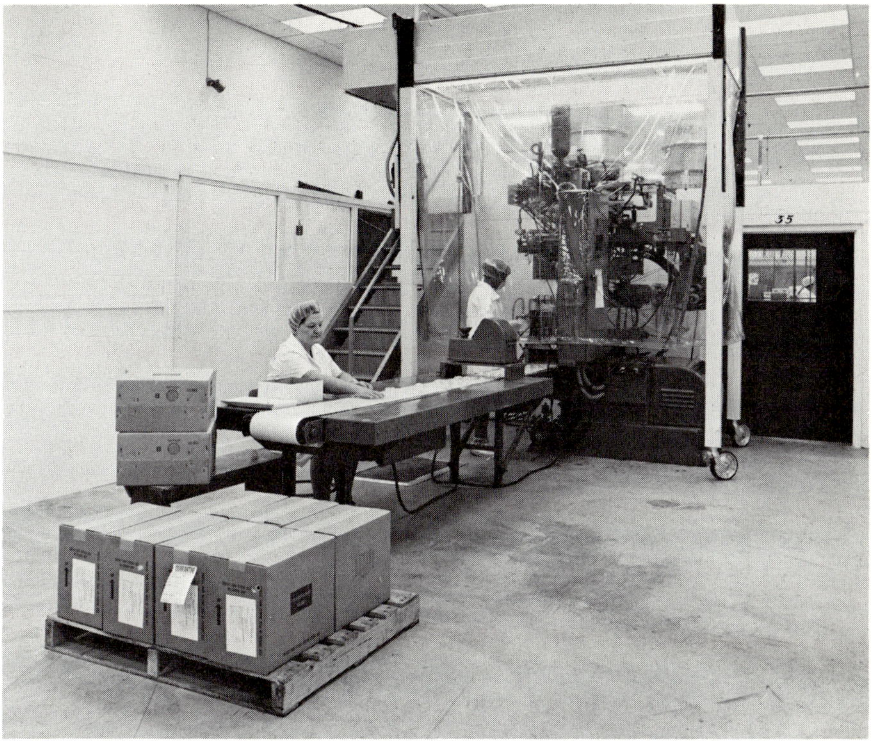

Fig. 8. *Portable downflow laminar unit over an aseptic packaging operation. Photo courtesy of IVERS-LEE, Division of Becton, Dickinson and Co.*

TABLE II

Air Cleanliness Classes

Class	Maximum number of particles 0.5 μ and larger per cu. ft	Maximum number of particles 5 μ and larger per cu. ft	Maximum number of viable particles per ft	Average number of viable of particles per sq. ft per week
100	100	[a]	0.1	1,200
10,000	10,000	65	0.5	6,000
100,000	100,000	700	2.5	30,000

[a]Counts below 10 particles per cubic foot are unreliable except when a large number of samplings are taken.

laboratory rooms should ideally be a single-pass, nonrecirculating system (Norman, 1965). To prevent cross-contamination and recirculation of odors and contaminants, each room should have air supply and exhaust systems separate from the other rooms. This one-pass air handling system is especially advantageous when an accident occurs because it makes possible the isolation of the area of the accident for decontamination without interference with the functioning of surrounding areas. However, for economical reasons, it is recognized that many geographical considerations sometimes preclude this approach. A compromise using 100% "fresh" air for animal rooms with filtered recirculated air in laboratories and production units has proved satisfactory in many instances. Movement of air under normal operating conditions should be directed from clean to less-clean spaces by progressively decreasing air pressures. "Fresh" air intakes should be located upwind and as far as practicable from exhaust ducts.

Today, "fresh" air as well as exhaust air will probably contain a variety of contaminants. The most economical method for the removal of particulates is air filtration, which is adequate in most circumstances. Air filtration techniques have been discussed extensively in the literature (Decker *et al.*, 1962); a classification of these devices by their efficiencies are presented in Table III.

TABLE III

Efficiency Range of Devices for Removing Biological Particles (1–5 μ) from Air

Cleaning device	Bacterial removal to be expected (%)
Ultrahigh-efficiency filters	99.99+
High-efficiency filters	90–99
Medium-efficiency filters	60–90
Roughing filters: fibrous, metallic, oiled, and screen types	10–60
Electrostatic precipitators	60–90
Air washers and scrubbers (low-pressure-drop type)	20–90

Absolute filters (HEPA filters) have been shown to have an efficiency of 99.999% for removal of biological particles of a size of less than 0.1 μ in diameter. Low-efficiency filters inserted upstream can prolong the usefulness of higher efficiency filters by removing the preponderance of larger particles and a fraction of smaller particles before they reach the more expensive filters. Filters should be fitted in ducts with tight seals. When infectious agents are involved, filters should be decontaminated before removal. The exhaust air can be diverted through a bypass filter by means of gasketed, gastight dampers located in a dual plenum at the filtration point during the filter changing process (Runkle and Phillips, 1967). After decontaminating materials have evaporated through the system, maintenance personnel can safely replace the used filters. To prevent a reverse airflow due to mechanical or electrical failure, all exhaust fans in contaminated areas (including those in primary barriers such as cabinets) should be interlocked with supply fans so that the failure of one will automatically stop the operation of the other. Redundant fans, motors, and electrical generators should be available for immediate replacement in critical areas. The effectiveness of incinerator and air filtration systems must be tested periodically.

The type of operation to be performed in the facility will determine the need for the extent of additional exhaust air treatment. Obviously, if the process involves production of infectious, toxic, caustic, flammable, noxious, or other hazardous substances, some final treatment of the exhaust will be required. Increased awareness of such problems by consumers and the federal government undoubtedly will result in more restrictive air pollution control measures at local, state, and national levels. It may be necessary to employ such devices as adsorbent beds, scrubbers, electrostatic precipitators, or other more expensive pollution control devices. Careful review of the process involved, the appropriate pollution control regulation, and the possible future requirements at the design stage should minimize the total cost of the facility.

For maximum comfort and flexibility, individual room temperature and humidity controls are recommended; there is not only a wide variation in heat production in different production operations, laboratories, and animal areas, but also a great fluctuation in the amount of heat produced within single rooms. Air change rate, humidity, and temperature parameters at any specific location will depend on the requirements of the particular activities. For instance, some species of animals are very susceptible to temperature changes. Their quarters and other sensitive areas should have emergency provisions for heating and cooling failures. Several recent publications discuss air-conditioning systems in detail (Norman, 1965; Ryan *et al.*, 1967; Harstad *et al.*, 1967; National Institute of Health, 1968a, b).

One of the most effective methods of maintaining control of contaminants in pharmaceutical operations involves the use of laminar flow techniques. Laminar flow of air is the unidirectional movement of the entire body of air within an enclosure along parallel lines at uniform velocity. Airborne particles are very effectively swept along in the laminar flow. Settling rates in horizontal laminar flow for particles ranging from 2 to 104 μ in diameter are shown in Table IV.

TABLE IV

Settling Rates of Sand and Clay Particles (Specific Gravity 2.65) in Laminar Airflow

Particle diameter, (μ)	Approximate floating distance (feet) of particles while falling 3 ft in cross-drafts of	
	60 fpm	90 fpm
104	1.1	1.66
76	2.0	3.1
53	4.3	6.4
40	7.5	11.3
20	30.0	45.0
10	120.0	180.0
2	> 750.0	> 1100.0

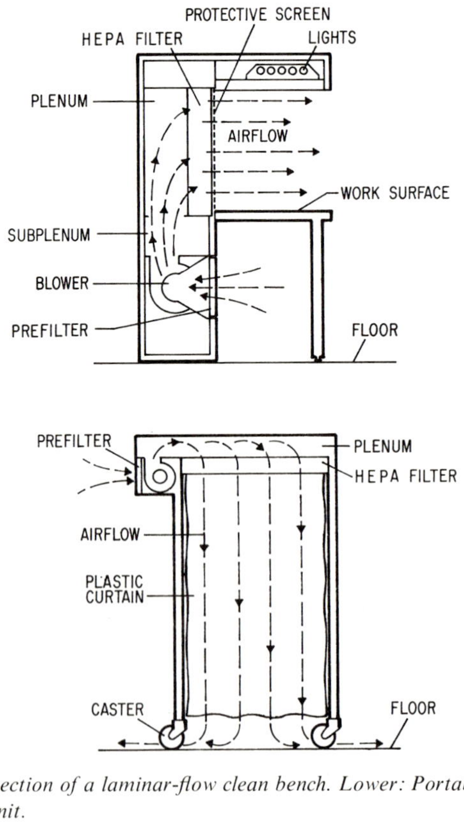

Fig. 9. *Upper: Cross section of a laminar-flow clean bench. Lower: Portable curtained downflow laminar-flow unit.*

Two diagrams of laminar-flow clean benches, one representing horizontal flow and the other representing a portable downflow unit, are presented in Fig. 9. The clean air entraps contaminants in the air stream and any turbulence caused by obstacles in its path is generally eliminated by the streamlining effect in a short distance (Whitfield and Morris, 1970). Judicious arrangement of equipment and control of personnel movements within the enclosed space is necessary for optimal protection. Laminar-flow devices and rooms are useful to the pharmaceutical industry in such operations as preparation of aliquot samples, siliconing containers, filling and packaging, chemical assay of antibiotics, bulk manufacturing, sterile filtration, and tissue culture work. A recent comparison of settling plate counts in laminar-flow cabinets and in turbulent clean rooms indicates that the use of laminar flow results in significantly fewer microorganisms settling out (Phillips, 1969) (see Table V).

TABLE V

Settling Plate Counts in a Laminar-Flow Hood and a Clean Room

Comparison	No. of plates exposed[a]	No. of colonies recovered	Significance
Room A laminar-flow hood	804	24	Highly significant
Room A clean room	786	1339	
Room B laminar-flow hood	775	14	Highly significant
Room B clean room	770	1141	

[a]Each plate exposed for 3.5 to 4.0 hours.

Germicidal UV radiation is useful as an adjunct to sterilization and decontamination procedures and is frequently used in maintaining separation between various critical areas in a clean production facility or in a laboratory area. The radiant energy dose required for inactivation varies with the nature of the microorganisms present (Phillips and Hanel, 1960) (see Table VI).

In general, spore forms require longer exposure than vegetative cells. The spectrum of radiation most destructive to bacteria is 2200–3000 Å with a peak effect at 2650 Å. Ultraviolet lamps available commercially emit rays at 2537 Å. Radiation at this wavelength has limited penetrating ability and is only partially effective for air and surface decontamination. Clumps of microorganisms and those shielded by dust and other debris are not destroyed. Any collection of dust, oil, and other extraneous matter on the bulbs will absorb the germicidal rays and must be removed periodically.

TABLE VI

Typical LD_{50} *Values for Representative Organisms*

Organism	LD_{50} (ergs/mm^2) (254 mμ)
Bacteria	
Escherichia coli	44–208
Micrococcus candicans	341
Pseudomonas pyocyanea	291
Staphylococcus aureus	86–275
Serratia marcescens	57
Fungi	
Saccharomyces cereviseae (dark)	503–900
Saccharomyces cereviseae (light)	1400
Neurospora crassa, microconidia (dark)	370
Neurospora crassa, microconidia (light)	1024
Neurospora crassa, microconidia (dark)	1440
Neurospora crassa, microconidia (light)	3000
Protozoa	
Amoeba proteus (dark)	2160

Since output of the germicidal radiation from ultraviolet lamps cannot be detected visually, checking of the lamps at regular intervals with a meter which registers the appropriate wavelength is required.

Ultraviolet radiation is used successfully in lowering viable counts of microorganisms in transfer air locks, safety cabinets, animal rooms, clean rooms (see Fig. 10), and other areas. Personnel working under direct radiation must be protected by appropriate shielding of face, eyes, and other exposed areas.

Pure water has only a momentary existence. Contaminants present should be identified by chemical and biological analysis. The nature and amount of impurities acceptable will vary with the purpose for which the water is used. Several recent articles provide information on methods of purifying and distributing water (Smith, 1964; Haight, 1972). Regular checking of the degree of purity and biological quality of the water is recommended.

Breaktank devices or backflow preventors should be installed in the water supply between control facilities and the central water supply to prevent accidental contamination by reverse water flow (Runkle and Phillips, 1969). Water supplied to safety showers, personnel showers, wash basins, water stills, and drinking fountains should come directly from the water main, bypassing the breaktank or backflow preventor. Safety showers should be installed within easy reach of chemical fume hoods and at other strategic locations. They should be operable by chain pulls, and drinking fountains

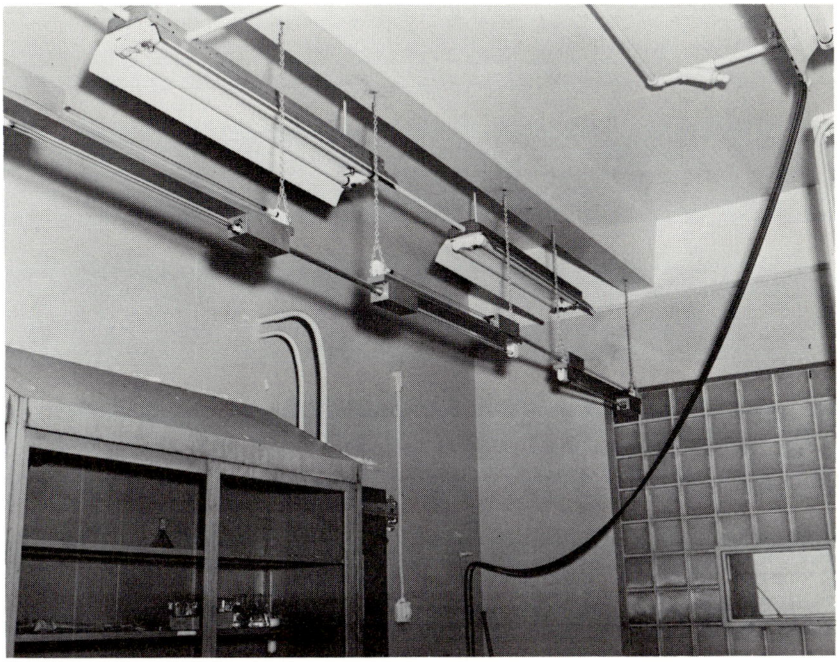

Fig. 10. *Germicidal UV lamps installed in a laboratory room. Photo courtesy of U.S. Army.*

should be foot-operated for safety purposes. When infectious microorganisms are to be used there should be one hot water system downstream from the breaktank to serve the contaminated area and another hot water system upstream from the breaktank to serve the clean areas.

Floor drains should be installed in all areas where liquid disinfectants will be used for washing walls, floors, and furnishings. They should be deep enough to prevent negative pressure from pulling the traps. Piped priming water should be supplied to each trap or some arrangement made to assure that the traps do not dry out. When drains are not in use, they should be closed with screw-type plugs. Floor drains in animal rooms should be the nonclog, bucket type to handle animal hair and other debris. Sewage from contaminated area drains, including shower drains in the contaminated change rooms, should run into the sewage treatment facility.

Various methods of sewage sterilization are discussed in a recent publication (Runkle and Phillips, 1969). The most reliable and efficient method is the constant-flow, heat-exchanger sterilization system (see Fig. 11). Contaminated sewage flows by gravity to a holding tank which should be located in a watertight pit large enough to accommodate all untreated sewage in the

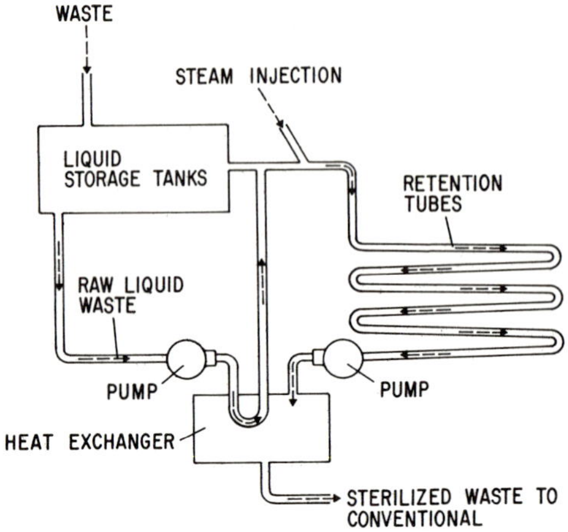

Fig. 11. *Constant-flow, heat-exchanger liquid waste sterilization system.*

system if the tank ruptures or a valve leaks. The second pump in the system is a safety measure added to prevent contaminated sewage from leaking into the sterile sewage if a leak occurs between the tube and shell side of the heat exchanger. Samples should be taken regularly from the discharge line for sterility testing. Air exhausted from this area should be passed through a filtration system. All precautions applicable to personnel safety in contaminated areas should be provided for the maintenance crew.

IV. Facility Monitoring

During the construction of the facility, the owner should require that the contractor submit all materials, parts, subsystems, and systems along with a certificate of compliance with design drawings and specifications to the architects and engineers or to the planners for approval (Runkle and Phillips, 1969). Constant vigilance is required to maintain the integrity of the secondary barrier, particularly by the inspection of masonry, metal surfaces, sealing techniques, plumbing and ductwork, and routine cleaning as the work progresses (Ballard, 1971). After construction is completed, the mechanical performance of the various systems incorporated for maintaining environmental control should be verified before final acceptance.

Surfaces of walls, floors, and ceilings should be free of troweling buildups, loose particles, and excess moisture, and should be nonporous (Runkle and Phillips, 1969). Cracks, leaks, and joints should not be sealed by taping or caulking but by the compression of a suitable gasketing material. Heli-arc welding is the preferred method for sealing ultrahigh efficiency filter frames to ductwork. Outlets and other penetrations should be internally sealed and isolated from the external environment by silicone rubber mastic. All metal surfaces including plumbing and ductwork should be anodized or treated by prime and seal methods that will prevent the shedding of rust, scale, and oxides. Careful application of epoxy coatings is acceptable for most surface finishing and joint sealing. Painted surfaces should be inspected for water blisters, cracks, flaking, and peeling. Lack of attention to these construction details will raise maintenance costs and imperil environmental control.

Built-in sources of particulate contaminants can be eliminated by thorough cleaning during construction of areas that will later become inaccessible under standard operating conditions (Runkle and Phillips, 1969). Examples of problem areas are: the interiors of stud partitions; walls prior to application of gypsum board; spaces above ceilings; interior and exterior surfaces of ductwork; and interior and exterior surfaces of all electrical fixtures, races, ducts, and boxes. Routine cleaning of collecting surfaces such as window sills, door frames, steps, and floors by wet and dry vacuuming will help in preventing the contamination of the problem areas during installation and will minimize the spoilage of finishing materials during application.

At the final inspection, the adequacy of the performance of all control features should be confirmed (Runkle and Phillips, 1969). Continuous air flow from high pressure spaces to low pressure areas with corresponding pressure drop distribution should be maintained, regardless of the amount of air filtration and fire control procedures in operation. Manometers measuring air velocity and pressure drops across filters must be checked. Filters, frame gaskets, and mating surfaces should be examined with a light-scattering photometer for leaks upon the introduction of smoke particles of the appropriate size into the filtration system. Gastight process equipment (tanks, cabinets, vessels, etc.) should be tested for leakage by the injection of Freon (chlorofluorohydrocarbon) gas into the interiors and checking for the escape of Freon molecules. This is done by injecting Freon gas into the unit to create 2–6 in. water gage of positive air pressure within the cabinet. The presence of this gas outside the cabinet as shown by a G.E. Type 2, Halogen Leak Detector indicates a leak which must be sealed (Runkle and Phillips, 1969). Temperature and humidity controls, fan efficiency, air-conditioning balance and capacity, illumination levels, temperature rise of all motors, and fire control and alarm sensitivity should at least meet all specifications. The overall efficiency of the air filtration systems employed should be tested over a period of several days by obtaining counts of particulate matter found in air samples taken at various locations.

No matter what barrier systems are used in the facility, their continued effectiveness will depend on constant monitoring of equipment and techniques; therefore, rigorous methods must be adopted at the outset to measure the level of contamination present. Environmental control of biological parameters is complicated by the rapid multiplication of microorganisms in moist areas and liquid aerosols, by the formation of spores resistant to germicides which destroy the vegetative forms, by the vulnerability of many pathogenic bacteria to adverse conditions which results in their death before they can be entrapped or cultured, by the widely differing growth requirements of different species, and by microbial mutation and consequent adaption to new conditions. If these complications are not understood, the interpretation of results obtained from inappropriately selected or improperly placed monitoring devices can be misleading even though the devices are functioning adequately.

In planning the environmental control program, the use of mathematical models can be very helpful. Death-rate reactions produced by the process employed should be studied before the selection of positive microbial controls to be used for the detection of low levels of contaminants. There are five categories of testing procedures in current use for environmental microbiological sampling: air sampling; surface and component sampling; physical and chemical tests and measurements; filter, incinerator, sewage, and water testing; and Freon leakage testing (Phillips and Brewer, 1968).

Air impaction samplers* and liquid impingers are used for determining viable particles per cubic foot of air. Settling plates are used to determine the count of viable particles per square foot per hour. Particle-size values may be obtained from liquid impinger samplers and from the Andersen cascaded sieve sampler. A particle counter that sounds an alarm when particles 0.5 μ or larger exceeding 100 per cubic foot of air are detected has been described (Fornabaio, 1970). Recent publications have discussed various aspects of air-sampling methods (Wolf *et al.*, 1959; McDade *et al.*, 1966) and air samplers (Phillips *et al.*, 1965). Surface contaminants are collected by the swab–rinse technique, the immersion of components in sterile fluids, the stainless steel strip method, direct surface agar plating, the agar contact method, the vacuum probe sampler, and ultrasonic treatment of rough surfaces. Viable counts are made of microorganisms per unit area of surface. The various techniques for sampling surfaces for microorganisms have been recently described. (Angelloti and Foter, 1958; Vesley and Michaelsen, 1964; Favero *et al.*, 1967; Puleo *et al.*, 1967; Farmer *et al.*, 1971). Steriliza-

*Developed originally by U.S. Army Biological Labs, Ft. Detrick, Maryland. Previously commercially available from Reyniers & Co. New version produced by Unit Electric Control, Orlando, Florida.

tion equipment, either wet- and/or dry-heat systems or gaseous systems such as ethylene oxide, should be monitored for temperature, period of exposure, and gas concentration. With the wet-treatment system, the monitoring of pressure is also required. In addition to the usual method for detecting the presence of viable microorganisms, the use of tracer microorganisms is advocated for monitoring sterilizers, air filters, air and solid-waste incinerators, and sewage- and water-treatment systems. Testing must not disrupt the continuity of the environmental control process. Gases and liquids used for area decontamination should be assayed periodically for germicidal potency. Checking for the migration of Freon gas through gas-tight barriers is considered an adequate test for leakage in microbiological safety enclosures or absolute barrier systems.

The periodic analysis of data obtained from testing and measurement programs can lead to improvement and/or modification of procedures for personnel safety, environmental control techniques, and comfort standards. Constant reevaluation of the results of the overall environmental-control system through analysis of sampling data, quality-control records, and other pertinent data can frequently result in reduced operating costs through the elimination of unnecessary criteria.

V. Personnel Training and Orientation

Management is responsible for the initiation, funding, and support of environmental-control programs (Phillips and Brewer, 1968). The hierarchy of individuals charged with the responsibility and corresponding authority for maintaining the environmental-control system should be established at the very beginning of the program. Employees should be selected on the basis of their technical competence and skills necessary for the performance of the tasks assigned to them. Although the impact of the Williams-Steiger Occupational Safety and Health Act of 1970 (Public Law 91–956) has not been fully realized, it is apparent that this will significantly affect all industries (Safety Standards, 1971). The planning team and A/E should become fully aware of the various aspects of Public Law 91–956 in order to properly design the facility. This act, when fully implemented, will define required healthful working environments with regard to air contaminants (including biological and chemical contaminants), noise, ionizing radiation, heat, and illumination. A carefully structured employee health program and detailed safety program such as that described briefly in the following paragraphs may be necessary to implement this regulation.

Applicants should be screened by preemployment medical examinations for physical conditions or diseases that might endanger themselves or the project. For some situations, new employees need thorough medical examinations including blood analyses, microbiological culture tests, biochemical function studies, and chest X-rays. Serum samples may sometimes need to be collected and stored for future diagnostic purposes and, in other instances, vaccination may be indicated. All employees should undergo periodic examinations similar to their preemployment examination and the medical findings compared with those recorded at previous examinations. Regular monitoring of personnel health may detect illnesses before overt symptoms appear. All individuals involved in biological accidents or having clinical symptoms should receive prompt attention and be observed clinically as long as the circumstances warrant medical care.

Some occupationally acquired illnesses are very slow to develop and difficult to diagnose. Any statistically significant increase in specific disease or general malaise occurring among the personnel which is above the incidence in the general community should be investigated assiduously. The investigation of the causative factors should not be discontinued until their source and mode of infection or irritation is revealed. This is particularly important for environments in which nonpathogenic microorganisms and substances believed to be nontoxic are present, because the connection between the illness and the etiologic agent is not easily apparent. Prolonged or unusual exposure to ordinarily innocuous materials may result in specific disease or may lower resistance to the extent that secondary illnesses not obviously related to occupational environments can develop. The most salubrious environment is that which is as free of contaminants (including decontaminating agents) as it is feasible to design, construct, and maintain.

Mental and physical stress or discomfort has a debilitating effect on human beings. High or low temperatures and humidities, excessive noise levels, and obnoxious odors produce fatigue and lower the efficiency of personnel. Some investigators have concluded that the performance of the employee in a closed ventilated system is affected by the psychological implications of barrier systems and by the physical restraints imposed, the restriction of movement, and the comfort of the operating position (Doxie and Ullom, 1967). These discomforts can be alleviated by thoughtful designing of the barrier. An impression of openness in windowless rooms may be provided by the use of color, paintings, murals, and drapes to offset possible claustrophobia-inducing effects.

All personnel must be thoroughly instructed in the safety regulations, contamination control systems, the nature of hazardous materials and their potential danger, the techniques developed for processing, and personal hygiene (Phillips and Brewer, 1968). The instruction should emphasize the reason for the adoption of each step of the contamination-control program in order that the necessity for adherence to the rules established is clearly understood. Periodic review may be helpful in maintaining alertness of employees.

Common laboratory practices that create unnecessary hazards are: mouth pipetting of hazardous materials, blowing out the last drop from a pipette, mixing dilutions by blowing air through a pipette into a culture, use of syringes without needle locks, and careless discarding of contaminated material. Personal habits to be avoided include: eating, drinking, and smoking in protected areas; improper washing; and transport of unsterilized papers, books, clothing, and other materials from protected areas (Phillips and Jemski, 1963).

Protective garments provided for personnel should be as static-free, nonlinting, and impervious to microorganisms as possible (Weisburd, 1969). Their use in bioclean areas is essential for personnel safety and product protection in many operations and a valuable aid in keeping airborne contaminants low in all situations.

VI. Summary

Designing facilities for pharmaceutical industries is a complex undertaking demanding the coordinated efforts of specialists in diverse professions. The management, legal counselors, production officers, research staff, architects, engineers, and building contractors must communicate their ideas and requirements in specific terms from the inception to the completion of the project. Frequent consultation with those experienced in the nature and control of contaminants is essential for planning a facility for the manufacture of high-quality products at the lowest level of expenditure. The efficiency of the environmental-control program and the initial building costs, maintenance expenses, and remodeling expenditures are directly related to the layout of the functional zones, the distribution of utility services, and the primary- and secondary-barrier systems incorporated. Thorough inspection of materials and methods used in construction should be made regularly while the work is in progress. Before final acceptance, the performance of systems intended to control environmental quality should be tested. Stringent monitoring and preventative maintenance programs are necessary for continued control. The selection of capable personnel and the execution of adequate training and health programs for employees are indispensable to the successful operation of the facility.

References

Angelotti, R., and Foter, M. J. (1958). *Food Res.* **23**, 175.

Ballard, D. W. (1971). "Checklist of Good Contamination Control Practices from a Manufacturing Viewpoint," Publ. SC-M-70-549. Sandia Corp.

Brewer, J. H., and Phillips, G. B. (1971). *Critical Rev. Environ. Control* **1**, 4.

Brewer, N. R. (1964). *Heat, Piping, Air Cond.* (Oct.) pp. 139–141.

Crossman, R. F., and Elsea, R. (1961). *Air Cond., Heat. Vent.* (July) pp. 71–76.

Decker, H. M. *et al.* (1962). "Air Filtration of Microbial Particles," U.S. Army and Dept. of Health, Education and Welfare.

Doxie, F. T., and Ullom, K. J. (1967). *West. Elec. Eng.* **11**, 24–32.

Farmer, F. H. *et al.* (1971). *J. Amer. Contam. Control* **3**, 15–18.

Faust, F. R. (1962). *J. Lab. Animal Care* **13**, 221–467.

Favero, M. S. *et al.* (1967). "Microbiological Sampling of Surfaces," Tech. Rep. Biol. Contam. Control Committee, Amer. Ass. Contam. Control.

Federal Standard No. 209A (1966). Gen. Serv. Admin., Washington, D.C.

Fornabaio, T. A. (1970). *Bull. Parenteral Drug. Ass.* **24**, 110.

Fox, G. W. (1964), "Specific Pathogen Free Animal Production—Selected References 1931–1964." Research Facilities Planning Branch, Div. Res. Serv. Nat. Inst. Health, Bethesda, Maryland.

Graham, W. R., and Feenstra, E. S. (1957). *Proc. Anim. Care Panel* (Nov.) 7–9.

Griffith, W. R. (1964). *Amer. Rev. Resp. Dis.* **89**, 240.

Haight, A. G. (1972). *Plant Eng.* (in press).

Harstad, J. B. *et al.* (1967). *Proc. 6th Annu. Tech. Meet. Amer. Ass. Contam. Control. Washington, D.C.*

Hill, B. F. (1962). *Lab. Anim. Care* **13**, 221–467.

Institute of Laboratory Animal Resources, National Academy of Sciences, National Research Council (1965). "Guide for Laboratory Animal Facilities and Care," Public Health Service, U.S. Dept of Health, Education and Welfare, Washington, D.C.

Jonas, A. M. (1965). *J. Amer. Vet. Med. Ass.* **146**, 6.

Kraft, L. M. *et al.* (1964). *J. Lab. Anim. Care* **14**, 16–19.

Livingston, J. R. (1965). "Special Problems in the Design of Research Laboratories," Nat. Inst. Health, Bethesda, Maryland.

Matson, G. C., and Baldwin, C. L. (1969). *Proc. 7th Annu. Tech. Meet. Amer. Ass. Contam. Control, Boston, Massachusetts.*

NASA Standard Procedures for the Microbial Examination of Space Hardware (1968). NHB 5340.1A, U.S. Govt. Printing Office, Washington, D.C.

NASA Standards for Clean Rooms and Work Stations for the Microbially Controlled Environment (1967). NHB 5340.2, Printing Office, Washington, D.C. Superintendent of Documents, U.S. Govt.

National Institute of Health (1962). "Planning and Design of Medical Research Facilities," Nat. Inst. Health, Bethesda, Maryland.

National Institute of Health (1968a). *U.S., Pub. Health Serv., Publ.* **1804**.

National Institute of Health (1968b). *U.S., Pub. Health Serv., Publ.* **1807**.

Norman, J. C. (1965). "Air Handling Objectives," pp. 37–42. Med. Diagnostic Lab. Planning and Design, U.S. Dept. of Health, Education and Welfare, Baltimore, Maryland.

Phillips, G. B. (1969). "Sterility Testing Environments: Equipment and Facilities in Federal Regulations and Practical Control Microbiology for Disinfectants, Drugs, and Cosmetics," Spec. Publ. No. 4. S.I.M.

Phillips, G. B., and Brewer, J. H. (1968), *Develop. Ind. Microbiol.* **9**, 105.
Phillips, G. B., and Hanel, E. (1960). *U.S. Govt. Res. Rep.* **34**, No. 2, 1–122.
Phillips, G. B., and Jemski, J. V. (1963). *J. Lab. Anim. Care* **13**, 13–20.
Phillips, G. B., and Runkle, R. S. (1967). *Appl. Microbiol.* **15**, 378.
Phillips, G. B. *et al.* (1965). "Microbiological Contamination Control—A State of the Art Report," Biol. Contam. Control Committee, Amer. Ass. Contam. Control.
Puleo, J. R. *et al.* (1967). *Contam. Control* **6**, 58.
Runkle, R. S. (1964). *Amer. Inst. Architects* **41**, 55–58 and 77–80.
Runkle, R. S., and Phillips, G. B. eds. (1969). "Microbial Contamination Control Facilities," Van Nostrand-Reinhold, Princeton, New Jersey.
Ryan, H. J. *et al.* (1967). *ASHRAE J.* pp. 36–50.
Safety Standards (1971). "Annotated Guide to the Williams-Steiger Occupational Safety and Health Act of 1970," Vol. 20, p. 3. U.S. Dept. Labor, Washington, D.C.
Smith, V. C. (1964). "Methods of Producing and Handling High Purity Water." Nat. Inst. Health, Bethesda, Maryland.
Snow, D. L. (1963). *U.S., Pub. Health Serv., Pub. Health Monogr.* **71**.
Vesley, D., and Michaelsen, G. S. (1964). *Health Lab. Sci.* **1**, 107–113.
Walter Kidde Constructors, Inc. (1965). "Planning for Laboratory Facilities," Walter Ridde Constructors, Inc., New York.
Weisburd, M. (1969). Unpublished manuscript.
Whitfield, W. J., and Morris, M. E. (1970). *Contam. Control* **9**, 10.
Wolf, H. W. *et al.* (1959). *U.S., Pub. Health Serv., Pub. Health Monogr.* **60**.
York, J. E. (1953). "Ventilation and Air Conditioning for Laboratories," Heating and Ventilating's Ref. Sect., pp. 80–86.

PRESERVATIVES IN PHARMACEUTICAL PRODUCTS

Donald Jaconia

Research Department,
CIBA-GEIGY Pharmaceutical Company,
Summit, New Jersey

I. Introduction

The function of a preservative in a pharmaceutical preparation is to prevent microbial contamination. The continuing efforts of the pharmaceutical industry to exclude harmful microbes from its products have received added impetus today, when governmental agencies and consumer groups alike insist on a high level of quality control. The regulatory agency particularly requires the use of preservative when there is a more than one-time use of active material in the same container. According to the "United States Pharmacopeia XVIII"

> a suitable substance or mixture of substances to prevent the growth of microorganisms must be added to preparations intended for injection that are packaged in multiple dose containers regardless of the method of sterilization employed, unless the active ingredients are themselves bacteriostatic. Ophthalmic solutions packaged in multiple dose containers must contain a suitable substance or mixture of substances to prevent the growth of or to destroy microorganisms accidentally introduced when the container is opened for use.

A. Topical Preparations

Included in this category are such pharmaceutical preparations as: lotions, creams, pastes, liniments, and various preparations intended for insertion into body cavities, e.g., ear, nose. Commonly used preservatives include most of those used in parenteral ophthalmic or oral products, such as:

Organic mercurials
Parabens
Phenols
Quaternary ammonium compounds.

B. Oral Preparations

These, preparations are classified as therapeutically active drugs, either solid or liquid, dispersed in a liquid called the vehicle. The types of preservatives commonly used for this type of product are:

Benzoic acid
Chloroform
Parabens (esters of *p*-hydroxybenzoic acid)
Sorbic acid (2,4-hexadienoic acid)
Sulfur dioxide and sulfites

C. Ophthalmic Solutions (Eye Drops)

It is generally agreed that eye drops should be sterile at the time they reach the consumer. The "United States Pharmacopeia" points out that the sterility of solutions applied to an injured eye is of the greatest importance.

Substances in use as preservatives for this type of product are:

Benzalkonium chloride
Chlorobutanol
Mercury compounds
Parabens
Phenylethyl alcohol

An examination of the literature reveals that some organisms have the ability to develop resistance to preservatives, while other preservatives exhibit toxic properties which limit their usefulness in pharmaceutical products. This would seem to indicate that the ideal preservative is not readily available and that the search for such a preservative must continue. In preparing this article, it is the author's intention to present as much information as possible on the work that is being done today in the field of preservatives as well as that which has been done in the past. This has been accomplished by referring to the findings of a great number of authors who are considered experts in their respective fields. It is the author's hope that, in this manner, the reader will be made aware of the present status of preservatives in pharmaceutical products.

D. Parenteral Preparations

The "International Pharmacopoeia" defines injections as a class of sterile pharmaceutical solutions, emulsions, or suspensions in containers which will maintain sterility and are intended for parenteral administration, that is, under or through one or more layers of skin or mucous membrane. Preservatives for this type of product are limited in number by their suitability for injection into the body. The most commonly used preservatives are:

Alcohols
Benzoic acid
Mercurials
Phenols
Quaternary ammonium compounds

II. Topical Pharmaceutical Preparations

The list of preparations included in this category are: aerosols, creams, emulsions, suspensions, solutions, liniments, jellies, ointments, and pastes. The pharmaceutical form of these various materials may be either liquid or solid and may be suspended in or mixed with either an aqueous or oily vehicle. In view of the fact that these products are formulated to treat a variety of skin infections and since many of them contain some form of antimicrobial agent to combat the infection, it can be assumed that many do not need a preservative. Nevertheless, there are times when a preservative is included in the formulation. Anderson (1970) states that emulsified systems seem to be very liable to microbial contamination and therefore adequate preservation is essential on both economic and toxicological grounds. Many of the components used in topical pharmaceutical emulsions readily support microbial growth.

In the preservation of these products, it should be pointed out that such antimicrobials must be nonirritating to the skin and must not produce sensitization. These are important aspects of a product which is in contact with the skin. In addition, the preservative should be compatible with the other ingredients in the formulation and should not have a strong odor or affect the color of the product.

Hjorth and Trolle (1962) found that primary sensitization from preservatives in creams is very rare when low concentrations are used. If, however, people are exposed to high concentrations of similar compounds, skin reactions may occur in these previously sensitized individuals. This has occurred with the paraben esters and organic mercury compounds. Primary sensitization to the parabens in creams had not been reported prior to the report of Hjorth and Trolle. Sorbic acid, which occurs naturally in cranberries and mountain ash, provoked an erythema, lasting more than 30 minutes, after use of an ointment containing this preservative.

The most commonly used antimicrobial agents in topical preparations are essentially many of those used for oral products and parenterals. This would include the parabens, organic mercurials, quaternary ammonium compounds, phenols, sorbic acid, chlorocresol, and hexachlorophene. The use of these agents in the various topical dosage forms is described as follows.

A. Emulsions and Creams

Tenenbaum (1967) states that "pseudomonads are bacterial organisms found in soil, water, air, and food, in and on the body. They break down emulsions, cause foul odors, and produce slime, while decomposing cosmetics and pharmaceuticals. These organisms have the capacity to develop resistance to agents inimical to other microorganisms." He feels that an essentially self-sterilizing preparation can be achieved.

Pettoruto (1970) points out that a preservative should be required whenever a system contains water and that it should be active and stable over a wide range of pH and temperature conditions and be nonvolatile.

Noble and Savin (1966) showed that when oily substances, such as cetomacrogol, emulsifying ointments, olive oil, or oleic acid were incorporated in a formulation, the inhibitory action of chlorocresol was reduced. They suggest that chlorocresol preferentially dissolves in the oily substance and is thus prevented from exerting antimicrobial action in the water phase in which *Pseudomas aeruginosa* is capable of growing. They feel that 0.02% chlorocresol is sufficient except when the aforementioned oily substances are present. Because most preparations formulated for application to the skin tend to be nutritive toward certain types of microorganisms, preservatives with lethal activity are more desirable than those which merely inhibit growth. Wedderburn (1964), in her excellent review of preservation of emulsions, studied 26 preservatives and many nonionic surfactants and showed that nonionics reduced the effectiveness of all preservatives when the ratio of surfactant to the preservative exceeded a critical value.

B. Solutions

The preservation of solutions is almost always accomplished by the use of one of a variety of preservatives available. In the choice of the proper preservative, one must take into consideration the question of compatibility with other ingredients, its stability, nonvolatility, and nonirritant qualities. The preservatives most widely used for this type of product are: chlorocresol, alcohol, quaternary ammonium compounds, phenylmercuric salts, and, occasionally, phenolic compounds.

C. Suspensions

Suspensions are preparations of finely divided, undissolved drug particles which are dispersed in a liquid vehicle. With this type of preparation, the problem of adsorption of the preservative onto the suspended material is always possible (McCarthy, 1969). Harris (1961) showed that a cationic antiseptic, such as chlorhexidine, was inactivated by 5% bentonite in suspension. USP XVIII states that suitable antimicrobial agents should be included to protect the preparations from bacterial and mold contamination.

D. Jellies

The uses of this type of product are varied, e.g., application to body orifices, such as the nose or vaginal canal, or use as a lubricant for insertion of instruments into a body opening. A jelly usually consists of about 1% to 5% of a gel-forming material, such as sodium alginate, gum tragacanth, gelatin, or methylcellulose. USP XVIII states that gelatin is subject to microbic decomposition when wet or in solution. The same may be said for most gel-forming substances. As has been pointed out, if sufficient water is available in a formulation, a preservative is needed in order to prevent microbial contamination.

There have been numerous reports of interaction between the preservative and the gel substances. Tillman and Kuramoto (1957) demonstrated the formation of a complex between methylcellulose 400 and methyl, propyl, and butyl parabens. An interaction also takes place between methyl and propyl parabens, gelatin, and polyvinylpyrrolidone. However, the authors did not find a significant degree of interaction between methyl paraben and gum tragacanth.

Eisman *et al.* (1957) found that gum tragacanth exerted a strong neutralizing effect upon the bactericidal activity of chlorobutanol, the *p*-hydroxybenzoates, and benzalkonium chloride. This was also true, but to a lesser extent, with phenol, phenylmercuric acetate, and merthiolate.

Taub *et al.* (1958) concluded that gum jellies can be effectively preserved. They felt that gum tragacanth exerted no marked deleterious effect upon the bacteriostatic activity of the parabens. Optimum conditions were obtained with a combination of methyl (0.2%) plus propyl (0.05%) parabens at a pH of 7.0 or below. They showed that in samples of preserved jellies that had been stored for 28 days before being contaminated with a test organism, no lessening of the antimicrobial activity of the preservative was exhibited.

E. Ointments and Pastes

These products are prepared with oily bases and microbial contamination seldom takes place and hence such preparations do not usually require a preservative. Nevertheless, it is felt that one should add a preservative when formulating this type of product as a general safety procedure. The preservative thus incorporated in the ointment should arrest the proliferation of a possible contaminant.

III. Oral Pharmaceutical Preparations

A. Liquid Medicinals

Liquid medicinals that are to be administered orally can be categorized and defined according to the listing in the USP XVIII.

a. Suspension. A suspension is a preparation of finely divided, undissolved drugs, dispersed in a liquid. Powders for suspensions are preparations of finely powdered drugs intended for suspension in liquid vehicles. Suitable antimicrobial agents should be included to protect the preparation from bacterial and mold contamination.

b. Gels. Gels are suspensions in an aqueous medium of insoluble drugs in hydrated form, the particle size of which approaches or attains colloidal dimensions.

c. Milks. Milks are suspensions of insoluble drugs in an aqueous medium. They are differentiated from gels in that the suspended particles are larger.

d. Syrups. Syrups are liquid preparations of medicinal or flavoring substances in concentrated aqueous solutions of sugar, usually sucrose. They may contain antimicrobial agents to prevent bacterial and mold growth.

e. Tinctures. Tinctures are alcoholic or hydroalcoholic solutions prepared from vegetable materials or from chemical substances.

One of the simplest mixtures possible to make is one in which the ingredients of a solid drug are dissolved in water. Since very few mixtures are made of only the drug and water, it becomes necessary to add other materials in order to make the medication palatable, as well as stable. In addition, it is sometimes necessary to adjust the pH of the mixture in order to maintain stability. When these adjustments are made, the possibility of microbial contamination exists. Since few materials used in making non-sterile products are sterile when received, those who manufacture such products must recognize their responsibility to ascertain that microorganisms present in the finished article are unlikely to cause harm to the user or to the product. If the taste of the drug is unpleasant, it is usually camouflaged by the addition of a flavor or sweetening agent, such as sucrose, sorbitol, glycerol, or propylene glycol. It has been shown by Barr and Tice (1957a) that growth of *Monilia albicans* was inhibited by 50% w/v glycerol and by 30% w/v propylene glycol. When there was more than 10% sorbitol present, the concentrations of glycerol and propylene glycol inhibiting growth were reduced. Other sugars were tested in the same manner by Barr and Tice (1957b) and they report that 60% w/w of invert sugar inhibited *Aspergillus niger*; however, solutions that contained 50% w/w of levulose or dextrose did not inhibit its growth. One can conclude that unless active ingredients contain a high concentration of glycerol or propylene glycol, it is necessary to have an antimicrobial agent in the sweetened aqueous mixture or solution. Prickett *et al.* (1961) point out that pharmaceutical formulations similar to simple syrups are difficult to preserve against microbial spoilage. These formulations sometimes require higher concentrations of preservatives, such as the parabens. Propylene glycol alone did not exhibit significant antimicrobial activity at either 2% or 5%, but low levels of propylene glycol potentiated the activity of the parabens to the point where practically all of the inoculants (except bacterial spores) were destroyed. The potentiating effects of propylene glycol on the antimicrobial activity of the parabens in liquid preparations may be applied practically to increase the preservative action in products that are difficult to protect against microbial spoilage and to reduce the concentration of parabens, thereby improving the flavor and consumer acceptance.

In the preparation of suspensions, it is often necessary to add an inert suspending agent to retard sedimentation. To enhance the physical stability of the suspension, suspending and possibly emulsifying agents may be added. One should be cognizant that suspending agents, such as gum tragacanth or gum acacia, as well as the cellulose derivatives, are subject to attack by microbes, thus destroying or diminishing their usefulness in pharmaceutical preparations. This would certainly indicate that the presence of an antimicrobial agent becomes a necessity for this type of product.

Having determined the necessity of an antimicrobial agent in a formulation, the producer may then be faced with the problem of the complexing of the celluloses with a number of preservatives. Tillman and Kuramoto (1957) showed that methylcellulose forms complexes in solution with *p*-hydroxybenzoic acid. They found the degree of interaction to be in the following decreasing order: *p*-hydroxybenzoic acid, *p*-aminobenzoic acid, methylparaben, propylparaben, and butylparaben. Synthetic nonionic surfactants of the fatty acid ester type (sorbitan esters and their polyoxyethylene derivatives) are used as emulsifying or solubilizing agents in pharmaceutical products. Barr and Tice (1957c) showed that *Penicillium notatum*, *P. aeruginosa*, *M. albicans*, and *A. niger* are capable of growing in solutions of nonionic surfactants of the above-named types. The fact that these organisms can grow on and degrade the surfactant becomes a real problem when one considers that these same organisms are common contaminants in pharmaceutical products. The splitting of the surfactant would most likely result in the destruction of its emulsifying and stabilizing properties and, in consequence, result in a breakdown of the product. In a follow-up publication, Barr and Tice (1957d) tested more than 50 substances and combinations for their effectiveness as preservatives for solutions containing nonionic surfactants of the above types. Those found to be effective were: sorbic acid, 0.1–0.2%; phenyl mercuric nitrate, 0.01%; phenylmercuric acetate, 0.007%; benzalkonium chloride, 0.1%; hexylene glycol, 3.0%. The phenols were not effective, due, most likely, to complexing with the surfactant. Anderson (1970) feels that the important question of the suitability of a preservative in this system would seem to be its chemical potential or thermodynamic activity rather than its overall concentration, and that the best, simple measure of preservative's activity in a complex system is the concentration of the preservative, unbound and undissociated, in the aqueous phase. As has been shown, preservatives may be bound to emulgents; for example, the interaction of phenols and simple carboxylic acids with polyoxyethylene chains of nonionic surfactants. A further illustration of the problems one may encounter is the partitioning of a preservative into an oil phase of a formulation. This may lead to a much greater loss of activity than interaction with surfactants. Bean *et al.* (1962; 1965; Bean and Heman-Ackah, 1964) have listed partition coefficients for some phenols in arachis oil–water and liquid paraffin–water systems. McCarthy (1969) states that insoluble powders in a suspension or emulsion can adsorb preservatives from the aqueous phase, thus allowing proliferation of microbial contaminants.

As stated earlier, Eisman *et al.* (1957) found evidence to prove that the presence of gum tragacanth exerts a strong neutralizing effect upon the *p*-hydroxybenzoates, benzalkonium chloride, and, to a lesser extent, upon phenol and phenylmercuric acetate. There exists an inverse relationship between the bactericidal activity of preservatives and the concentration of gum tragacanth contained in the preparation. The greater the concentration of the gum, the less effective is the preservative agent. Taub *et al.* (1958) demonstrated that the combination of methyl and propyl parabens was much more effective than chlorobutanol or benzoic acid in preserving gum tragacanth. The gum exerted no marked deleterious effect on the bacteriostatic activity of the parabens. Benzoic acid at pH 5.0 or below, at a concentration of 0.2%, is effective but to a lesser degree than parabens.

The general consensus concerning the desirable properties of a preservative are: (a) it should not be unpleasant to the taste; (b) it should be free from odor; (c) it should be compatible with other ingredients in the formulation; (d) it should be effective in the selected concentration against a number of microorganisms; (e) it should not interfere with or change the pH of the formulation; (f) it should definitely be nontoxic or nonirritating at the concentration normally used in a formulation.

B. Preservatives

1. Benzoic Acid

Benzoic acid is generally accepted as a safe preservative and most often is used in concentrations of 0.05 to 0.1%. This compound is ordinarily effective at pH 4.0 (Entrekin, 1961). Patel and Foss (1965) studied benzoic acids and found that they all exhibited reversible association with surfactants of the polyether type. The binding affinity of polysorbate 80 for benzoic acid decreased with an increase of the pH. While it is used as a safe preservative in foods, its use in pharmaceuticals has been displaced by other compounds (Elowe, 1955).

2. p-*Hydroxybenzoic Acid Esters (Parabens)*

The esters of *p*-hydroxybenzoic acid are tasteless, stable, and have been shown to be nontoxic. Aalto *et al.* (1953), in their studies, demonstrated that the methyl, ethyl, propyl, and butyl esters were effective in low concentrations against fungi and gram-positive bacteria and less active against gram-negative bacteria. The esters are more fungistatic than fungicidal. They suggest that the effects of the esters are additive and therefore the use of combinations to achieve higher concentrations in water is desirable. The *p*-hydroxybenzoates are equally effective in acid or neutral solutions in the pH range from 4 to 8. Growth of *A. niger* in a procaine penicillin suspension was inhibited by 0.02% propyl ester of *p*-hydroxybenzoic acid. Neidig and Burrell (1944) did a thorough review of the literature of these compounds through the 1940s. Prickett *et al.* (1961) demonstrated that syrups could be preserved with the parabens and that the addition of small amounts of propylene glycol (usually 2% to 5%) potentiated the antimicrobial activity of the parabens. Pisano and Kostenbauder (1959) demonstrated that *p*-hydroxybenzoates can be employed as efficient preservatives in the presence of nonionic surfactants, but the proper concentration must be employed. Hydrophobic esters, such as propyl and butyl, are usually effective in lower concentrations; but in the presence of surfactants of the polyoxyethylene type, this relationship may be reversed.

3. Sorbic Acid (2,4-Hexadienoic Acid)

Sorbic acid is a naturally occurring compound which may be obtained from the berries of mountain ash (Merck Index, 1968). Puls *et al.* (1955) found sorbic acid superior to benzoic acid as a fungistatic agent against *A. niger*. Sorbic acid, in a concentration as low as 0.05%, preserved 1% guar gum solution, and 26% sucrose solution when stored at 5°C, 25°C, and 37°C for 30 days. This compound may be used in combination with other preservatives but its use in pharmaceuticals has been displaced by other compounds (Elowe, 1955).

IV. Ophthalmic Preparations

It is generally agreed that an ophthalmic solution should be sterile when it reaches the consumer. The USP XVIII, in its initial statement, points out that the sterility of ophthalmic solutions to be applied to the injured eye is of the utmost importance. It further states that

> ophthalmic solutions are sterile solutions that are compounded and packaged for instillation into the eye. Preparation of an ophthalmic solution requires careful consideration of such factors as the inherent toxicity of the drug itself, the isotonicity value, the need for buffering agents, the need for an antimicrobial agent (and, if needed, its selection), sterilization, and proper packaging.

The preparation of an ophthalmic solution involves the dissolution of the medicament in an aqueous vehicle, which, in some cases, may or may not be a buffering agent. The purpose of the buffer is to prevent an increase in pH caused by the slow release of hydroxyl ions by glass. Such a rise in pH can affect both the solubility and stability of the drug. The solution is then sterilized by heating in an autoclave at 121°C, providing the ingredients are unaffected by heat. Heat-labile solutions are sterilized by membrane filtration, provided caution be exercised in the selection, assembly, and use of the equipment.

Sterile preparations in special containers for single use on one patient should be available in every hospital, office, or other installation where accidentally or surgically traumatized eyes are treated.

The USP XVIII states that ophthalmic solutions may be packaged in multiple-dose containers when intended for the individual use of one patient and where ocular surfaces are not damaged. Even though sterile when dispersed, a suitable antimicrobial agent must be added to each solution in order to prevent the growth of, or to destroy, microorganisms accidentally introduced when the container is opened for use. Benzalkonium chloride 0.01% (1:10,000) is frequently used for this purpose, but it is not always satisfactory because it is incompatible with anionic drugs or nonionic surfactants in high concentrations. Where nitrates or salicylates are used, benzalkonium chloride should be replaced with phenylmercuric nitrate or phenylmercuric acetate 0.002% (1:50,000). Chlorobutanol and phenylethyl alcohol, in a concentration of 0.5%, are alternative preservatives.

At concentrations tolerated by the tissue of the eye, all of the foregoing agents discussed are ineffective against some strains of *P. aeruginosa*, an organism that can invade the abraded cornea and cause ulceration and blindness. Ophthalmic solutions intended for use in surgical procedures must be sterile but should not contain antimicrobial agents since they may be irritating to the ocular tissues.

The "British Pharmaceutical Codex" (BPC, 1968) lists the following as suitable antibacterial and antifungal substances: 0.002% w/v phenylmercuric nitrate, 0.002% w/v phenylmercuric acetate, 0.002% w/v benzalkonium chloride, and 0.01% w/v chlorhexidine acetate.

According to Anderson (1970) and also Foster (1965), the ideal antimicrobial agent should possess the following properties: (a) it should be compatible with other ingredients in the formulation; (b) it should have a wide bacteriostatic and preferably bactericidal activity; (c) it should have no toxicity or cause irritation to ocular tissues; (d) it should be able to withstand heat sterilization, as well as prolonged storage; (e) it should show little or no absorption into the rubber closure, and, added to these properties; (f) it should have a sterilizing time of less than 1 hour as proposed by Kohn *et al.* (1963). It was Kohn's feeling that an antibacterial substance that has a sterilizing time of more than 1 hour may be arbitrarily considered too slowacting for use as a preservative in multiple-dose vials. An additional desirable characteristic of the preservative would be that it should not alter the pH and toxicity of ophthalmic solutions (Lawrence, 1955).

A. Antimicrobial Substances Used in Ophthalmic Solutions

1. Mercury Compounds

The most popular mercury compounds used as preservatives in ophthalmic solutions are phenylmercuric acetate, phenylmercuric nitrate, and thimerosal. Klein *et al.* (1954) considered thimerosalate (0.005%), phenylmercuric acetate (0.005%), and phenylmercuric nitrate (0.005%) as safe substances to use.

Riegelman (Riegelman *et al.*, 1956) pointed out that phenylmercuric nitrate is considered to be a suitable bacteriostatic agent for providing "self-sterilizing" solutions. He further states that phenylmercuric nitrate may not be used in concentrations greater than 1:10,000 in ophthalmic solutions, since the presence of halide ions would result in a precipitate of the insoluble phenylmercuric halide. Riegelman feels that the safe use of a bacteriostatic preservative at a given concentration in ophthalmic solutions requires knowledge of the time period required to sterilize the solution after contamination. Brown *et al.* (1964) states that when suitably formulated, solutions for ophthalmic use may be acceptably preserved with thimerosal. On the other hand, Kohn (Kohn *et al.*, 1963) considers thimerosal 1:5000 too slow-acting because, in his experiments, it took 6 hours to destroy the test organism, *P. aeruginosa*. Phenylmercuric nitrate also took six hours to sterilize the test solution. Foster (1965) pointed out that eye solutions can and have become contaminated with microorganisms (fungi, molds, bacteria, and viruses). He feels that these solutions must be sterilized immediately and in a manner similar to parenterals and should therefore contain an efficient bacteriostat or bactericide. He stated that the Pharmacopeia "Austrian" specifies the use of 0.002% phenylmercuric acetate, among other preservatives. Lawrence (1955) did not recommend the use of mercury compounds as suitable preservatives since, in the presence of ophthalmic material in the solution, the activity of phenylmercuric nitrate or thimerosal was of a lower order than of other preservatives against strains of *P. aeruginosa.*

With organic mercury compounds as preservatives for ophthalmic solutions, their possible toxicity must be taken into consideration. Foster (1965) indicated that even though mercurialentis (deposit of mercury on the lens of the eye) was caused by prolonged use of phenylmercuric nitrate, nevertheless, such a reaction should not detract from the usefulness of phenylmercuric nitrate as a preservative for ophthalmic solutions.

2. *Benzalkonium Chloride*

A number of authors have shown that benzalkonium chloride is an effective preservative for ophthalmic solutions. Lawrence (1955), in testing seven commonly used chemical compounds as preservatives, found benzalkonium chloride to be the most effective against *P. aeruginosa* and *Proteus*. Riegelman (Riegelman *et al.*, 1956) showed that benzalkonium chloride, at a concentration of 1:5000, revealed the most rapid bactericidal activity against *P. aeruginosa.* Nevertheless, he felt that this compound should be restricted to a concentration of not higher than 1:5000, since chronic use of such solutions is irritating to the eye. Kohn's work (Kohn *et al.*, 1963) concurs with that of Riegelman as far as rapidity of action of benzalkonium chloride against *P. aeruginosa* is concerned. Brown (Brown and Norton, 1965; Brown and Richards, 1965) considers suitably formulated benzalkonium chloride to be a most effective preservative for ophthalmics. Among those favoring benzalkonium chloride is Foster (1965) who, while agreeing that it is an excellent preservative, considers 0.02% rather high and recommends a concentration of 0.01%. Klein (Klein *et al.*, 1954), on the other hand, does not recommend the use of quaternary ammonium compounds because of their effect upon the cornea of the eye. However, Anderson (1970) states that the "Australasian Pharmacopeia" and the "British Pharmaceutical Codex" recommend benzalkonium chloride as a suitable ophthalmic solution preservative. The "Australasian Pharmacopeia" also includes disodium edetate whenever benzalkonium chloride is used in order to increase its antipseudomonal activity. Benzalkonium chloride, being a quaternary ammonium compound, is less active against gram-negative organisms than against gram-positive bacteria. Ethylenediaminetetra acetate has been shown by MacGregor and Elliker (1958) to reduce the resistance of *P. aeruginosa* to quaternary ammonium compounds. In 1965, Brown and Richards demonstrated that the activity of polymyxin B sulfate, chlorhexidine diacetate, and benzalkonium chloride against *Pseudomonas* was increased by the addition of EDTA to the solution. It has been postulated that EDTA is synergistic with these antimicrobial agents. The antimicrobial activity of EDTA is associated with the removal of Mg^{2+} and/or Ca^{2+} ions from the cytoplasmic membrane (Russell *et al.*, 1967).

In an interesting experiment, Adair *et al.* (1969) showed that *P. aeruginosa* was able to multiply in minimal salts solutions containing various concentrations of commercially prepared benzalkonium chloride in which ammonium acetate was present as a buffer and served as a nitrogen source. Minimum salts solutions of pure benzalkonium chloride (PBC), containing no ammonium acetate, did not support the growth of *P. aeruginosa*. When $(NH_4)_2SO_4$ was added to PBC, the solution supported the growth of both benzalkonium chloride-resistant and -sensitive organisms. Adair feels that the regulation allowing the presence of ammonium acetate in commercially prepared benzalkonium chloride should be reconsidered, since ammonium acetate is carried over by such preparations into drug formulations and disinfectant solutions where it has the potential to support the growth of resistant bacteria and thus introduces a risk of serious infection.

Adair *et al.* (1972) make the further observation that the addition of EDTA to quaternary ammonium compounds (QAC) will definitely prevent the growth of QAC-resistant *P. aeruginosa.* QAC-resistant cells were not cross-resistant to organic mercurials.

3. Chlorobutanol

Klein *et al.* (1954) considered chlorobutanol as a safe preservative at a concentration of 0.8% (a saturated solution). Riegelman *et al.* (1956) indicated that, while chlorobutanol may not have an adequate rate of action for many ophthalmic uses, it was nevertheless his second choice as a preservative. On the other hand, Kohn *et al.* (1963) found that 0.5% chlorobutanol required a 12-hour contact period to sterilize the test solution. Brown and Norton (1965) found chlorobutanol to be an effective but slow sterilizing agent. Lawrence (1955) found it effective in destroying *Pseudomonas* and *Proteus* cultures if left in contact for a sufficient length of time (usually several hours). It must be pointed out that chlorobutanol, when heated, hydrolyzes to hydrochloric acid, thus causing a decrease in the pH of the solution. This also takes place at room temperature but at a slower rate.

4. Chlorhexidine

This compound was first described in 1954 by Davies *et al.* as a potent antibacterial compound. The mode of action of this drug, as described by Hugo and Longworth (1964), seems to be that it reacts with the cell, causing a disorientation of the lipoprotein membrane. The result is that the membrane no longer can fulfill its function as an osmotic barrier. According to Anderson (1970), the "British Pharmaceutical Codex" and the "Australasian Pharmaceutical Formulary" APF recognize chlorhexidine acetate (as well as other compounds) as a preservative for ophthalmic solutions. Unfortunately, this compound is incompatible with some of the active ingredients of ophthalmic solutions, as was shown by Humberstone (1961). The compound causes a precipitate when in contact with sulfate ions. Chlorhexidine is not listed as a suitable ophthalmic preservative by the USP (1970).

5. Parabens

Aalto *et al.* (1953) showed that the methyl, ethyl, propyl, and butyl esters of *p*-hydroxybenzoic acid were effective in low concentrations against fungi and gram-positive bacteria and less so against gram-negative bacteria. They showed that the esters were more fungistatic than fungicidal and they suggested the use of combinations to achieve higher concentrations in aqueous solutions. The *p*-hydroxybenzoates are equally effective against microorganisms in acid or neutral solutions in the pH range from 4 to 7.

Hugo and Foster (1964a) discerned that a strain of *P. aeruginosa*, obtained from an infected human eye, grew in solutions of esters of *p*-hydroxybenzoic acid without any previous adaptation. Montgomery and Halsall (1964) disagreed with the findings of Hugo and Foster, stating that the concentrations used (methyl 0.02% + propyl 0.01%) were insufficient. They found that with 0.08% (total ester concentration), the combination was at least bacteriostatic and probably bactericidal. Foster (1964) pointed out that 0.08% (methyl–propyl ratios of 2:1) total ester concentration was bacteriostatic for *P. aeruginosa*. In order to produce bactericidal activity, it was necessary to have a combined total of 0.2% parabens, and, at this concentration, the esters were irritating to the eye. The "Australasian Pharmacopeia" specifies the use of 0.1% *p*-hydroxybenzoates (Foster, 1965). Anderson (1970) indicates that hydroxybenzoate esters are now considered unsatisfactory and are no longer recommended as preservatives for eye solutions.

Brown and Norton (1965), interestingly, indicate that *P. aeruginosa* has the capacity to utilize the *p*-hydroxybenzoates as a source of carbon, which seems to preclude their widespread use as an eye solution preservative. Lawrence (1955) and Kohn *et al.* (1963) have also shown that the parabens are virtually inactive against *P. aeruginosa.*

6. *Chlorocresol*

Klein (Klein *et al.*, 1954) states that 0.1% solutions of this agent are safe but cause smarting of the eyes. Brown and Norton (1965), in their list of suitable preservatives, recommend chlorocresol 0.05%. According to Russell *et al.* (1967), chlorocresol is not unduly irritating to the intact, noninflamed eye and is known to be an effective antibacterial agent. Further, Russell and his colleagues (1967) state that this compound was deleted from the "British Pharmaceutical Codex" as an ophthalmic preservative. He feels that this compound should be reinvestigated, since it is an effective antimicrobial agent.

7. *Alcohols*

Brewer (Brewer *et al.*, 1953) tested 43 ophthalmic solutions containing phenylethyl alcohol and showed that 2 had a minimum growth in 7 days and were sterile in 14 days. Twenty-six solutions without phenylethyl alcohol were found to contain viable *P. aeruginosa*. He advises the use of phenylethyl alcohol as a preservative. According to Brown and Norton (1965), available evidence offers little support for the use of phenylethyl alcohol as an ophthalmic preservative. Kohn *et al.* (1963) pointed out that phenylethyl alcohol took more than 24 hours to destroy *P. aeruginosa* placed in an ophthalmic solution.

8. *β-Phenylethyl Alcohol*

Grote and Woods (1955) found that β-phenylethyl alcohol is not irritating to the rabbit eye. A 0.3% solution does not destroy the natural antiseptic action of the lysozyme normally present in the lacrimal fluid. A 0.3% solution has a slightly lower surface tension than water and would thus allow better penetration of the ophthalmic solution. Rose water (which contains natural phenylethyl alcohol) has been used in ophthalmic preparations for centuries.

9. Combination of Preservatives

Kvamme (1969) reported that, after the use of 0.05% tetracemin and 0.01% of a quaternary ammonium compound, such as cetylpyridinium chloride, benzalkonium chloride, or cetrimmonium bromide for 2 years, there has been no report of allergy or sensitization. He further states that good chemical stability and water solubility are the advantages of this combination.

B. Conclusions

As can be seen from the foregoing, there is no single chemical substance that is capable of meeting all the requirements of the ideal preservative for ophthalmic solutions at the present time. A promising look into the future is indicated by the work of Adair *et al.* (1969, 1972) in their studies on the nature of resistance of *P. aeruginosa* to QAC. In addition, the work of Brown and Richards (1965) on the effects of Tween 80 and EDTA in reducing the resistance of *P. aeruginosa* to chemicals, is an encouraging factor for possibly obtaining good preservative activity against *P. aeruginosa*.

V. Parenteral Pharmaceutical Preparations

A. Definitions

Injections, as defined in the USP XVIII, are sterile preparations for parenteral use and are grouped into five distinct classes:

(1) medicaments, or solutions or emulsions thereof suitable for injection;
(2) dry solids or liquid concentrates containing no buffers, diluents, or other added substances, and which, upon the addition of suitable solvents, yield solutions conforming in all respects to the requirements for injections;
(3) preparations the same as those described under (2) except that they contain one or more buffers, diluents, or other added substances;
(4) solids which are suspended in a suitable fluid medium and which are not to be injected intravenously or into the spinal canal;
and
(5) dry solids, which, upon the addition of suitable vehicles yield preparations conforming in all respects to the requirements for sterile suspensions.

There are a number of reasons why some medications are administered by the injection method (parenteral), e.g., the medication may be destroyed when given by mouth, and the drug usually acts more quickly when injected. Many times, a drug formulated with the proper vehicle produces a prolonged action which could not be attained by oral administration. Injections may be administered by any of the following routes: intradermal, subcutaneous, intramuscular, intravenous, intrathecal, and intracisternal. There is no question that medicines to be injected into the human body must be sterile. Injection of nonsterile or contaminated material into a patient is a grave hazard and must be avoided at all times. In addition, the presence of non-pathogenic microbes may cause the breakdown of the drug with a concomitant loss of antimicrobial activity (Kedzia *et al.*, 1961). Injectable materials are most often of the aqueous type but at times they may also be in fixed oils of vegetable origin. According to the USP XVIII, the addition of substances to increase stability of the product is permitted provided it can be shown that they are harmless and do not detract from the therapeutic efficacy of the drug. "Unless otherwise directed, maximum limits for agents containing mercury and cationic surface-active compounds are 0.01%; for chlorobutanol, cresol, and phenol, 0.5% is permitted. Sulfur dioxide or an equivalent amount of the sulfite, or metabisulfite of potassium, or sodium, 0.2% is permitted."

Materials for parenteral use may be packaged in either single- or multiple-dose containers. A single-dose container is one in which the vial or ampul is sealed so that none of the material can be withdrawn without destroying the container. A multiple dose container is one in which the product is protected from contamination by a rubber closure, thus allowing for more than one removal of the medication. The possibility of contamination of the contents with the use of multiple-dose containers is always present. Kohan *et al.* (1962), in a study of multiple dose vials, found that 13 out of 490 had become contaminated while in use. The USP XVIII states that "a suitable substance or mixture of substances to prevent the growth of microorganisms must be added to preparations intended for injection that are packaged in multiple dose containers, regardless of the method of sterilization employed."

B. Sterilization

Despite the addition of antimicrobial substances, sterilization of the injectable is an indisputable step which may be accomplished in a number of ways. The method used is generally determined by the character of the product. The USP XVIII lists five methods of sterilization herein summarized.

1. Steam

Products that can withstand steam under pressure should be sterilized by this method. The temperature most often used in this process is 121°C and the time of exposure depends upon the type of product and the container. The "British Pharmacopoeia" (1968) recommends 115°C to 116°C for 30 minutes. With this method, some type of device should be used to ascertain the even distribution of heat throughout the chamber.

2. Dry Heat

A gas oven, designed for this method of heating, is utilized to sterilize such products as oils and powders. The USP XVIII recommends 160°C to 170°C for a period of 2 to 4 hours for this type of sterilization; whereas, the "British Pharmacopoeia" recommends 150°C for 1 hour.

3. Filtration

When a product that is sensitive to heat must be sterilized, the filtration method may be utilized. This process is dependent upon the adsorption of the organisms on the filtering mechanism. The sterilized material is then transferred asceptically into previously sterilized containers.

4. Gas

Heat-sensitive products may be sterilized by exposing them to ethylene oxide or propylene oxide gas. The possible formation of toxic substances from the use of this type of sterilization must be taken into consideration, particularly when a product contains chloride ions. Tests for gas residues and toxic products are essential.

5. Penetrating Radiation

Gamma or cathode rays can be used to sterilize certain types of pharmaceuticals. The utilization of the energy from 2.5 Mrad, distributed to all parts of the product, is usual for this type of sterilization. It is essential that stability tests be performed upon the sterilized product.

C. Water for Injection

A great many injectable solutions are aqueous; therefore, the water used in their preparation is of importance. Eisman *et al.* (1949) clearly indicated that deionized water differs from distilled water with respect to its bacterial content. If deionized water is to be used, the frequent regeneration of the resin bed is essential in order to remove the small number of microorganisms contained in raw water. Taylor and Burrman (1956) point out that potable water may contain a wide range of bacterial contaminants which may be sufficient to make it unsuitable for injectable solutions. In view of this, it would seem that deionized water is unsuitable for injectable solutions. Sterile water for injection is water that has been purified by distillation, made sterile, and is nonpyrogenic. Saunders and Shotten (1956) state that bacterial breakdown products in water can cause pyrogenic reactions; they, therefore, recommend that solutions for injection be prepared from freshly distilled water.

D. Antimicrobial Substances (Preservatives)

Of the available antimicrobial compounds, many are not acceptable for use in injectables because they cannot be applied parenterally. When the choice of a preservative is being decided upon, a number of factors must be taken into consideration. e.g., its chemical properties (pH) and its compatibility with the other ingredients of the formulation. Felix (1964) suggests a number of properties that the ideal preservative should possess in the normally used concentration: effectiveness against a wide range of microorganisms; solubility unaffected at either normal or subnormal temperatures; unaffected by the container, which should be nontoxic and non-irritating. Royce and Sykes (1957) point out that loss of antimicrobial agent by absorption by and volatilization through the rubber closure is a serious problem. The selection of rubber material with low absorbency may be of some help. Soaking the rubber stoppers in a solution of the antimicrobial before use is a possible countermeausre against the initial absorption of the antimicrobial agent. Furthermore, an antimicrobial agent with a more favorable partitioning between runner and water plus a small diffusion loss should be most acceptable. Both phenol and benzyl alcohol are in this class; however, the phenylmercuric salts are contraindicated. Sykes (1958) lists a number of bacteriostats according to their partioning ratios and confirms the work of Royce and Sykes (1957). Lachman *et al.* (1962) showed a greater loss of preservative from rubber-stoppered vials than from sealed ampuls containing the same preservatives. Natural rubber stoppers were the least harmful to the preservative content, and butyl rubber was least compatible with the preservative solutions. The authors felt that this might be due to the leaching of an accelerator residue. Chlorobutanol suffered degradation in solution and was absorbed by the rubber closure, as was *p*-chloro-β-phenylethyl alcohol (Lachman *et al.*, 1963).

When an antimicrobial substance has been considered for use, questions concerning its effectiveness under a number of conditions must be answered, e.g., its stability after storage under different conditions for various lengths of time. Sykes (1958) suggests that it should be reasonable to expect an antimicrobial to be effectively lethal, as well as inhibitory to all types of organisms, including molds; but the same cannot be expected with regard to lethal action against bacterial spores. It must be borne in mind that there are limitations and disadvantages in certain antimicrobial agents. Many are absorbed into rubber with the exception of phenol, which has a low partitioning ratio between rubber and water. Hess (1965) points out that commonly used bacteriostats do not have the same degree of activity, e.g., 0.1% chlorocresol is more active than 0.3% cresol. An added factor governing the choice of a preservative is its effect upon erythrocytes. Ansel and Cadwallader (1964) showed that among the preservatives studied, the parabens and thimerosal did not cause total hemolysis of rabbit and human erythrocytes within the concentrations normally employed in parenteral solutions; however, low concentrations of quaternary ammonium hemolyzed human erythrocytes. The authors suggest that hemolytic activities of quaternary ammonium compounds might be indicative of their bacteriolytic activity. Chlorhexidine diacetate destroyed rabbit erythrocytes at concentrations close to the antimicrobially effective range. Polyethylene glycols reduced the hemolytic activity of chlorhexidine diacetate and dimethylsulfoxide.

When an antimicrobial agent has been selected, its antimicrobial effectiveness in a formulation should be determined. The usual procedure is to select samples of the product randomly and subject them to a sterility test. Rdzok *et al.* (1955) developed a test procedure in which the preserved product was insulted by the introduction of common contaminants, followed by tests to determine the death or survival of the contaminants. Eisman *et al.* (1963) described a microbiological turbidimetric assay method for preservative content with *Escherichia coli* as the indicator organism. Kenny *et al.* (1964) further developed the test used by Rdzok and applied it to a wide range of products. The USP XVIII provides an official test for the estimation of viable organisms in a preserved product. This test procedure employs five test organisms: *Staphylococcus aureus*, *E. coli*, *P. aeruginosa*, *Candida albicans*, and the spores of *A. niger*. After the product has been deliberately contaminated with the test organism, samples are removed for survivor determination at various intervals of time up to 28 days.

E. Antimicrobial Agents Commonly Used in Parenterals

1. Phenol

For many years, this well-known substance has been used as an antimicrobial agent at a strength of 0.5%. According to Sykes (1958), this compound does not act rapidly and bacterial spores may survive treatment with this compound. This was confirmed by Loosemore and Russell (1963). It was demonstrated by Royce and Sykes (1957) that, in a multiple-dose vial, the distribution ratio of phenol between rubber and water is of the order of 25 to 75, which is indicative of its high concentration exponent. The antimicrobial activity of phenol is increased in acid solutions but decreased in alkaline solutions. Some of the disadvantages of phenol are: its volatility, odor, toxic properties, and occasional incompatibility with other components of the formulation.

2. Cresol

Cresol, which is not listed as an antimicrobial agent in the USP XVIII but is accepted as an antimicrobial agent by the "British Pharmacopoeia" is normally used in concentrations up to 0.5%. Royce and Sykes (1957) point out that the distribution ration of this compound between rubber and water is 33 to 67. This indicates the amount of the compound in the aqueous solution available for antimicrobial action. Halogenated cresols have been found to be more active than the nonhalogenated substances. Chlorocresol has the same type of disadvantages as phenol, e.g., volatility, odor, etc. Royce and Sykes (1957) and Sykes (1958) showed that the distribution ratio between rubber and water of chlorocresol is 85 to 15, thus indicating high dissolution in the rubber.

3. Chlorobutanol

Chlorobutanol at 0.5% is an acceptable antimicrobial agent (USP, 1970). The compatibility of this substance with drugs is acceptable; in addition, the compound has some analgesic qualities. Nair and Lach (1959) pointed out that chlorobutanol decomposes during sterilization at 115°C for 30 minutes and suggest keeping the pH at or below 4.0 when chlorobutanol is used in a formulation. The half-life period in a solution at 25°C and pH 3.0 was 90 years, whereas, at pH 7.5, it was 0.23 years. Gladbart *et al.* (1955) did not recommend the use of chlorobutanol because of its breakdown upon autoclaving. Royce and Sykes (1957) indicated that up to 90% could be absorbed by rubber stoppers. Hydrolysis of the compound above pH 3.0, causing release of hydrochloric acid, is a distinct disadvantage.

4. Organic Mercury Compounds

Phenylmercuric nitrate, phenylmercuric borate, and thimerosal are the most commonly used mercurial antimicrobials in parenteral preparations at concentrations ranging from 0.001% to 0.005%. While these compounds are recognized as strong antimicrobial agents, they have the disadvantage of being slow-acting (Riegelman *et al.*, 1956); Lawrence, 1955). These compounds also have the disadvantage of having up to 95% of the mercurial absorbed by the rubber closure (Royce and Sykes, 1957). Elowe (1955) points out that thimerosal is not stable in acid solutions; nevertheless, thimerosal is the preservative of choice in biological products. This will be covered more fully under the appropriate heading.

5. *Benzyl Alcohol*

This substance has wide use in parenteral solutions, both for its antimicrobial effectiveness and for its anesthetic properties. In 1% to 3% concentrations it demonstrates high antimicrobial activity. The advantages of this type of agent are its pleasant odor, solubility in water, and its effectiveness over a varied pH range. Vasani and King (1969) point out that in aqueous solutions containing benzyl alcohol and Tween 80, the development of cloudiness was a function of concentration and temperature. Turbidity in autoclaved samples is reversible when the solution is initially clear, but not if the solution is initially cloudy.

6. p-*Hydroxybenzoic Acid Esters*

Aalto *et al.* (1953) suggest that the parabens are probably the closest to what may be considered the ideal preservative. This observation has also been made by Neidig and Burrell (1944), Elowe (1955), and Gottfried (1962). Of the four homologous esters, the methyl and propyl parabens are the most widely used. Several authors suggest that there is synergistic activity when combinations of parabens are used (Barr and Tice, 1957b; Aalto *et al.*, 1953). In a great number of pharmaceutical formulations, the parabens are stable, although they are more active when the pH of the solution is acidic rather than neutral or alkaline (Entrekin, 1961). When the pH of a solution containing parabens reaches 10.0, they hydrolyze so rapidly that they are no longer effective (Wickliffe and Entrekin, 1964). The rather poor solubility of these compounds in water can be overcome by the use of combinations, for example, methyl paraben 0.18%, and propyl paraben 0.02%. The incompatibilities of these compounds with other agents in the formulation has been extensively covered in other parts of this chapter.

In retrospect, it should be fairly clear that the most suitable preservative for a given parenteral may be found among those discussed in this section of the article. Until the problems of absorption, odor, irritation, incompatibility, etc. are solved, the manufacturing pharmacists have to select from the available antimicrobials that which is most likely to fill their needs.

7. Combinations of Antimicrobials

Deeb and Boenigk (1958) point out that concentrated chlorobutanol can be prepared in Tween 20 and readily diluted with water or isotonic sodium chloride solution to form a suitable antimicrobial solution. Chlorobutanol is readily soluble in benzyl or phenylethyl alcohol and these combinations can be readily diluted with water to a sufficient concentration of preservative. Chlorobutanol 0.5% with either 0.5% benzyl or phenylethyl alcohol have a greater antimicrobial activity than 0.5% chlorobutanol alone.

F. Injectables (Biologics)

The list of products that come under the heading of biologics requiring preservation with an antimicrobial agent include: antitoxins, antivenins, blood derivatives, immune serums, toxoids, and vaccines. The USP XVIII states, "the choice of antimicrobial agents for use in biologics requires special care and a demonstration of effectiveness with respect to both suppression of microbial growth and relative freedom from inactivation of the therapeutic principle." In general, one of the antimicrobial agents very often used for these products is thimerosal (merthiolate). When this agent is used, it should be recognized that certain deficiencies do exist. For example, Birner and Garnet (1964) found that, upon storage, the concentration of the agent is lowered. The authors suggest that this may be due to partial absorption by the rubber closure.

1. Antitoxin

An example of this type of product is botulism antitoxin; the preservative generally used is 0.4% phenol and 0.004% phenyl mercuric borate (PDR, 1971).

2. Toxoids

When grown under favorable conditions, gram-positive organisms produce soluble toxins. These toxins are treated with formaldehyde to produce a substance known as a toxoid. Thimerosal is the antimicrobial agent of choice for this type of product.

3. Vaccines of Viral Origin

Under the heading of this group is listed: poliomyelitis (Sabin), a living vaccine; poliomyelitis (Salk), an inactivated vaccine; and smallpox, a living vaccine.

Numerous investigators have tested a number of antimicrobial agents for these products. In the preservation of the Salk vaccine, Pivnick *et al.* (1963) determined that formaldehyde, if not neutralized by bisulfite, is sufficiently antibacterial. They found that benzethonium chloride inhibited the growth of gram-positive bacteria, yeasts, and molds but was less active against gram-negative organisms. Antibiotics were not adequate in themselves in preventing gross bacterial contamination. If 2-phenoxyethanol was added to the vaccine along with the antibiotics, the combination was effective in destroying contaminants. Tracy *et al.* (1964) found that formaldehyde is sufficiently antibacterial but, in the concentration used in the vaccine, has insufficient antimycotic activity. The parabens 0.16%, when mixed with residual formaldehyde, are effective antimicrobial agents except that, upon prolonged storage, they cause a lowering of the pH. Gardner and Pittman (1965) found that the mercurials decreased the potency of inactivated polio vaccine. The addition of ethylenediaminetetracetic acid prevented the breakdown of merthiolate, thus permitting the maintenance of its antimicrobial effectiveness.

Smallpox vaccine is supplied in dry form to which is added the sterile solvent. The antimicrobial agent generally used in this product is 0.5% phenol. Influenza vaccine and rabies vaccine must contain an antimicrobial agent (USP, 1970). The acceptable preservative for these products is merthiolate.

4. *Immune Serum*

These substances, in general, are obtained from immunized animals, except for antiviral serums, which are obtained from patients who have recovered from the disease. Merthiolate and phenol are acceptable as antimicrobials for this type of product.

5. *Bacterial Vaccines*

These are preparations of killed, attenuated, or avirulent organisms, or any of their products which are used to produce immunity. When an antimicrobial agent is chosen for the preservation of this type of product, it must be ascertained that no damage is inflicted upon the organisms, such that the antigenic potency is impaired. Thimerosal and phenol are usually acceptable antimicrobial agents for this group of products. The influence of the preservative upon the stability of the vaccine is of importance. Gardner and Pittman (1965) showed that the stability of pertussis vaccine preserved with benzethonium chloride or the parabens (methyl and propyl) was less stable than with thimerosal. The use of formaldehyde as a preservative in pertussis vaccine had a deleterious effect upon the potency of the vaccine (Pittman and Cox, 1965). With the addition of inactivated Salk polio to diphtheria, tetanus, and pertussis vaccine, a combination of four antigenic vaccines was formed under the name of DTPP vaccine. In combinations of vaccines, instability of one or more components of the vaccine is caused by the preservative, e.g., the deleterious effect of thimerosal upon the potency of inactivated polio vaccine. Another example of incompatibility would be the instability of the pertussis portion of the combination due to the use of the parabens as a preservative (Gardner and Pittman, 1965).

6. *Diagnostic Preparations*

Purified protein derivative (PPD), a substance used in testing a subject for tuberculin reactivity, is normally preserved with 0.5% phenol. Pivnick *et al.* (1965) demonstrated that phenol reduced the potency of diluted PPD solutions. Magnusson *et al.* (1958) reported that 8-hydroxyquinoline sulfate was an effective antimicrobial agent for PPD. This was confirmed by Pivnick *et al.* (1965), who showed that this compound was effective against small numbers of *P. aeruginosa*, yeasts, and molds.

ACKNOWLEDGMENTS

The author wishes to express his gratitude for the assistance given him in the preparation of this chapter. Dr. Frank Adair, Dr. Jerome Harris, and Dr. Hans Heymann applied themselves to scientific and editorial matters. I am obliged to Mrs. Elizabeth Meylan for help in surveying the literature and to Mrs. Ruth Blatchford for her invaluable assistance in producing this manuscript.

References

Aalto, T. R., Firman, M. C., and Rigler, N. E. (1953). *J. Amer. Pharm. Ass.* **42**, 449–457.
Adair, F. W., Geftic, S. G., and Gelzer, J. (1969). *Appl. Microbiol.* **18**, 299–302.
Adair, F. W., Geftic, S. G., and Gelzer, J. (1972). *Appl. Microbiol.* (in press).
Anderson, R. A. (1970). *Australas. J. Pharm.* [N.S.] **51**, Suppl. 94, 592–594.
Ansel, H., and Cadwallader, D. (1964). *J. Pharm. Sci.* **53**, 169–172.
Barr, M., and Tice, L. F. (1957a). *J. Amer. Pharm. Ass., Sci. Ed.* **46**, 217–218.
Barr, M., and Tice, L. F. (1957b). *J. Amer. Pharm. Ass., Sci. Ed.* **46**, 219–221.
Barr, M., and Tice, L. F. (1957c). *J. Amer. Pharm. Ass., Sci. Ed.* **46**, 221–223.
Barr, M., and Tice, L. F. (1957d). *J. Amer. Pharm. Ass., Sci. Ed.* **46**, 442–445.
Barr, M., and Tice, L. F. (1957e). *J. Amer. Pharm. Ass., Sci. Ed.* **46**, 445–451.
Bean, H. S., and Heman-Ackah, S. M. (1964). *J. Pharm. Pharmacol.* **16**, 58T-67T.
Bean, H. S., Richards, J. P., and Thomas, J. (1962). *Boll. Chim. Farm.* **101**, 339–346.
Bean, H. S., Heman-Ackah, S. M., and Thomas, J. (1965). *J. Soc. Cosmet. Chem.* **16**, 15–30.
Birner, J., and Garnet, J. R. (1964). *J. Pharm. Sci.* **53**, 1424–1426.

Brewer, J. H., Goldstein, S. W., and McLaughlin, C. B. (1953). *J. Amer. Pharm. Ass., Sci. Ed.* **42**, 584–585.
BPC, (1968). "British Pharmaceutical Codex."
Brown, M. R. W., and Norton, D. A. (1965). *J. Soc. Cosmet. Chem.* **16**, 369–387.
Brown, M. R. W., and Richards, R. M. E. (1965). *Nature (London)* **207**, 1391–1392.
Brown, M. R. W., Foster, J. H. S., Norton, D. A., and Richards, R. M. E. (1964), *Pharm. J.* **192**, 8.
Davies, G. E., Francis, J., Martin, A. R., Rose, F. L., and Swain, G. (1954). *Brit. J. Pharmacol.* **9**, 192–196.
Deeb, E. N., and Boenigk, J. W. (1958). *J. Amer. Pharm. Ass., Sci. Ed.* **47**, 807–809.
Eisman, P. C., Kull, F. C., and Mayer, R. L. (1949). *J. Amer. Pharm. Ass., Sci. Ed.* **38**, 88–91.
Eisman, P. C., Cooper, J., and Jaconia, D. (1957). *J. Amer. Pharm. Ass., Sci. Ed.* **46**, 144–147.
Eisman, P. C., Ebersold, E., Weertz, J., and Lachman, L. (1963). *J. Pharm. Sci.* **52**, 183–185.
Elowe, L. N. (1955). *Bull. Ont. Coll. Pharm.* **4**, 45–47.
Entrekin, D. N. (1961). *J. Pharm. Sci.* **50**, 743–746.
Felix, R. I. (1964). *J. Soc. Cosmet. Chem.* **16**.
Foster, J. H. S. (1964). *Pharm. J.* **192**, 429.
Foster, J. H. S. (1965). *Mfg. Chem.* **36**, 45–47.
Gardner, R. A., and Pittman, M. (1965). *Appl. Microbiol.* **13**, 564–569.
Gladbart, W. R., Jr., Wood, R. M., and Purdum, W. A. (1955). *Bull., Amer. Soc. Hosp. Pharm.* **12**, 534–539.
Gottfried, N. S. (1962). *Amer. J. Hosp. Pharm.* **19**, 310–314.
Grote, I. W., and Woods, M. (1955). *J. Amer. Pharm. Ass.* **44**, 9–11.
Harris, W. (1961). *Australas. J. Pharm.* **42**, 583–584, and 587–588.
Hess, H. (1965). *Soap, Perfum. Cosmet.* **38**, 955–961.
Hjorth, N., and Trolle, L. C. (1962). *Amer. Perfum.* **77**, 43–45.
Hugo, W. B., and Foster, J. H. S. (1964). *J. Pharm. Pharmacol.* **16**, 209.
Hugo, W. B., and Longworth, A. R. (1964). *J. Pharm. Pharmacol.* **16**, 655–662.
Humberstone, B. (1961). *Australas. J. Pharm.* [N.S.] **42**.
Kedzia, W., Lewon, J., and Wisnieuski, T. (1961). *J. Pharm. Pharmacol.* **13**, 614–616.
Kenny, D. S., Grundy, W. E., and Otto, R. H. (1964). *Bull. Parenteral Drug Ass.* **18**, 10–19.
Klein, M., Millwood, E. G., and Walther, W. W. (1954). *J. Pharm. Pharmacol.* **6**, 725–732.
Kohan, S., Carlin, H., and Whitehead, R. (1962). *Amer. J. Hosp.* **36**, 78.
Kohn, S. R., Gershenfeld, L., and Barr, M. (1963). *J. Pharm. Sci.* **52**, 967–974.
Kvamme, R. (1969). *Norg. Apotekerforen. Tidsskr.* **77**, 468–479.
Lachman, L., Weinstein, S., Hopkins, G., Slack, S., Eisman, P. C., and Cooper, J. (1962). *J. Pharm. Sci.* **51**, 224–232.
Lachman, L., Weinstein, S., Urbanyi, T., Ebersold, E., and Cooper, J. (1963). *J. Pharm. Sci.* **52**, 241–243.
Lawrence, C. A. (1955). *J. Amer. Pharm. Ass., Sci. Ed.* **44**, 457–464.
Loosemore, M., and Russell, A. D. (1963). *J. Pharm. Pharmacol.* **15**, 558.
McCarthy, T. (1969). *J. Mond. Pharm.* **12**, 321–329.
MacGregor, D. R., and Elliker, P. R. (1958). *Can. J. Microbiol.* **4**, 499–503.
Magnusson, M., Guld, J., Magnus, K., and Waaler, H. (1958). *Bull. W.H.O.* **19**, 799 and 828.
Merck Index. (1968). "Merck Index of Chemicals and Drugs," 7th ed.
Montgomery, W. F., and Hallsall, K. C. (1964a). *Pharm. J.* **192**, 407.
Montgomery, W. F., and Hallsall, K. C. (1964b). *Pharm. J.* **192**, 461.
Nair, A. D. and Lach, J. L. (1959). *J. Amer. Pharm. Ass., Sci. Ed.* **48**, 390–395.
Neidig, C. P., and Burrell, H. (1944). *Drug Cosmet. Ind.* **54**, 408–410 and 481–489.
Noble, W. C., and Savin, J. A. (1966). *Lancet* **1**, 347–349.
Patel, N. K., and Foss, N. E. (1965). *J. Pharm. Sci.* **54**, 1495–1499.

Pettoruto, N. (1970). *Drug Cosmet. Ind.* **106**, 46–50 and 138–141.
PDR (1971). "Physicians' Desk Reference."
Pisano, F. D., and Kostenbauder, H. B. (1959). *J. Amer. Pharm. Ass., Sci. Ed.* **48**, 310–314.
Pittman, M., and Cox, C. B. (1965). *Appl. Microbiol.* **13**, 447–456.
Pivnick, H., Tracy, J. M., and Glass, D. G. (1963). *J. Pharm. Sci.* **52**, 883–888.
Pivnick, H., Siebenman, C. D., Landi, S., and Ashford, W. R. (1965). *J. Pharm. Sci.* **54**, 640–642.
Prickett, P. S., Murray, H. L., and Mercer, N. H. (1961). *J. Pharm. Sci.* **50**, 316–320.
Puls, D. D., Lindgren, L. F., and Cosgrove, F. P. (1955). *J. Amer. Pharm. Ass., Sci. Ed.* **44**, 85–87.
Rdzok, E. J., Grundy, W. E., Kirchmeyer, F. J., and Sylvester, J. C. (1955). *J. Amer. Pharm. Ass., Sci. Ed.* **44**, 613–616.
Riegelman, S., Vaughn, D. G., Jr., and Okumoto, M. (1956). *J. Amer. Pharm. Ass., Sci. Ed.* **45**, 93–98.
Royce, A., and Sykes, G. (1957). *J. Pharm. Pharmacol.* **9**, 814–822.
Russell, A. D., Jenkins, J., and Harrison, I. H. (1967). *Advan. Appl. Microbiol.* **9**.
Saunders, L., and Shotton, E. (1956). *J. Pharm. Pharmacol.* **8**, 832–847.
Sykes, G. (1958). *J. Pharm. Pharmacol.* **10**, 40T–46T.
Taub, A., Meer, W. A., and Clausen, L. W. (1958). *J. Amer. Pharm. Ass., Sci. Ed.* **47**, 235–239.
Taylor, E. W., and Burrman, N. P. (1956). *J. Pharm. Pharmacol.* **8**, 817–831.
Tenenbaum, S. (1967). *J. Soc. Cosmet. Chem.* **18**, 797–807.
Tillman, W. J., and Kuramato, R. (1957). *J. Amer. Pharm. Ass., Sci. Ed.* **46**, 211–214.
Tracy, J. M., Glass, D. G., Nicholson, M. J., and Pivnick, H. (1964). *J. Pharm. Sci.* **53**, 659–663.
USP (1970). "United States Pharmacopeia," 18th rev. ed. Mack Publ. Co., Easton, Pennsylvania.
Vasani, J., and King, R. E. (1969). *Amer. J. Pharm.* **141**, 177–185.
Wedderburn, D. L. (1964). *Advanc. Pharm. Sci.* **1**, 195–268.
Wickliffe, B., and Entrekin, D. N. (1964). *J. Pharm. Sci.* **53**, 769–773.

THE PRACTICE OF QUALITY ASSURANCE IN THE HOSPITAL PHARMACY

William E. Hassan, Jr.

Peter Bent Brigham Hospital,
Boston, Massachusetts

I. Introduction

In a statistical profile of the nation's hospitals for 1970, the American Hospital Association reported that there were 7123 hospitals in the United States registered by that body. These hospitals had 1,615,771 beds, admitted 31,7759,124 in-patients, and spent over $25 billion to provide services for both in-patients and ambulatory patients. These statistics represent one admission for every 15 residents of the United States and expenditures equal to $127 for each resident of the country (Guide Issue, 1971).

Clearly, the above statistics place the hospital industry in the top five industries of the nation. As such, it has an effect upon every citizen, whether hospitalized or not, and it owes to him the assurance of quality care in return for his support. In this regard, hospitals make every effort possible to maintain high standards of medical care. They invite outside agencies to enter the premises and inspect them in order to assure the public that the physical plant meets the standards set by fire, sanitation, environmental, and radiation safety codes. Where possible, employees performing specialized tasks such as nursing, pharmacy, laboratory technology, and radiation technology are required to be registered by the state and are required to participate in a program of continuing education to maintain a high degree of competence. Outside accreditation bodies, such as the Joint Commission for the Accreditation of Hospitals and the American Association of Blood Banks, are invited to review the institution's staff and procedures in order to assure the public of high quality performance. Even the hospital's educational programs are subject to scrutiny and evaluation by such agencies as the American Medical Association, National League for Nursing, American Society of Hospital Pharmacists, and the American Dietetic Association, to mention a few.

Internally, hospitals maintain an on-going program designed to provide assurance that the quality of care is being monitored. Consider the fact that most hospitals have many of the following committees examining special activities of the institution:

Antibiotics Committee. Reviews the use of antibiotics within the hospital.
Environmental Safety Committee. Reviews all environmental hazards including fire, electrical, and sanitary.
Operating Room Committee. Reviews all procedures and policies of this highly specialized area.
Current Practices Committee. Reviews all procedures in use on the nursing floors and standardizes techniques and equipment.
Blood Bank Advisory Committee. Reviews all procedures and techniques in use in collecting, testing, preserving, and distributing of

blood and its components.
Laboratory Committee. Reviews all requests for new laboratory procedures and monitors the quality of laboratory performance.
Pharmacy and Therapeutics Committee. Maintains surveillance over the selection and use of drugs within the hospital.
Nursing Advisory Committee. Reviews current nursing protocols and recommends improved methods of performance.
Medical Records Committee. Reviews the quality of the patient's medical record.
Utilization Review Committee. Reviews patient admissions as well as length of stay in order to prevent unnecessary utilization of hospital beds.
Research Committee. Reviews all applications for research to be conducted within the hospital.
Human Subjects Committee. Reviews all research projects intending to use human beings as research subjects to assure that the procedure is safe and that informed consent has been obtained.
Radiation Committee. Assures that radiation safety is practiced throughout the hospital and its laboratories.
Tissue Committee. Insures that surgery of the highest standard is practiced in that healthy tissue is not routinely excised.

Without a doubt, hospitals make every effort to provide assurance of overall quality care. Yet, what assurance do they give relative to the quality of pharmaceutical service?

One of the greatest contributions made by the hospital pharmacists of today, to the institution, its staff, and its patients is a quality control system that insures the integrity of the pharmaceutical service and its products. This has been accomplished through the use of drug formularies, automatic stop orders, control of research drugs, prepackaging of drugs, unit-dose dispensing, analytical control of in-hospital manufactured products, and the development of a Pharmacy and Therapeutics Committee to monitor the department's programs.

Accordingly, the purpose of this chapter is to provide an overview of how these systems provide an assurance of quality of the products dispensed by and the services rendered by the hospital pharmacy staff.

The Pharmacy and Therapeutics Committee

The Pharmacy and Therapeutics Committee is a tool for maintaining medical staff self-government. It is responsible to the medical staff as a whole and its recommendations are subject to medical staff approval. The

Committee assists in the formulation of broad professional policies regarding the evaluation, selection, procurement, distribution, use, safety procedures, and other control matters relating to drugs in hospitals.

In 1959, The American Hospital Association and the American Society of Hospital Pharmacists approved a statement on the Pharmacy and Therapeutics Committee which states (1959):

> Preamble*
>
> Hospitals organize and marshal the best professional skills and judgment available to provide care and treatment of patients. The treatment of these patients in many cases is dependent upon the effective use of drugs. The multiplicity of drugs available today makes it mandatory that an organized sound program of activity be developed within the hospital to ensure that patients receive the best care and protection possible. One of the most effective ways of providing this kind of care and protection is by organizing a pharmacy and therapeutics committee. This committee is designed to make maximum use of available professional skills and judgment. The establishment of a pharmacy and therapeutics committee is strongly recommended to all hospitals. It is a measure which supports and enhances the principle of self-government in the area of high drug standards and practices for the medical staff connected with a hospital. Ultimate benefits accrue to the patient in improved patient care and treatment as established voluntarily by the medical staff.
>
> The Pharmacy and Therapeutics Committee
>
> The Pharmacy and Therapeutics Committee is an advisory group of the medical staff and serves as the organizational line of communication or liaison between the medical staff and the pharmacy department. This committee is composed primarily of physicians and the pharmacist and is selected under the guidance of the medical staff. It is also a policy-recommending body to the medical staff and to the administration of the hospital on all matters related to the use of drugs. (This committee does not have intrinsic authority or power of action unless specifically granted such authority.)
>
> Purposes
>
> The primary purposes of the pharmacy and therapeutics committee are:
>
> A. Advisory—The committee recommends the adoption or assists in the formulation of broad professional policies regarding evaluation, selection, procurement, distribution, use, safe practices, and other matters pertinent to drugs in hospitals.
>
> B. Educational—The committee recommends or assists in the formulation of programs designed to meet the needs of the professional staff (doctors, nurses, and the pharmacist) for complete current knowledge on matters related to drugs and drug practices.
>
> Organization
>
> While the composition of the pharmacy and therapeutics committee may vary from hospital to hospital, the following is offered as a guide:
>
> A. The pharmacy and therapeutics committee of the medical staff should be composed of no less than three physicians and the pharmacist, appointed by a governing unit or elected official of the organized medical staff. The hospital administrator or his designated representative should be an *ex officio* member of the committee.

B. A chairman from the physician representatives should be appointed. The pharmacist is generally designated secretary.

C. The pharmacy and therapeutics committee should meet regularly, no less frequently than twice per year, and should meet on call when necessary.

D. The committee should feel free to invite to its meetings persons within or without the hospital who can contribute from their specialized knowledge or experience.

E. An agenda is desirable and should be prepared and submitted to members of the committee in sufficient time before the meeting.

F. Minutes should be kept by the secretary and should be maintained in the permanent records of the hospital.

G. Recommendations of the pharmacy and therapeutics committee should be presented to the medical staff or its appropriate committee for adoption or recommendation.

Functions and Scope

The basic organization of the hospital and medical staffs will determine the functions and scope of the pharmacy and therapeutics committee. The following list, which is not necessarily comprehensive, is offered as a guide:

A. To serve in an advisory capacity to the medical staff and hospital administration in all matters pertaining to the use of drugs.

B. To serve in an advisory capacity to the medical staff and the pharmacist in the selection or choice of drugs which meet the most effective therapeutic quality standards.

C. To evaluate objectively clinical data regarding new drugs or agents proposed for use in the hospital.

D. To prevent unnecessary duplication of the same basic drug or its combinations.

E. To recommend additions to and deletions from the list of drugs accepted for use in the hospital.

F. To develop a basic drug list or formulary of accepted drugs for use in the hospital and to provide for its constant revision.

G. To make recommendations concerning drugs to be stocked in hospital patient units or services.

H. To establish or plan suitable educational programs for the professional staff on pertinent matters related to drugs and their use.

I. To recommend policies regarding the safe use of drugs in hospitals, including a study of such matters as investigational drugs, hazardous drugs, and others.

J. To study problems involved in proper distribution and labeling of medications for inpatients and outpatient s.

K. To study problems related to the administration of medications.

L. To review reported adverse reactions to drugs administered.

M. To evaluate periodically medical records in terms of drug therapy.

A. Adverse Drug Reaction Control

In addition to the responsibility for selection of drugs to be used within the hospital, the committee plays an important role in developing adverse drug reaction programs and in formulating automatic stop orders for all categories of dangerous drugs. With respect to the adverse drug reaction program, it is the responsibility of the committee to define, for the purposes of the institution, the phrase "adverse drug reaction." Once the definition has been promulgated, then the committee develops a methodology for the reporting of these adverse reactions. In addition, the adverse reactions are studied by the committee and when necessary data are forwarded to national agencies that are interested in the accumulation of this data. The adverse drug reaction report form can take many different formats and none is recommended here. However, one should be careful to see that whatever the format is, it includes space for the provision of the following information:

a. Drug or agent involved;
b. Type of reaction;
c. Age of patient;
d. Sex of patient;
e. Color of patient;
f. Other drugs in use concomitantly with the offending agent;
g. Corrective action taken.

Since one of the functions of the Pharmacy and Therapeutics Committee is "to serve in an advisory capacity to the medical staff and hospital administration in all matters pertaining to the use of drugs," many such committees have also become involved in such endeavours as drug–interactions, drug–laboratory test interactions, and drug utilization review (Visconti, 1969; Rucker, 1970).

B. Automatic Stop Order

Because certain drugs should not be used for long periods of time without adequate control of the patient, the Pharmacy and Therapeutics Committee generally develops for hospital use what is known as an "automatic stop order for dangerous drugs." By adopting such a policy, patients who are receiving such agents as narcotics, hypnotics, anticoagulants, etc., must be reviewed at predetermined periods of time and the medication order rewritten to prevent its expiration. Although this may seem cumbersome, it is clear that this is a means whereby dangerous drugs may be properly administered under medical staff control.

C. The Hospital Formulary

Another major responsibility of the Pharmacy and Therapeutics Committee is the development of the hospital formulary. Although there are those who denounce the formulary system, it does have a valid and valuable use within the institution. At the least, it serves as a means of controlling the medicinal agents to be used within the hospital by having the various products evaluated by a group of physicians who demonstrate an interest in the area of therapeutics. Thus, in an institution where there are large numbers of students—medical and nursing—it is of importance to utilize the hospital formulary as a control over the types of medication that are available for use in the hospital. In addition, the meticulous review by each member of the Pharmacy and Therapeutics Committee assures the physician and the patient of the fact that the product he is receiving is considered to be the most efficacious available at that time.

Because of the importance of the operation of a hospital formulary system, the American Medical Association, the American Pharmaceutical Association, the American Hospital Association, and the American Society of Hospital Pharmacists have agreed upon the following Statement of Guiding Principals on the Operation of the Hospital Formulary System. The following is the statement:

> Preamble*
>
> The treatment of patients in hospitals in many cases is dependent upon the effective use of drugs. The multiplicity of drugs available makes it mandatory that a sound program of drug usage be developed within the hospital to ensure that patients receive the best care and protection possible.
>
> In the interest of better patient care, there should be a program of objective evaluation, selection, and use of medicinal agents in the hospital. This program is the basis of rational drug therapy. The hospital formulary concept is a method for providing such a program in hospitals and has been utilized as such over the years.
>
> The hospital formulary system is based upon its approval by the organized medical staff, the concurrence of individual staff members, and the functioning of a properly organized pharmacy and therapeutics committee of the staff. The basic policies and procedures governing the hospital formulary system should be incorporated in the medical staff bylaws, or in the medical staff rules and regulations.
>
> The pharmacy and therapeutics committee, composed of physicians and pharmacists selected under the guidance of the medical staff, represents the official organizational line of communication and liaison between the medical staff as a whole and its recommendations are subject to approval by the organized medical staff, as well as to the normal process of administrative approval.
>
> This committee assists in the formulation of broad professional policies relating to drugs in hospitals, including their evaluation or appraisal, selection, procurement, storage, distribution, use and safety procedures.
>
> Definition of Hospital Formulary and Hospital Formulary System
>
> The hospital formulary is a continually revised compilation of pharmaceuticals which reflects the current clinical judgment of the medical staff.
>
> The hospital formulary system is a method whereby the medical staff of a hospital,

*"Statement of Guiding Principles on the Operation of the Hospital Formulary System." Reference manual on hospital pharmacy, pp. 186–190. American Hospital Association, Chicago, Illinois.

working through a pharmacy and therapeutics committee, evaluates, appraises, and selects from among numerous available medicinal agents and dosage forms those that are considered most useful in patient care.

The hospital formulary system provides for the procuring, prescribing, dispensing, and administering of drugs under either their nonproprietary or proprietary names in instances where drugs have both names.

Guiding Principles.

The following principles may serve as a guide to physicians, pharmacists, and administrators in hospitals utilizing the hospital formulary system:

1. The medical staff shall appoint a pharmacy committee composed of physicians and pharmacists and outline its purposes, organization, function, and scope.

2. The hospital formulary system shall be sponsored by the medical staff based upon the recommendations of the pharmacy and therapeutics committee. The medical staff should adapt the principles of the hospital formulary system to the needs of the particular hospital.

3. The medical staff shall adopt written policies and procedures governing the hospital formulary system as developed by the pharmacy and therapeutics committee. Action of the medical staff is subject to the normal process of administrative approval.

These policies and procedures shall afford guidance in the evaluation or appraisal, selection, procurement, storage, distribution, safety procedures, and other matters relating to drugs in the hospital and shall be published in the hospital's formulary or other media available to all members of the medical staff.

4. To ensure the maintenance of the responsibility and prerogatives of the physician in the exercise of his professional judgment, the hospital formulary system shall not contain any policies or procedures which, prior to the time of prescribing, provide for consent by the physician to the dispensing of a nonproprietary drug or to the dispensing of a proprietary brand different from the brand which he prescribed. However, it shall be within his discretion at the time of prescribing to approve or disapprove the dispensing of a nonproprietary drug or the dispensing of a different proprietary brand.

5. The medical staff shall adopt the policy of, and formulate the procedure for, including drugs in the formulary by their nonproprietary names, even though proprietary names are and will continue to be in common use in the hospital. Physicians may be encouraged to prescribe drugs under their nonproprietary names, although the nomenclature used is entirely a matter of the individual medical practitioner's discretion.

6. In the absence of written policies approved by the medical staff relative to the operation of the hospital formulary system, and authorization from the prescribing physician, the pharmacist must dispense the brand prescribed, bearing in mind his professional prerogative to confer with the physician should the prescribed brand be unavailable.

7. A hospital shall make certain that its nursing personnel are informed in writing (through its established means of communication) about the existence of the formulary system in the hospital and the procedures governing its operation.

8. In the formulation of policies and procedures, the terms "substitute" and "substitution" should be avoided, since these terms have been used to imply the unauthorized dispensing of a brand different from that prescribed or the dispensing of an entirely different drug, neither of which takes place under a properly operated hospital formulary system.

9. Provision shall be made to apprise the medical staff of changes in the working of the hospital formulary system or in the content of the hospital formulary.

10. Provision shall be made for the appraisal and use by members of the medical staff:

(a) of drugs not included in the formulary, and (b) of investigational drugs.

11. The pharmacist, with the advice and guidance of the pharmacy and therapeutics committee, shall be responsible for specifications as to quality, quantity, and source of supply of all drugs, chemicals, biologicals, and pharmaceutical preparations used in the diagnosis and treatment of patients, and for assuring that quality is not compromised for economic considerations. When applicable, such products shall meet the standards of quality of the United States Pharmacopeia or National Formulary.

12. The labeling of a medication container with the nonproprietary name of the contents is always proper. The use of a proprietary name other than that describing the actual contents is improper if it is used in a manner that can be taken as descriptive of the contents, even though personnel familiar with the hospital formulary system may understand that it is not descriptive. The following format is recommended for labeling individual patients' containers used within hospitals:

(Nonproprietary name)
(Name of manufacturer or distributor)
Note for information of staff:
Prescription or order for
(Proprietary name)
Dispensed as per formulary policy;
contents are same basic drugs as
prescribed but may be of another
brand

Recommendation

A hospital formulary system, based upon these guiding principles, is considered to be important in drug therapy in hospitals. In the interest of better patient care, its adoption by hospital medical staffs is recommended.

D. Investigational Use of Drugs

Of all drugs introduced into the hospital system, the investigational use drug requires the greatest control. In addition to hospital controls, the Federal Government and the manufacturer require that certain restricted protocols be followed by the principal investigator.

The American Hospital Association, the American Society of Hospital Pharmacists, and the American Nurses Association have combined to develop the following Statement of Principles involved in the Use of Investigational Drugs in Hospitals. In reading the statement, it should be borne in mind that no specific method for the control of these drugs is recommended and the methodology for their control is left to the ingenuity of the Pharmacy and Therapeutics Committee. Thus, some hospitals have developed physician's data sheets on investigational drugs, nurse's data sheets on investigational drugs, pharmacist's data sheets on investigational drugs, and new drug forms (Hassan, 1967a).

The Statement*

Hospitals are the primary centers for clinical investigations on new drugs. By definition these are drugs that have not yet been released by the Federal Food and Drug Administration for general use.

Since investigational drugs have not been certified as being for general use and have not been cleared for sale in interstate commerce by the Federal Food and Drug Administration, hospitals and their medical staffs have an obligation to their patients to see that proper procedures for their use are established.

Procedures for the control of investigational drugs should be based upon the following principles:

1. Investigational drugs should be used only under the direct supervision of the principal investigator, who should be a member of the medical staff and who should assume the burden of securing the necessary consent.
2. The hospital should do all in its power to foster research consistent with adequate safeguards for the patient.
3. When nurses are called upon to administer investigational drugs, they should have available to them basic information concerning such drugs—including dosage forms, available strengths, actions and uses, side effects, symptoms of toxicity, and so forth.
4. The hospital should establish, preferably through the pharmacy and therapeutics committee, a central unit where essential information on investigational drugs is maintained and whence it may be made available to authorized personnel.
5. The pharmacy department is the appropriate area for the storage of investigational drugs, as it is for all other drugs. This will also provide for the proper labeling and dispensing in accord with the investigator's written orders.

The Department of Health, Education, and Welfare has determined that the rights and welfare of human subjects involved in activities supported by this agency must be protected and such protection is the responsibility of the institution receiving the support of the agency. In order to enforce this policy, HEW has specifically stated that no grant will be funded until such time as the institution has complied with this requirement. The compliance review shall specifically state that the rights and welfare of the subjects involved are adequately protected, that the risks to an individual are outweighed by the potential benefits to him or by the importance of the knowledge to be gained, that an informed consent is to be obtained by methods that are adequate and appropriate. In addition, the institution must show evidence that there exists a mechanism for continuing review of the activity in keeping with these determinations.

In reviewing the federal regulations, the following defintions are of relevance:

*"Statement of Principles Involved in the Use of Investigational Drugs in Hospital." Reference manual on hospital pharmacy, p. 179. American Hospital Association, Chicago, Illinois.

a. *Subject*
This term describes any individual who may be at risk as a consequence of participation as a subject in research, development, demonstration, or other activities supported by DHEW funds.

b. *At Risk*
An individual is considered to be "at risk" if he may be exposed to the possibility of harm—physical, psychological, sociological, or other—as a consequence of any activity which goes beyond the application of those established and accepted methods necessary to meet his needs. The determination of when an individual is at risk is a matter of the application of common sense and sound professional judgment to the circumstances of the activity in question. Responsibility for this determination resides at all levels of institutional and departmental review. Definitive determination will be made by the operating agency.

c. *Informed Consent*
Informed consent is the agreement obtained from a subject or his authorized representative, to the subject's participation in an activity. The basic elements of an informed consent are:
(1) A fair explanation of the procedures to be followed, including an identification of those which are experimental;
(2) A description of the attendant discomforts and risks;
(3) A description of the benefits to be expected;
(4) A disclosure of appropriate alternative procedures that would be advantageous for the subject;
(5) An offer to answer any inquiries concerning the procedures;
(6) An instruction that the subject is free to withdraw his consent and to discontinue participation in the project or activity at any time. In addition, the agreement, written or oral, entered into by the subject, should include no exculpatory language through which the subject is made to waive, or to appear to waive, any of his legal rights, or to release the institution or its agents from liability for negligence. Informed consent must be documented.

E. Institutional Responsibility

In view of the fact that the grantee or contracting institution is accountable to the Department of Health, Education and Welfare (HEW) for effectively carrying out the provisions of the institutional assurance for the protection of human subjects as accepted and recognized by the department, most hospitals have formulated a committee with this responsibility assigned to it. In many institutions this committee is called the Human Subjects Committee, Research Committee, or Committee for the Use of Human Subjects in Research.

Irrespective of the name assigned to the committee, it has the responsibility of complying with the federal regulations. The committee members are generally selected from a representative group of the medical disciplines. The committee members appointed are identified by name, occupation or position, and by other pertinent indications of experience and competence in areas pertinent to the areas of review such as earned degrees, board certifications, licensures, memberships, etc.

Once formed, it is the responsibility of the committee to adopt a statement of principles that will assist it in the discharge of its responsibilities. In addition, most committees generally adopt a series of guidelines which are published and distributed to all individuals on the medical staff interested in the use of human subjects for research purposes. These guidelines usually spell out the parameters which the department of HEW requires in order that the institution be in compliance. In addition, it provides for such basic information as the forms that require the type of informed consent that will be accepted by the committee, dates of committee meetings, types of reviews to be held, appeal procedures, and penalties for noncompliance.

III. Bulk Compounding

Most pharmacists believe that the future of pharmacy depends upon practitioners who are patient-oriented rather than product-oriented. However, there are those who agree with Provost (1969) that the above philosophy be modified to "patient oriented *as well* as product oriented."

Product orientation goes far beyond the knowledge of dosage form, dose, toxicity, incompatabilities, and adverse reactions. It includes the scientific knowledge associated with product formulation and compounding. While physicians and clinical pharmacologists can invade the former aspect of product orientation, the biopharmaceutical phase is an area reserved only for the pharmacist.

Reference to "Mirror to Hospital Pharmacy" (Francke *et al.*, 1967) reveals that approximately 40% of hospitals with pharmacies operate a bulk compounding program; three out of four short-term general hospitals with 500 or more beds and a similar percentage of all long-term hospitals engage in some type of manufacturing. The same publication also reveals that a large proportion of the hospitals with bulk compounding programs produce products that are commercially unavailable. The reason given for this is as follows:

> This may be explained, perhaps, by the close relationship between physicians and pharmacists in hospitals. Another major factor is the unsuitability of many commercially available dosage forms for the treatment of certain types of unusual illnesses often encountered in hospital practice. . . . Whatever form the product takes, its origin lies in the desire of the physician to find a better therapeutic agent for his patient. Thus, many hospital pharmacists have considerable opportunity to utilize the fundamental processes of manufacturing pharmacy and to offer characteristic professional services to the physician and patient. (p. 122).

It is doubtful that the above has changed significantly in the past decade. Thus, since hospital pharmacists do manufacture, it is imperative that the manufacturing program be coordinated with a program for quality control.

This view is emphasized by other writers (Bowles, 1969) who state that hospital-produced drug products pose a contamination problem. Accordingly, it is imperative that the hospital pharmacist should review critically compounding techniques for hospital-produced products. Included in this review should be the following:

a. Suitability of the area for the manufacturing program;
b. Cleanliness of the area;
c. Condition of the equipment;
d. Control of personnel;
e. Evaluation of formulae giving special attention to preservatives and stabilizers;
f. Labeling and dispensing methods;
g. Adequacy of assay procedures.

In addition, hospital pharmacists should, where possible, follow the guidelines of the policy statement of the Pharmaceutical Manufacturer's Association—General Principles of Control of Quality in the Drug Industry—as well as the new regulation of the Federal Food and Drug Administration on the same subject.

A. Equipment

Equipment used in bulk compounding within the hospital is often a matter of economic consideration although, at times, it may be one of personal preference. For this reason it is not possible to provide for a listing of all of the available equipment. As individuals publish data concerning manufacturing programs, suggested equipment lists are generally included (Martin, 1965; Schumacker, 1969).

One aspect of control which is generally overlooked is that of mechanical equipment maintenance. Clean, efficiently functioning equipment does contribute to the quality of the hospital manufactured product. A method of control is via the Equipment Maintenance Record (Hassan, 1967b). Such a record, in addition to providing the equipment name, vendor, serial number, cost, and acquisition date also discloses a history of repairs and preventive maintenance endeavors. Coupled with the ordinary inspection prior to use by the pharmacist and routine cleaning after each use, the Equipment Maintenance Record assures that clean functional equipment is available when needed.

B. Quality Control

Because the majority of the hospital pharmacies in this country are not large enough to warrant a separate quality control division, manufacturing of bulk compounding in these institutions is being eliminated in favor of the purchased product. This trend is an acknowledgment of the often stated assertion that every lot of every shipment of raw material and every lot of finished product which can be controlled by chemical, physical, and biological testing should be tested in the laboratories of the quality-control sector of the organization. Clearly, most hospitals are not in a position to retain the personnel necessary to perform such procedures and in most instances are not capable of acquiring the hardware necessary to carry out these determinations adequately.

However, whenever hospitals do practice manufacturing an effort is made to build some controls into the procedure. Raw materials as well as the finished product are often subjected to chemical and biological testing. These tests are generally performed in laboratories outside of the department of pharmacy and in some instances outside of the hospital proper. Many of the control procedures listed within the United States Pharmacopeia and the National Formulary are amenable to spectrophotometric and titration type analysis. In view of the fact that the hospital's chemical laboratories are accustomed to performing these types of determinations on sera and other body fluids, it is not unusual to have the director of the pharmacy service work in cooperation with the director of the laboratory services towards the development of an analysis suitable to the product being manufactured. Cooperation is obtainable from the bacteriological laboratory of the institution relative to the testing of certain products for sterility. Generally, the department of pathology of the institution is equipped to handle pyrogen testing on a limited basis. Accordingly, it is not unusual to have the department of pathology perform pyrogen testing on large-volume solutions produced by the department of pharmacy.

Products manufactured within the hospital pharmacy are held in quarantine until such time as the reports from the various testing laboratories have been received and indicate that the product is suitable for general distribution. At this time, appropriate labeling is provided, which provides for the addition of the quality control number and batch number to the information generally found on products manufactured within the institution. The application of the quality control and batch lot numbers to the packages thus provides the department of pharmacy with the capability of recalling any product for any reason.

IV. Prepackaging Control

With the availability of compact low-cost prepackaging equipment, many hospital pharmacists find it economically feasible to purchase drugs in bulk or large lot containers and prepackage it into small quantities suitable to the prescribing practices of the medical staff. Such an undertaking requires the development of adequate safety controls and checks. Failure to build these into the prepackaging operation can result in such embarrassing situations as medication errors on the pavilions, the inability to locate and remove containers of drugs involved in a drug recall by the manufacturer, and improper or inadequate labeling which may be misleading to the prescriber or nurse and therefore become the subject of unnecessary telephone calls to the pharmacy. Generally, all of the preceding situations indicate a lack of control only in the prepackaging operation; however, human tendency is to assume that the entire operation is equally sloppy.

A. Purchase and Inventory Control

Much has been published on the issue of generic *vs.* brand-named drugs. Therefore, little space will be devoted to the issue other than to state that it is the responsibility of the pharmacist to make available to the patient and prescriber a therapeutically effective product. This can be achieved by the purchase of products from reliable manufacturers or through the purchase of products that comply with the standards of the "United States Pharmacopeia" or the "National Formulary." Where neither of the above is practical, then the pharmacist should require the manufacturer to provide him with copies of the appropriate assay and control documents.

Once the product is received by the hospital pharmacy, it should be inspected prior to storage. In addition, a control card showing the following information should be created; (a) generic or chemical name, (b) proprietary name, (c) strength, (d) dosage form, (e) manufacturer's control number, (f) acquisition date, and (g) cost per unit of dose.

With respect to storage of drugs and biologicals, proper temperature is essential in order to maintain product potency. Thus, reference to the pharmacopeia (USP, 1970) provides the appropriate definitions for the following storage temperatures; "cold," "cool," "room temperature," "controlled room temperature," "excessive heat," and "protection from freezing." Once the proper storage environment is made available it is essential to control it in order to be assured that major fluctuations have not occurred and thereby impaired the quality of the drug or biological.

This is accomplished by the installation of a recording thermometer and an alarm which gives auditory notice of when the temperature within the area has exceeded certain limits. Also, the refrigeration system in the pharmacy is generally wired to the emergency electrical system as further assurance of safety.

B. Prepackaging and Labeling

Once the decision is made to prepackage a particular product, thought must be given to the requirements of the official compendia regarding preservation, packaging, storage, and labeling (USP, 1970, pp. 9–10). These provide definitions of "container," "closure," "light-resistant container," "well-closed container," "tight container," "hermetic container," "single-dose container," and "multiple-dose container." Injectable products and irrigating solutions are also provided for (USP, 1970, pp. 9–10 and 798). Paper or cellophane bags, cardboard boxes, certain plastic vials, some strip-packaging materials, and any combination thereof should not be used in place of the proper glass container if the purchased drug is to continue to meet the specifications stated in the official compendia.

The pharmacopeia (USP, 1970) also makes provision for storage in bulk and under nonspecific conditions. Note the following:

> Bulk packages are exempt from the storage requirements when the products are intended for manufacture or for subsequent re-packaging for the dispenser or distributor. Where no specific storage directions or limitations are provided, it is to be understood that the storage conditions include protection from moisture, freezing and excessive heat.

The pharmacopeia also provides a monograph on the labeling of drugs and drug products (USP, 1970, pp. 10–11 and 799). Included therein are the definitions of "label" and "labeling" (USP, 1970, p. 799).

Once the purchased drug is prepackaged (this applies to the hospital-manufactured product as well), it is important to apply a control label to the container until such time as the package is labeled in the conventional manner. This is accomplished by printing, within the pharmacy, self-adhering labels containing the following primary information:

a. Date of prepackaging by month and year—upper left corner;
b. If the item is dated, the expiration date is in the upper-right corner;
c. Name and strength of the drug;
d. Name of manufacturer;
e. Manufacturer's control number.

This label is then affixed to the container and remains on it even though a prescription label is later applied. In order to obviate temptation to remove this label, some pharmacists affix it to the inside of the cap of the tablet or capsule vial. With this information on each container, it becomes possible to remove all drug-recall products from the hospital pavilions and thereby assures physician and patient alike that total control over the product is being exercised by the pharmacist.

Some hospitals use color-coded labels for dispensing rather than the standard prescription label (Crider, 1969). This system involves the use of a 2-part medication card-label form, color-coded for time of administration, so that medication labels and nursing drug administration cards are identical. This saves the nurses' time in preparing the medication card and assures that no inaccuracies will creep into the system during transcription. Directions for use and termination of medication dates are also included on the card in addition to such standard information as patient's name, hospital number, room and bed number, drug name, strength, and dose.

Much has been published in the lay and scientific press relative to drug labeling. Some writers have demonstrated the need for placing the generic name of the drug on the prescription container.

Hospital pharmacists in many areas have been labeling drug packages in this manner for many years. However, the mere application of the generic name to a container does not totally resolve the problems of insuring the safe use of medications in the hospital.

Thus, it seems appropriate at this time to review the following three sections of the American Society of Hospital Pharmacists *Guidelines Relative to the Safe Use of Medications in Hospitals** (Anderson, 1962):

SECTION I
LABELING AND MEDICATION CONTAINERS—GENERAL

1.1 Drug labeling should be performed by a pharmacist or under the supervision of a pharmacist. Prescription labels and pharmacy stock labels should be used only by the the hospital pharmacy. (See 1.16 and 4.14).

1.2 The pharmacist should be consulted and should make recommendations concerning labeling, containers and storage of housekeeping items, insecticides, cleaners, and such.

1.3 Medication labels should be typed or machine-printed. Labeling with pen or pencil, use of adhesive tape or china marking pencils should be prohibited. A label should not be superimposed on a label.

1.4 The label should be legible, easily read, and free from erasures and strikeovers. It should be firmly affixed to the container. The label for stock containers should be protected from chemical action or abrasion.

1.5 Labels should bear the name, address, and telephone number of the hospital.

1.6 One order or prescription should be filled and labeled at a time.

1.7 The following or similar accessory labels and caution statements should appear where indicated:

a. Poison
b. Not to be taken internally
c. Shake well before using
d. For external use only
e. For the eye
f. For the nose
g. For the ear
h. Refrigerate at 2°–10°C (35°–50°F)
i. Refrigerate after reconstitution
j. Warning: Not for injection
k. Do not use after ________________
l. Not to be swallowed
m. Keep out of reach of children
n. Keep from freezing
o. Keep below freezing
p. Caution: Potent Drug
q. Research Drug
*r. NONPROPRIETARY NAME
Note for information of staff: Prescription or order for (Proprietary Name) filled as per formulary policy; contents are same basic drug as prescribed, but may be of another brand.
*s. NONPROPRIETARY NAME
Note for information of staff: Contents may be used, per formulary policy, to fills prescriptions or order for any of the following brands of the same basic drug:
(Proprietary Name, Brand 1)
(Proprietary Name, Brand 2)
(Proprietary Name, Brand 3).
t. Note change in color, size, or shape
u. Other accessory labels providing special information such as dosage, side effects, or contraindications for investigational drugs may be used where necessary.

1.8 The metric system should be given prominence on all labels where both metric and apothecary systems are commonly used.

1.9 The name of the therapeutically-active ingredients should be indicated in compound mixtures.

1.10 Labels for medications should indicate the amount of drug or drugs in each dosage form unless otherwise indicated.

1.11 Drugs and chemicals in forms intended for dilution or reconstitution should carry directions for so doing. Whenever possible, dilutions and labeling should be done in the pharmacy.

1.12 Perishable drugs, such as antibiotics and biologicals, should clearly indicate the expiration date on the label.

1.13 The routes of administration should be indicated for parenteral medications whenever possible.

1.14 Numbers, letters, coined names and unofficial synonyms and abbreviations should

*Applicable to those hospitals operating under the formulary system as outlined in AHA–ASHP Statement of Guiding Principles on the Operation of the Hospital Formulary System (1960).

not be used to identify medications with the exception of approved letter or number codes for investigational drugs.

1.15 Only light-resistant, tight containers meeting USP standards should be used.

1.16 Medications if brought into the hospital by the patient or physician should be positively identified before use. Such medications should be checked by the hospital pharmacist with the originating pharmacy by prescription serial number. A supplemental label should be attached in the hospital pharmacy providing information required in Section II. Where no pharmacist is on duty, the physician should check with the issuing pharmacy and attach the supplemental label described above.

1.17 Containers presenting difficulty in labeling, such as small tubes, should be labeled with no less than the prescription serial number, name of drug, strength, and name of patient, and should then be placed in a larger carton or container bearing a label with the necessary information indicated in Sections II and III.

1.18 The label should conform with all applicable Federal, state, and local laws and regulations.

1.19 Floor stock medication labels should carry codes to identify source and lot number of medication.

SECTION II
Labeling and Dispensing In-Patient Prescriptions

2.1 In addition to the recommendations outlined in Section I, the in-patient prescription labels should bear, as a minimum, the following information:

a. Patient's full name
b. Nonproprietary and/or proprietary name of the drug actually dispensed
c. Strength
d. Date of issue
e. Name or initials of dispenser

2.2 The prescription or in-patient order should have noted thereon, at the time dispensed, the source and batch identifying number of the medication and the initials of the dispenser.

2.3 For in-patient self-care medications, label as in Section III.

SECTION III
Labeling and Dispensing Out-Patient Prescriptions

3.1 Medications to be dispensed to in-patients who are being discharged should be returned to the pharmacy for relabeling.

3.2 The out-patient prescription label should bear the following information:

a. Patient's full name
b. Prescription identification number
c. Specific directions for use
d. Date of issue
e. Name or initials of dispenser
f. Name of prescribing physician
g. Where physician requests or hospital policy dictates, identity and strength should be on the label
h. A "Keep out of reach of children" label
i. Name, address, and telephone number of hospital.

3.3 Prescriptions should have noted thereon, at the time dispensed, the source and batch identifying number of the medication and the initials of the dispenser.

3.4 An identifying check system to insure proper identification of out-patients should be established.

The above guidelines should not be considered to be restrictive to the hospital environment. They are ideally suited for use in extended-care facilities, nursing homes, and clinics, and represent one more example of control in drug handling and dispensing.

C. Unit-Dose Packaging

Most hospital practitioners now agree that the unit dose package is one of the better means for the control of drugs as well as for assuring that the quality of the contents has not been altered by contamination.

It has been shown (Tester, 1967) that a unit dose system is instrumental in: (a) providing identification of each unit of medication by complete labeling; (b) reducing preparation and dispensing time; (c) preventing contamination of the medication; (d) permitting more accurate inventory control in the pharmacy and on the nursing station; (e) eliminating waste by allowing return and reuse of unused medications; (f) permitting more accurate medication charging methods; and (g) decreasing medication errors.

Addition criteria, entitled, *Guidelines for Single Unit Packages of Drugs** (1971) have been developed. The following is a direct reproduction of the Guidelines:

Introduction

These guidelines have been formed with the hope that they will be sufficiently directive to be useful guides to pharmaceutical manufacturers and packagers. It is hoped that they will encourage the continued exploration of new packaging ideas and techniques.

Pharmaceutical manufacturers can package single unit packages more efficiently and economically than can hospitals; however; standardization of packages would provide even greater efficiency and greater economic savings. Even though manufacturers are not expected to package all items in all doses needed in the hospital, they should make an effort to package as many items as possible in single unit packages. The major premise of these guidelines is that a need continues to exist in the hospital for packaging materials and techniques which will provide the hospital a flexibility that permits available packages to fit into existing and future drug distribution systems.

A single unit package is one which contains one discrete pharmeceutical dosage form, i.e., one tablet, one capsule, one 2-ml quantity of a liquid, etc. A single unit package becomes a unit dose package when the physician happens to order that particular amount for a particular patient. In either case the packages should be

*Approved by the Board of Directors, American Society of Hospital Pharmacists December 2, 1966. Revised October 26–27, 1970. Revised statement appears in the February 1971 issue of *Amer. J. Hosp. Pharm.*

labeled and patient-ready so that the contents can be administered directly from the package. General Considerations.

1. Packaging material

The characteristics of the packaging material which are essential in protecting the drug dosage form are the responsibility of the pharmaceutical manufacturer to determine and provide for each produce. Comparable packaging material, equipment and devices should be commercially available to the hospital pharmacist to use in completing the hospital's packaging program.

2. Shape and form

By definition, the contents must be deliverable directly to the patient without any repackaging into another container or device. In performing this function the single unit package should be easy to open and easy to use, and its use should require no additional education or experience.

3. Label copy

Current Federal Government requirements for "Labeling" should be adhered to and particular attention given the following special considerations. The desired copy and format are as follows:

NONPROPRIETARY NAME
(and proprietary name, if to be shown)
(dosage form, if special)
STRENGTH
CONTROL NUMBER
(special notes, e.g., "Refrigerate").

a. Nonproprietary (generic, official or established name) and proprietary (trade name) names: The nonprietary name and the strength should be the most prominent part of the label. It is not necessary to have the proprietary name, if any, on the package. However, if one does appear, in compliance with requirements set forth in the Food, Drug and Cosmetic Act, the established name of any prescription drug or ingredient shall be printed in letters that are at least half as large as the letters comprising the proprietary name, and the established name shall have a prominence commensurate with the prominence of the proprietary name. The style of type should be chosen to provide maximum legibility, contrast and permanence.

b. Special characteristics of the dosage form should be a part of the label, e.g., extended release. Packages should be labeled as to the route of administration if other than oral, e.g., topical use. In a package containing an injection, the acceptable injectable route(s) of administration should be stated. The route of administration should appear on the innermost package.

c. Strength should be stated in accordance with terminology in the American Hospital Formulary Service. The metric system should be used, with dosage forms formulated to provide the rounded-off figures in the USP and NF tables of approximate equivalents and expressed in the smallest whole number.

Micrograms should be used through 999, then milligrams through 999, then grams. Thus,

300 mg, not 5 gr, nor 325 mg, nor 0.32 g;
60 mg, not 1 gr, nor 0.06 g, nor 64.5 mg, nor 65 mg;
400 mcg, not 1/150 gr, nor 0.4 mg, nor 0.0004 g;
ml (milliliters) should be used instead of cc (cubic centimeters).

d. The control number should appear on the label. The name of the manufacturer should be included if there is no proprietary name on the package.

e. Special notes such as conditions of storage (e.g., 2–10°C.; expiration date), preparation (e.g., shake well; moisten), and administration (e.g., not to be chewed) that are not obvious from the dosage form designation are to be included at the bottom of the label. When possible, all arbitrary expiration dates should become effective only during the months of January and July to simplify product location and recall.

f. The use of identification codes (that appear directly on the dosage form) for individual identification is encouraged.

4. Minimum quantities of unit package products available from manufacturers should be within reason for hospitals for all sizes.

5. Each unit package should be so designed that it is evident when the package is still intact, that it has never been entered or opened.

Specific Considerations

1. Oral Solids

a. Blister package. A blister package should:

—have an opaque and nonreflective backing (flat upper surface of package) for printing and be square in shape of the dimensions $1\frac{1}{4} \times 1\frac{1}{4}$ inches;—have a blister (dome or bubble) of a see-through material that is a flat bottomed, round, nonangular cup with a top diameter of $\frac{7}{8}$ inch tapering to bottom diameter of $\frac{5}{8}$ inch with a depth of $\frac{3}{8}$ inch;

—be easily peelable;

—peel from all sides and have opening tabs at multiple locations;

—be in single cut units.

b. Pouch package. A pouch package should:

—have one of its sides opaque and nonreflective for printing and the other a see-through side;

—be one of the following two outside dimensions: $1\frac{1}{4}$ by $1\frac{1}{4}$ inches or $1\frac{1}{2}$ by 2 inches.

—be easily deliverable (large tablets in large pouches, small tablets in small pouches);

—tear from any point or multiple locations;

—be in single cut units.

c. The packages should be such that contents can be delivered directly to the patient's mouth or to the patient's hand.

2. Oral Liquids

a. The unit package should be filled to deliver the labeled contents. It is recognized that overfilling will be necessary, depending on the shape of the container, the container material, and the formulation of the dosage form.

b. The label should state the contents as follows:

Delivers ________ mg (or g or mcg) in ________ ml

3. Injectables

a. The device shall be appropriately calibrated in milliliters and scaled from the tip to the fill line. Calibrated space may be built into the device to permit addition of other drugs. the label should state the contents as follows:

Delivers ________ mg (or g or mcg) in ________ ml

b. An appropriate size needle should be an integral part of the device. The needle sheath should not be the plunger. The plunger should be mechanically stable in the barrel of the syringe.

c. The device should be of such a design that it is patient-ready and assembly instructions are not necessary.

d. The sheath protecting the needle should be a nonpenetrable, rigid material to protect personnel from injury. The size of the needle should be indicated on the sheath.

e. The device shall be of such a design that easy and visible aspiration is possible.

It should be as compact as possible and of such a size that it can be easily handled.

4. Intravenous Solutions (large volume)

The pH of the solution and the amount of overfill in the intravenous infusion container should be stated on the label.

5. Intravenous Additives

Drungs that are to be compounded into intravenous infusion solutions should be packaged so that the contents do not have to be withdrawn into a syringe in order to be added to an intravenous bottle. "Partial fills" (partially filled intravenous solution units) for intravenous additives should be made commercially available.

6. Other Dosage Forms—ophthalmics, topical preparations, suppositories, etc.

Dosage forms other than those specifically discussed above should be adequately labeled to indicate their use and route of administration and should adhere to the above and other required labeling criteria.

Future Considerations

1. Outpatient Dispensing

Dispensing packages for outpatient use should be developed. Packages should provide convenience and protect the integrity of the product regardless of the specialty or location of practice.

2. Pediatric Packages

Packages for pediatric doses and for use in providing special pediatric doses should be developed.

3. New Packages

In developing packages, concern for waste and for the eventual disposal of the package should be considered. Packages should be of lightweight, nonbulky, materials that produce nontoxic fumes when incinerated. Materials that are reusable as raw materials should be considered. It is hoped that new lightweight packaging that is more patient acceptable, easily disposable and more economical will be developed, made available and released for use.

The present and future use of computers and automation should be a consideration when developing new packages. It should be possible for hospital pharmacists to duplicate and process such packages themselves if necessary.

4. Materials Available

Information should be available to practitioners indicating the stability, compatibility and possible drug interactions with various materials and films used.

D. Dated Pharmaceuticals

Because biological products and many of the newer pharmaceuticals are "dated" it is imperative that the hospital pharmacist maintain a control over these items in the form of a Record of Dated Pharmaceuticals (Hassan, 1967c). Such a record provides for a sheet with the name of the product, date of purchase, source, control number, and a year calendar by month. Thus, a simple check mark under the number of the month on the same line of the product indicates that the drug life expires in the checked month. Some pharmacists prepare a separate sheet for each dated product.

Once the system is in effect, a glance at the control sheet at the end of the month indicates what products will soon be outdated and, should be either used or removed from inventory and returned for credit—if the manufacturer honors such a policy.

V. Conclusion

The Drug Product Quality Statement (Anonymous, 1970) issued by the Academy of Pharmaceutical Sciences of the American Pharmaceutical Association includes within its text some important concepts relative to drug product quality. The word "quality" is applied to a drug or drug product provided that it:

> Contain the quantity of each active ingredient claimed on its label, within the applicable limits of its specifications;
> Contain the same quantity of active ingredient from one dosage unit to the next;
> be free from extraneous substances;
> maintain its potency, therapeutic availability, and apperance until used.

Certainly these criteria are important and are so recognized by the hospital pharmacist. This is evidenced by the fact that these institutional practitioners have developed equipment and analytical control programs to assure the quality of products manufactured by the pharmacy; to enforce adherence to control procedures associated with prepackaging programs; and to ensure the safety of the patient via the activities of the pharmacy and therapeutics committee.

References

AHA–ASHP Statement of Guiding Principles on the Operation of The Hospital Formulary System (1960). *Amer. J. Hosp. Pharm.* **17**, 609.
Anderson, R. D. (1962). *Amer. J. Hosp. Pharm.* **19**, 577.
Anonymous (1970). *J. Amer. Pharm. Ass.* [N.S.] **10**, 107–116.
Bowles, Go. C., Jr. (1969). *Mod. Hosp.* **112**, 126.
Crider, H. F. (1969). *Hosp. Top.* **47**, 86–88.
Francke, D. E., Latiolais, C. J. Francke, G. N., and Ho, N. F. H. (1964) "Mirror to Hospital Pharmacy, p. 122. Amer. Soc. Hosp. Pharm. Washington, D.C.
Guide Issue (1971). *Hospitals* **45**, 447.
Guidelines For Single Unit Packages of Drugs (1971). *Amer. J. Hosp. Pharm.* **28**, 110.
Hassan, W. E. (1967a). "Hospital Pharmacy," 2nd ed., pp. 95–96. Lea & Febiger, Philadelphia, Pennsylvania.
Hassan, W. E., Jr. (1967b). "Hospital Pharmacy," 2nd ed., p. 267. Lea & Febiger, Philadelphia, Pennsylvania.

Hassan, W. E., Jr. (1967c). "Hospital Pharmacy," 2nd ed., p. 120. Lea & Febiger, Philadelphia, Pennsylvania.

Martin, E. W. (1965). "Remington's Pharmaceutical Sciences," 13th ed., pp. 417–671. Mack Publi. Co., Easton, Pennsylvania.

Pharmacy and Therapeutics Committee (1959). *Amer. J. Hosp. Pharm.* **16**, 122.

Provost, G. P. (1969). *Amer. J. Hosp. Pharm.* **26** , 69.

Rucker, T. D. (1970). *Amer. J. Hosp. Pharm.* **27**, 654.

Schumacker, G. E. (1969). *Amer. J. Hosp. Pharm.* **26**, 71.

Tester, W. W. (1967). "A Study of Patient Care Involving A Unit Dose System," Final Rep. College of Pharmacy and University Hospitals of the University of Iowa, Iowa City, Iowa.

USP (1970). "United States Pharmacopeia," 18th ed., p. 10. Mack Publ. Co., Easton, Pennsylvania.

Visconti, J. A. (1969). *Amer. J. Hosp. Pharm.* **26**, 378.

SAFETY TESTING OF PHARMACEUTICALS

R. Banziger and W. Pool

Research Division, Hoffmann-La Roche, Inc.,
Nutley, New Jersey

I. Introduction

The importance of assuring an aware public that pharmaceuticals are both safe and effective is obvious. Pharmaceutical manufacturers, therefore, have an obligation not only to assay constantly chemical purity, but also to determine the safety and efficacy of their drugs.

Great amounts of time and money are expended in investigating the pharmacologic and toxicologic effects of a therapeutic agent during the initial stages of development; however, it is also imperative that a continuing program be established to insure the safety and effectiveness of production-lots of marketed products.

Modern chemical analyses utilizing thin-layer chromatography, gas–liquid chromatography, and fluorimetry can detect minute quantities of impurities. However, chemical determinations cannot measure the biologic effects of small amounts of impurities or degradation products. There may be situations where chemical analyses may not be able to differentiate between degradation products and the original substances whereas biologic tests may show decreased or increased pharmacologic effects because of degradation products. The latter is of great importance during initial stages of product development because it is during this time that many problems may arise. During the early stages, chemical analytical procedures may not be yet refined to the point of complete identification of all possible degradation products. The biologic testing group should work closely with the product development group at this stage. Following development of the final formulation for eventual clinical trials, biologic and chemical testing procedures usually become routine.

Safety tests must answer these two questions:

1. Is the formulation free of deliterious effects?
2. Does the formulation produce the desired pharmacologic effect?

To be practical, these tests must be simple, rapid and reliable. Each lot of drug substance and experimental formulation, as well as preparations destined for clinical trial, and final marketed products must be evaluated. In other words, a continuing program of scrutinization is necessary during the entire process of drug development. By the time the FDA approves a drug for marketing, an enormous body of information has been accumulated with which to assess the safety and efficacy of the final product.

II. Types of Biological Tests Performed

The most commonly used biological test is the LD_{50} determination. The LD_{50} is that dose of drug which is lethal to 50% of the treated animals. Experimentally the LD_{50} is determined by administering the drug to groups of animals at several dose levels. The cumulative mortality is recorded over a period of 1 to 5 days and used to calculate the LD_{50} dose. The animals are placed in observation cages for the first few hours after drug administration to observe any signs or symptoms. Table I is a list of typical symptoms which may occur during an acute toxicity test. Careful observations of these signs may reveal characteristic pharmacologic and toxicologic effects of the drug. For example, a stimulant such as *d* amphetamine produces increased motor activity, Straub reaction, and salivation, whereas phenobarbital decreases motor activity and causes loss of righting reflex, hypnosis, muscle relaxation, and respiratory depression. A minimum of 3 dose levels is used, the high dose resulting in the death of most of the animals and the low dose causing only a few deaths. At least 2 of the 3 dose levels should produce mortality to some but not all of the animals tested. A typical dose-response of several drugs is shown in Table II. The dose-response profiles are used to calculate the LD_{50}. Although several methods are available to calculate LD_{50} values, the ones most commonly used are graphic methods based on probit analysis (Miller and Tainter, 1944; Litchfield and Wilcoxon, 1949). Figure 1 shows several typical plots of data using the Miller and Tainter method. This method also gives an estimate of the standard error. The LD_{50} is simply that dose level at which the dose-response curve crosses the 50% mortality line on the graph. The standard error is dependent on the

TABLE I

Symptoms Recorded during Acute Toxicity Tests

Increased motor activity	Sedation	Diarrhea
Tremors	Muscle relaxation	Writhing
Clonic convulsions	Hypnosis	Respiration
Tonic extensor	Analgesia	depression
Straub reaction	Anaesthesia	stimulation
Piloerection	Arching and rolling	respiratory failure
Catatonia	Ptosis	Skin color
Opisthotonos	Lacrimation	blanching
Hyperaesthesia	Exophthalmos	flushing
Loss of righting reflex	Salivation	cyanosis
Decreased motor activity	vicid	
Ataxia	watery	

TABLE II

Acute Toxicity: Dose–Response in Rats

Compound	Dose p.o. (mg/kg)	No. Dead/ No. Dosed	LD_{50} ± S.E.
Strychnine sulfate	6.3	4/10	7.2 ± 0.5
	8.0	7/10	
	10.0	10/10	
Caffeine	300	0/10	470 ± 15
	400	4/10	
	600	8/10	
Thioridazine hydrochloride	250	2/10	480 ± 83
	500	5/10	
	1000	9/10	
Diphenylhydantoin sodium	2500	2/10	3350 ± 390
	3200	5/10	
	4000	6/10	

slope of the dose–response curve and the number of animals tested. Drugs B and C have approximately the same LD_{50}, but the slope of the dose–response curve for drug C is much flatter, thereby indicating a larger standard error. With drug C, it would be difficult to detect 2- to 3-fold differences. Figure 2 illustrates several LD_{50} determinations with different lots of the same drug. Although the LD_{50} indicates that all the lots are equivalent, it is apparent from the dose response curves that toxicity is produced at lower doses with lot C than with lots A or B.

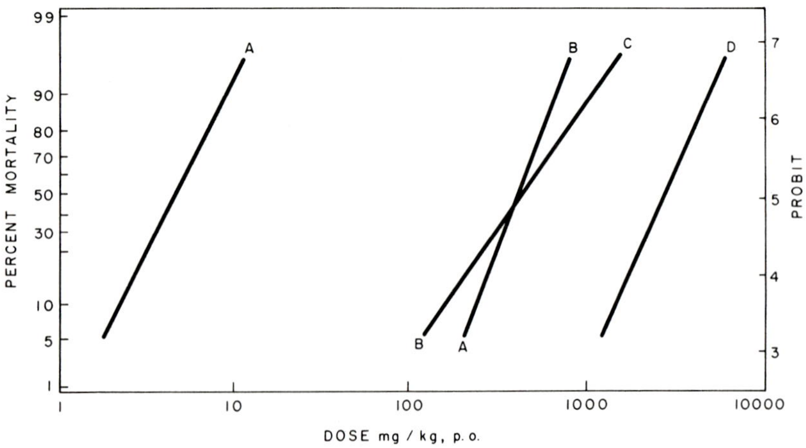

Fig. 1. *A typical dose-response profile of 4 drugs plotted on a semilog probit graph.*

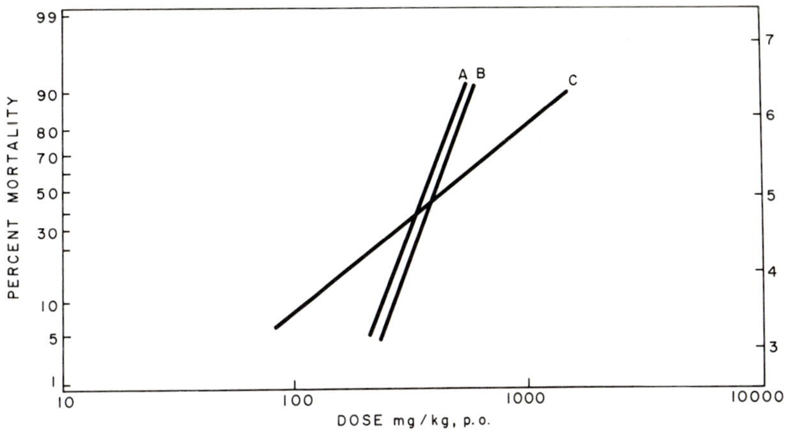

Fig. 2. *The dose–response profile of 3 lots of the same compound illustrate that even with identical* LD_{50}*'s the lots may not be biologically equivalent.*

Often the route of drug administration has a profound effect on the LD_{50}. In general, the least toxic route of drug administration is topical. Increasing toxicity is seen in the following order: oral, subcutaneous, intramuscular, intraperitoneal, and intravenous. A comparison of the oral route of administration to a parenteral route provides useful information about the relative rate of absorption of drug from the gastrointestinal tract. In Table III, drug A is almost equally toxic by all routes of administration while drug B is nontoxic when given orally but quite toxic when injected intraperitoneally. However, most drugs resemble drug C, which shows only a slight increase in toxicity by the parenteral route. The ratio of oral to parenteral LD_{50} values is an indication of the extent of absorption from the gastrointestinal tract. A compound such as drug B is obviously poorly absorbed when administered orally whereas drug A is well absorbed after oral administration.

TABLE III

Effect of Route of Administration on Acute Toxicity

	LD_{50} Mice (mg/kg)		
Route	Drug A	Drug B	Drug C
p.o.	274	> 4000	720
s.c.	235	> 2000	350
i.p.	—	124	154
i.v.	266	—	34

The choice of animal species is an important consideration in acute toxicity testing. In the early phases of the development of the drug, acute toxicity studies are carried out in at least four species, one being a nonrodent. Usually the drug is tested in mice, rats, rabbits, and dogs. LD_{50}'s are determined for mice, rats and rabbits; however, in the dog, doses are doubled each day until toxic signs appear. Hematology and clinical chemistries are monitored before, during, and after drug administration to the dog. Routinely, mice are the animals of choice for acute toxicity studies because they are small and inexpensive, and therefore relatively large numbers can be used. The size of the animal is especially important when quantities of drug are limited.

Numerous factors may influence LD_{50} determinations even within the same species. For example, the metabolic state of the animal can have profound effect. Animals that have been denied food are usually more sensitive to drugs than fed animals, this effect being partially due to the increased absorption from the gastrointestinal tract after oral administration (Peters, 1966). Higher levels of drug-metabolizing enzymes in the liver also may increase the LD_{50} (Burns *et al.*, 1965). Some hypnotic drugs, for instance, have been shown to stimulate the induction of liver metabolizing enzymes and because of this metabolism, the drugs pharmacologic activity is lessened (Remmer, 1962). This may be of great importance if a drug is being administered more than once to an animal. On the other hand, SKF 525A has been shown to inhibit the activity of liver metabolizing enzymes thus causing decreased metabolism of the drug administered (Axelrod *et al.*, 1954).

The age of the animals may also influence the toxicity of the compound. The effect of age on the acute toxicity of several drugs is illustrated in Table

TABLE IV

Effect of Age on Acute Toxicity[a]

	Age of rats			
Compound	< 24 Hours	5 Days	10 Days	40 Days[b]
Chlorpheniramine maleate	225	235	158	680
Chlorpromazine hydrochloride	480	330	190	136
Cocaine hydrochloride	98	120	114	280
Diphenylhydantoin sodium	215	500	1100	3350
Iproniazid phosphate	600	510	600	810
Meprobamate	420	340	345	1060
Phenobarbital sodium	124	140	136	162
Strychnine sulfate	22	17	9	7

[a] LD_{50} (mg/kg), p.o.
[b] Adult.

IV. Many drugs resemble chlorpheniramine, diphenylhydantoin, and meprobamate, becoming less toxic as the animals mature. The toxicity of some drugs, such as iproniazid and phenobarbital, is not appreciably affected by age. Chlorpromazine and strychnine are exceptions to the rule and are less toxic to neonates than to adults.

The sex of the animals used may also influence the acute toxicity. For example, procaine was found to be considerably more toxic in the female rat than in the male rat (Munoz *et al.*, 1961).

Even the caging of animals can have significant effects on the acute toxicity of some compounds. When administered equal doses of a CNS stimulant such as amphetamine, animals grouped together have a higher mortality than those caged individually. Presumably, this is due to the continual excitation and stimulation of animals caged together, whereas these stimuli are reduced when the animals are caged individually.

Because of the possible influence of all these factors on acute toxicity, routine testing is standarized as much as possible. The strain, sex, age, caging of animals, as well as consumed food and room temperature are all factors that should be carefully standardized and controlled.

Some drugs are relatively nontoxic. In such cases, a high dose of drug (4–5 gm/kg) is administered to ensure that a toxic contaminant has not been introduced.

III. Pharmacologic Tests

Pharmacologic tests are generally a much more sensitive means of measuring biologic activity than acute toxicity tests. The most commonly reported parameter is the ED_{50}, the dose which is effective in producing a specific pharmacologic action in 50% of the animals tested. The ED_{50} is calculated in much the same manner as the LD_{50}, but the end point of the test is simply some pharmacologic effect rather than mortality. Pharmacologic screening tests may be used but, like toxicity tests, they should be simple, rapid, and reliable. Table V lists several classes of drugs and pharmacologic tests which can be used to assess their actions. With some drugs, it is often easier and more reliable to measure a related effect or a side effect rather than the prime pharmacologic action of drug. For example, phenothiazines may be evaluated for their antihistaminic activity and benzodiazepines for their antimetrazol activity rather than for their psychopharmacologic effects.

By measuring the pharmacologic activity as an ED_{50} in addition to the acute toxicity as an LD_{50}, further information is gained about drug absorption. Onset and duration of action of drugs can be studied only with pharma-

TABLE V
Pharmacological Tests Employed in Quality Control

Compound	Test
Benzodiazepines	Antimetrazol
Antihistamines	Protection against intracardial administration of histamine
Sympathomimetics	Reserpine reversal, motor activity
Anticholinergics	Pilocarpine salivation
Anticonvulsants	Antimetrazol, anti-electroshock
Sedatives and hypnotics	Acute hexobarbital sleeping time, chlorprothixene hypnosis
Muscle relaxants	Inclined screen
Tricyclic antidepressants	Reversal of tetrabenazine ptosis
Estrogens	Uterine weight
Androgens	Seminal vesicle weight
Anti-emetics	Inhibition of apomorphine-induced gnawing

cologic tests. It is often useful to compare results obtained by oral administration of a drug with those produced by the intravenous administration to determine if the drug is well absorbed. Drug A (Table VI) is an example of a typically well-absorbed drug. After oral administration of drug A, the antimetrazol activity increases with time, and after 1 hour it is as active as when it is administered intravenously. After intravenous administration, drug A becomes less active with time indicating reduction of the drug activity either by metabolism or by excretion. The relatively slow onset of action of drug B after both oral and intravenous administration suggests that it is metabolized before the desired effect is produced. The comparison of the oral route versus the intravenous route of administration of drug C reveals poor oral absorption, since, at all time intervals, drug C is much

TABLE VI
Onset of Antimetrazol Activity[a]

Drug	Route	5 Minutes	15 Minutes	60 Minutes
Drug A	p.o.	3.60	1.60	0.70
	i.v.	0.20	0.90	1.20
Drug B	p.o.	97.00	11.80	5.70
	i.v.	27.00	2.80	2.40
Drug C	p.o.	17.30	12.10	12.40
	i.v.	0.90	0.70	0.80

[a] ED_{50} (mg/kg).

more active after intravenous administration than after oral administration. The antimetrazol activity of drug C does not decrease appreciably with time indicating slow metabolism and excretion.

Many of the factors which affect LD_{50} determinations can also influence pharmacologic testing. Age, sex, and strain of animals can be important considerations. Often only male mice weighing 17–25 grams are used, simply to eliminate any possible influences of age and sex. Even the concentration of drug itself in the vehicle can affect the ED_{50}. As shown in Table VII, the tenfold decrease in the concentration of the 3 drugs produces a twofold increase in antimetrazol activity. Other factors which can affect the ED_{50} are hepatic detoxifying enzyme levels, intake of food and water, and the temperature of the room in which the animal tests are carried out.

TABLE VII

Effect of Concentration on Antimetrazol Activity

Compound	Concentration (%)	ED_{50} (mg/kg)
Drug A	0.5	4.0
	0.05	2.1
Drug B	0.05	1.2
	0.005	0.6
Drug C	0.05	1.4
	0.005	0.3

IV. Miscellaneous Tests

In addition to acute toxicity and pharmacologic tests, there are a variety of other tests which are routinely performed depending on the compound and dosage form.

A. Hemolysis Testing

Hemolysis tests are performed in dogs on all parenteral formulations (Banziger, 1967). A control blood sample is taken from the jugular vein, and the drug is then injected into the cephalic vein. The injection is given slowly, usually over a 30-second period. One minute after the injection, a second blood sample is taken from the jugular vein. The blood samples are centrifuged and the plasma hemoglobin is determined by a colormetric method. The hemolysis produced by several drugs and vehicles are shown in Table VIII. Isotonic saline does not produce any hemolysis, while water for

TABLE VIII
Hemolysis Testing

Preparation	Dose (i.v.) (ml/dog)	gm/100ml Hb Control	gm/100ml Hb 1 Minute
Sodium chloride 0.9%	5	0.015	0.015
Water for injection	10	0.015	0.023
Digoxin injectable	2	0.011	0.015
Hydroxyzine HCl injectable	2	0.006	0.160
Propylene glycol 40% + alcohol 10%	2	0.023	0.045
Propylene glycol 20% + alcohol 10%	2	0.006	0.015

injection has a slight hemolytic effect due to hypotonicity. Digoxin causes essentially the same degree of hemolysis as water for injection; however, hydroxyzine produces a relatively high degree of hemolysis. Vehicles containing organic solvents such as propylene glycol and alcohol also produce hemolysis and should be considered a factor in formulating parenteral preparations.

B. Irritation Tests

1. Eye Irritation

Eye irritation tests are performed not only on ophthalmic preparations but on any topical or cosmetic preparation that might accidently get into the eye. The drug is instilled into one conjunctival sac of each of three rabbits in quantities of 0.1 ml or 0.1 gm. The other eye is left untreated to serve as a control. Observations are made immediately and 1, 2, 4, 24, 48, and 72 hours later. The extent of the eye irritation is scored by the method of Draize (1955). Table IX illustrates the irritation rating of the irritation produced by a typical drug after instillation into a rabbit's eye.

2. Skin Irritation

Skin irritation is tested by applying 0.1 ml or 0.1 gm to abraded and nonabraded skin areas of three rabbits. Untreated intact and abraded skin on the same rabbits serve as controls. The skin is examined for signs of irritation after 24 and 72 hours and scored by the method of Draize (1955). The skin irritation shown in Table X is typical for many topical preparations. Often, as in this example, both the erythema and the edema persist through 72 hours.

TABLE IX
Rabbit Eye Irritation[a]

	At instillation			1 Hour			2 Hours			4 Hours			24 Hours			48 Hours			72 Hours		
	A	B	C	A	B	C	A	B	C	A	B	C	A	B	C	A	B	C	A	B	C
Cornea																					
Opacity	0	0	0	0	0	0	0	0	0	0	0	0	0	0	0	0	0	0	0[b]	0[b]	0[b]
Area involved	0	0	0	0	0	0	0	0	0	0	0	0	0	0	0	0	0	0	0	0	0
Pupil reaction	+[c]	+	+	+	+	+	+	+	+	+	+	+	+	+	+	+	+	+	+	+	+
Conjunctiva																					
Redness	1	1	1	1	1	1	2	1	1	1	1	1	2	2	1	0	0	0	0	0	0
Chemosis	0	0	0	1	1	0	1	1	0	0	1	0	0	0	0	0	0	0	0	0	0
Discharge	—	—	—	2	2	1	2	2	1	1	2	0	1	0	0	0	0	0	0	0	0

[a]*Grading scale*: 0 = normal, 1 = very slight, 2 = well-defined, 3 = moderate, 4 = severe.
[b]Tested with Fluorescein.
[c]+ = Normal reaction to light present. – = Normal reaction to light absent.

TABLE X
Primary Skin Irritation Rabbits

	24 Hours						72 Hours					
	Abraded			Nonabraded			Abraded			Nonabraded		
	A	B	C	A	B	C	A	B	C	A	B	C
Erythema	2[a]	2	2	2	2	2	2	2	2	2	2	2
Edema	0	1	1	1	1	1	1	0	1	1	0	0

[a]Grading scale: 0 = normal, 1 = very slight, 2 = well-defined, 3 = moderate, 4 = severe.

3. *Muscle Irritation*

Muscle irritation is usually tested in rabbits, although occationally rats are used. In the typical test, nine rabbits are used per dose level. Intramuscular injections of high (1.0 ml) and low (0.1 ml) doses of the preparations are made into the sacrospinalis muscle of each animal. Groups of three rabbits are sacrificed at 24, 48, and 72 hours after injection. The

TABLE XI
Muscle Irritation (Rabbits)

Time	Dose (cc)	Swelling	Edema	Hemorrhage	Necrosis
24	1.0	0[a]	0	1	2
24	1.0	0	0	2	3
24	1.0	1	0	2	3
48	1.0	0	0	2	2
48	1.0	0	0	1	2
48	1.0	0	0	1	3
72	1.0	0	0	2	1
72	1.0	0	0	1	2
72	1.0	0	0	2	2
24	0.1	0	0	1	0
24	0.1	0	0	1	1
24	0.1	0	0	1	0
48	0.1	0	0	1	1
48	0.1	0	0	1	0
48	0.1	0	0	1	1
72	0.1	0	0	0	1
72	0.1	0	0	1	1
72	0.1	0	0	1	1

[a]Grading scale: 0 = normal, 1 = very slight, 2 = well-defined, 3 = moderate, 4 = severe.

sites of injection are grossly examined for incidences of swelling, edema, hemorrhage, and necrosis (Table XI). The degree of necrosis and, to a lesser extent, hemorrhage are the most important considerations. Organic solvents contained in many parenteral preparations may produce a considerable degree of irritation.

4. Venous Irritation

Venous irritation is routinely checked as a part of the hemolysis testing. The legs of the dogs are grossly examined 24 hours after injection for irritation. Dog cephalic vein is relatively resistent to many drugs and further testing is often necessary. One of the most sensitive tests utilizes rabbit marginal ear vein. Table XII shows the effect of rate of injection on venous irritation. When the drug is injected rapidly into the marginal ear vein of rabbits, a considerable degree of edema and erythema is produced. However, a slow injection results in only slight irritation. Saline is nonirritating when given as either a slow or a rapid injection.

TABLE XII
Rabbit Ear Vein Irritation

			24 Hours						48 Hours					
			Edema			Erythema			Edema			Erythema		
Preparation	Dose (ml/kg)	Rate of injection (seconds)	A	B	C	A	B	C	A	B	C	A	B	C
Drug	0.5	10	3[a]	3	2	3	3	4	3	3	3	3	3	4
		60	1	0	1	1	1	1	1	0	1	1	1	1
Isotonic saline	0.5	10	0	0	0	0	0	0	0	0	0	0	0	0
		60	0	0	0	0	0	0	0	0	0	0	0	0

[a]Grading scale: 0 = normal, 1 = very slight, 2 = well-defined, 3 = moderate, 4 = severe.

5. Mammary Gland Irritation

Whenever possible, it is advisable to test a preparation at the site of intended use. For mastitis preparations, the only appropriate site is the lactating mammary gland. Lactating female rats are separated from their litters 24 hours before the mastitis preparations are administered. The rats are anesthetized with sodium pentobarbital and the hair clipped from the mammary gland area. A volume of 0.3 ml of the preparation is injected into each mammary gland. The rats are examined after 24, 48, and 72 hours for

TABLE XIII
Mammary Gland Irritation

Preparation	Time (hours)	Average score: Irritation[a]	Average score: Necrosis[b]
Water	24	3	—
	48	0	—
	72	0	0
Drug in acacia solution	24	17	—
	48	12	—
	72	9	0.3
Mastitis formulation of drug	24	23	—
	48	14	—
	72	11	1.0
Mastitis formulation + β-carotene	24	23	—
	48	22	—
	72	20	3.0
Mastitis formulation + vitamin K	24	16	—
	48	8	—
	72	6	1.7

[a] Irritation: 0 = normal, 1–9 = slight, 10–18 = moderate, 19–27 = severe.
[b] Necrosis: 0 = normal, 1 = slight, 2 = moderate, 3 = severe.

swelling and hardening of the mammary glands. After the 72-hour examination, the rats are sacrificed and the injection sites examined grossly for necrosis and drug residue. Each preparation is injected into three glands so that each rat receives a total of six injections. In this way, two preparations can be tested per rat. In the examples shown in Table XIII, the mastitis formulation produced more irritation and necrosis than a suspension of the drug in acacia solution. Water was not irritating when injected into mammary glands. The addition of β-carotene to the mastitis formulation increased both irritation and necrosis whereas the addition of vitamin K reduced the degree of irritation but increased the necrosis.

6. *Vaginal and Rectal Irritation*

Vaginal and rectal irritation tests are performed with suppositories. In this test, the preparation, or a portion of it, is placed into the vagina or rectum of rats or rabbits. The animals are sacrificed after 24 hours and the tissue grossly examined for erythema and edema. It is often necessary to suture the opening of the vagina or rectum to prevent the loss of the preparations.

7. Skin-Sensitization Testing

Occasionally topical preparations are tested to determine the development of skin sensitivity. For this test guinea pigs are employed. The preparations is applied to the shaved backs of 10–20 guinea pigs every other day for 3 weeks. After a 2-week period without drug, the animals are challenged with the final application of the drug. The site of application is graded for the degree of edema and erythema (Draize *et al.*, 1944).

V. Testing of Drug Substance

Each lot of drug substance is tested prior to its use in the formulation of a dosage form. An LD_{50} and, if an appropriate pharmacologic test is available, an ED_{50} is determined before the drug is certified as biologically acceptable. In cooperation with the chemical analyst, the effects of contaminants or degradation products are studied. Pharmacologic and toxicologic tests are helpful in detecting small quantities of contaminants. The effects of a toxic degradation product on the LD_{50} of a compound is illustrated in Table XIV. The drug itself was quite nontoxic; however, a contaminant was found to be extremely toxic. Chemical testing identified the contaminant as a degradation product of the drug. When the drug was subjected to basic hydrolysis, both chemical and biological testing confirmed the presence of the toxic contaminant.

In order to determine the extent of contamination necessary to produce a change in the LD_{50}, a drug was deliberately contaminated with sodium fluoride, oxalic acid, or potassium cyanide (Table XV). With these contaminants, it was possible to measure changes in the mortality rate when the contaminants were present in concentrations of less than 1%. These results

TABLE XIV
The Effect of Degradation Products on Acute Toxicity

	LD_{50} (mg/kg, p.o.)
Drug	>4000
Contaminant	24
Acid hydrolysis product (<1% contaminant)	>4000
Basic hydrolysis product extracted from basic solution (50% contaminant)	82
Basic hydrolysis product extracted from neutral solution (10% contaminant)	2000–4000

TABLE XV

The Effect of Added Contaminants of Acute Toxicity

Compound	Dose (mg/kg, p.o.)	Contaminant	Percentage contamination	No. Dead/ No. dosed
Drug	400	—	—	0/10
Drug	400	Sodium fluoride	0.5	0/10
			1.0	2/10
			1.5	6/10
			2.0	10/10
Drug	400	Potassium cyanide	0.125	3/10
			0.250	10/10
Drug	400	Oxalic acid	0.500	1/10
			1.000	0/10
			2.000	7/10
			4.000	10/10

support the assumption that toxicity tests can detect accidental contamination of formulations by potentially toxic materials.

Table XVI notes the influence a small quantity of a contaminant can produce on the pharmacologic effect of the dosage form. In this case, one of the contaminants is considerably more potent than the drug while the other is less potent; however, with either contaminant being present, the ED_{50} is shifted from the original value, indicating problems at contamination. The physical characteristics of the compound, such as crystal form, material density, micronization, and solubility can have profound effects on the toxicity and pharmacologic activity. The antimetrazol activity of drug A (Table XVII) is enhanced by micronization and increased even

TABLE XVI

Effect of Contaminants on Pharmacologic Activity

Compound	Pilocarpine salivation test (ED_{50}, mg/kg)
Anticholinergic drug	16
Contaminant A	0.88
Contaminant B	>200
Drug + 1% contaminant A	12
Drug + 10% contaminant A	4.7
Drug + 1% contaminant B	16
Drug + 10% contaminant B	19

TABLE XVII

Effect of Drug Solubility and Particle Size on Biologic Activity

	Acute toxicity $LD_{50} \pm$ S.E. (mg/kg, p.o.)		Antimetrazol activity $ED_{50} \pm$ S.E. (mg/kg, p.o.)	
	Drug A	Drug B	Drug A	Drug B
Nonmicronized Drug	1770	610	4.0	2.7
Micronized drug	1380	595	2.8	2.5
Soluble salt of drug	960	570	2.1	2.3

further by converting the drug to a soluble salt. Other drugs, such as drug B, derive little benefit from either procedure, suggesting that the nonmicronized drug is well absorbed. In those cases in which the pharmacologic activity is increased, the acute toxicity is usually also increased to approximately the same extent. Naturally, combinations of drugs provide a further problem. The combination may be more toxic, less toxic, or equally as toxic as the individual drugs alone. The best way to determine the effects of combinations of drugs is to do a "sliding" LD_{50}. In this test, various ratios of the two drugs are administered to the animals to determine the LD_{50}'s. Figure 3 illustrates three possibilities. Curve 1 shows two drugs interacting to produce a supra-additive toxicity, curve 2 illustrates a simple additive toxicity, and curve 3 is an infra-additive toxicity.

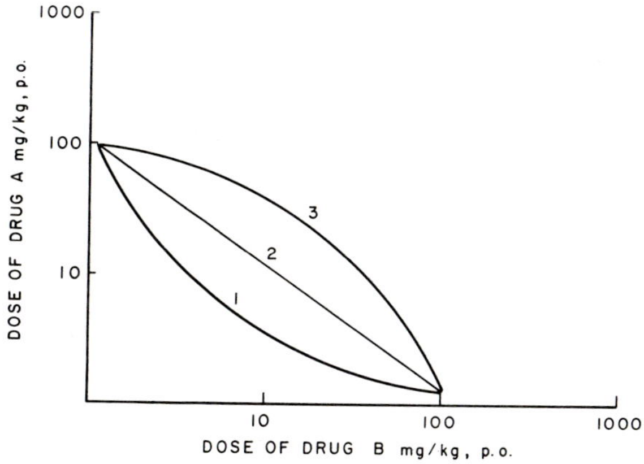

Fig. 3. *The three possibilities of combining two drugs are shown on this graph. Curve 1 represents a supra-additive toxicity, curve 2 illustrates a simple additive toxicity, and curve 3 demonstrates an infra-additive toxicity.*

VI. Oral Dosage Forms

Capsules and tablets are the most common dosage forms used. Acute toxicity and pharmacologic activity are determined for each lot of substance as well as experimental formulations, medical orders for clinical trial, and production lots.

In order to test capsules and tablets in mice, they must be converted into a liquid form for administration. Capsules are simply emptied and tablets are ground into a powder with a mortar and pestle; the powdered formulation is then suspended in a solution of gum acacia or carboxymethyl cellulose. Many capsules and tablets contain larger quantities of excipients than of active drug and, due to the volume limitations, it is often impossible to administer sufficient quantities of the formulations to produce mortality. This situation is especially common with very active drugs that are relatively nontoxic. In these cases, the pharmacologic activity is the only means of biologically measuring the content of active compound.

In Table XVIII, only the acute toxicity can be determined for the 10-mg tablets and capsules; however, the antimetrazol activity can be easily measured for all preparations. When an LD_{50} cannot be determined, a sufficiently large dose is administered to insure that a toxic contaminant has not been accidently introduced. The ED_{50} usually is not affected by excipients and, therefore, serves as a reliable test of activity. The onset and duration of action of capsules and tablets are difficult to study in small animals since the intact formulation cannot be administered to them. Since

TABLE XVIII

Acute Toxicity and Pharmacologic Activity of Capsules and Tablets

		Acute toxicity		Antimetrazol activity	
		LD_{50} (mg/kg, p.o.)		ED_{50} (mg/kg, p.o.)	
Formulations	Total weight of preparation (mg)	As active compound	As total weight	As active compound	As total weight
Drug substance	—	780	—	2.8	—
10 mg Capsule	180	785	14,000	2.7	49
5 mg Capsule	180	> 400	> 14,000	2.7	97
2 mg Capsule	180	> 160	> 14,000	2.9	243
10 mg Tablet	210	770	16,000	2.8	60
5 mg Tablet	210	> 380	> 16,000	2.7	120
2 mg Tablet	210	> 150	> 16,000	2.8	290

the onset and duration are especially important with enteric-coated and other time-release preparations, it is necessary to study them in either rabbits or dogs, to which intact formulations can be administered.

VII. Suspensions, Elixers, and Syrups

As with capsules and tablets, the oral liquid dosage forms are tested for acute toxicity and pharmacologic activity. Many liquid oral dosage forms contain large amounts of sweetners and/or solvents. When the preparations contain small quantities of very active drugs, the LD_{50} is often simply due to the toxicity of these relatively nontoxic agents, such as sucrose or sorbitol. The toxicity of the two suspensions listed in Table XIX is due entirely to the sucrose and sorbitol contained in the preparation. Again, the only way to determine the quantity of active compound present is to perform a pharmacologic test.

TABLE XIX

Effect of Excipients on the Acute Toxicity of Suspensions

	LD_{50}[a] (mg/kg, p.o.)		
Preparation	Active drug	Sucrose	Sorbose
Drug substance	970	—	—
5 mg/5 cc Suspension	45	24,750	6,300
2 mg/5 cc Suspension	17	23,200	5,880
Placebo suspension	—	23,925	6,090
Sucrose	—	33,300	—
Sorbitol	—	—	31,050
Sorbitol + sucrose (1:2)	—	21,000	10,000

[a] LD_{50}'s calculated in terms of individual components of the suspensions.

Another problem has been with adsorbants used to reduce the bitter taste of drugs. Some of these agents adsorb the drug very tightly and prevent the release of the drug in the gastrointestinal tract, resulting in a slow onset of activity.

VIII. Parenteral Formulations

The acute toxicity and pharmacologic activity of parenteral formulations are routinely tested by the intravenous route in mice. As previously men-

TABLE XX
Acute Toxicity of Parenteral Preparations

Preparation	LD_{50} p.o. (mg/kg)[a]	LD_{50} i.v. (mg/kg)[a]	LD_{50} (ml/kg)	LD_{50} Ratio (p.o./i.v.)
Drug A substance	1100			14
Parenteral preparation		78	1.6	
Vehicle (isotonic saline)			> 20	
Drug B substance	1500			8
Parenteral		197	7.9	
Vehicle (isotonic saline)			> 20	
Drug C substance	2350			170
Parenteral		14	5.5	
Vehicle (10% ethyl alcohol + 40% propylene glycol)			4.8	
Drug D substance	2600			46
Parenteral		57	4.6	
Vehicle (40% propylene glycol)			6.2	

[a]As active ingredient.

tioned, most drugs are more toxic and more active by the intravenous route compared to oral administration. Quite often the drugs are insoluble in simple aqueous vehicles and must be dissolved in various organic solvents such as ethyl alcohol or propylene glycol. In addition, preservatives and chelating agents are often added for stability purposes. It is not uncommon for the acute toxicity of parenteral preparations to be due primarily to the organic solvents contained in the vehicle. Table XX compares the oral and intravenous toxicity of several drugs as well as the toxicity of the vehicles alone. The acute toxicity of drugs A and B is obviously the result of the drugs themselves and not due to the vehicle. The toxicity of the vehicle for drug C is sufficient to account for the entire toxicity of the parenteral preparations. A third possibility is illustrated by drug D, where the toxicity of the parenteral preparation is the result of both drug and vehicle. The pharmacologic activity is usually also enhanced by intravenous administration and the drug shows a shorter onset of activity. To measure the onset of activity after intravenous administration, a pharmacologic test must be quite rapid. All parenteral preparations are tested for muscle irritation, hemolysis, and pyrogenicity.

IX. Suppositories

Due to volume limitations, the acute toxicity and pharmacologic activity of suppositories usually cannot be determined by the intended route of administration. Consequently, most suppositories are tested by the oral route. As a safety test, it can generally be assumed that rectal or vaginal administration will be less toxic than oral administration. Melting and dissolution times are measured in the dog by inserting the suppositories and making observations with a proctoscope at intervals of 1, 5, 10, 15, and 20 minutes. Either vaginal or rectal irritation studies are performed on all suppositories and are rated for the degrees of edema and erythema.

X. Topical Preparations

Topical preparations are tested for acute toxicity both topically and orally. The preparations are tested by applying the preparation to the shaved backs of rats, rabbits and dogs. An occlusive covering is used to increase absorption. Most topical preparations are poorly absorbed through the skin and evidence of systemic toxicity is seldom observed. Eye and skin irritation tests are carried out on all topical preparations. Skin sensitivity tests are performed on only a limited number of preparations.

XI. Aerosol Preparations

Inhalation acute toxicity, as well as oral toxicity, is determined for aerosol preparations. Inhalation toxicity is determined by placing animals in a closed chamber and introducing the aerosol into the chamber at different concentrations. If the compound is sufficiently toxic, an LD_{50} may be calculated as parts per million. For oral testing, the aerosol is either sprayed into a container or the concentrate is obtained before the addition of the propellant. If the preparation is collected by spraying into a container, sufficient time must be allowed for the propellant to evaporate or it will expand after dosing. All aerosols are tested for eye and skin irritation.

XII. Summary

The need for safety testing of pharmaceuticals is well established. A thorough program of biological testing in conjunction with analytical control procedures is imperative during the entire process of drug development and marketing. Biological tests, such as acute toxicity and pharmacological activity measurements, are necessary to ensure the safety and efficacy of all experimental and marketed drugs. The testing procedures described in this article reflect the current status of safety testing in the pharmaceutical industry. It is believed that the program presented is adequate to ensure both safety and efficacy. However, it should be emphasized that testing procedures are continually reviewed and modified as new information becomes available, permitting the investigator to provide an evaluation of safety and efficacy consistent with current knowledge.

References

Axelrod, J., Reichenthal, J., and Brodie, B. (1954). *J. Pharmacol. Exp. Ther.* **122**, 49.
Banziger, R. (1967). *Bull. Parenteral Drug Ass.* **21**, 148.
Burns, J. J., Cucinell, S. A., Koster, R., and Conney, A. H. (1965). *Ann. N.Y. Acad. Sci.* **123**, 273.
Draize, J. H. (1955). *Food Drug Cosmet. Law J.* **10**, 722.
Draize, J. H., Woodard, G., and Calvery, H. (1944). *J. Pharmacol. Exp. Ther.* **82**, 387.
Litchfield, J., Jr., and Wilcoxon, F. (1949). *J. Pharmacol. Exp. Ther.* **96**, 299.
Miller, L. C., and Tainter, M. L. (1944). *Proc. Soc. Exp. Biol. Med.* **57**, 261.
Munoz, C., Guerrero, S., Pacile, C., and Campos, I. (1961). *Toxicol. Appl. Pharmacol.* **3**, 445.
Peters, J. M. (1966). *Toxicol. Appl. Pharmacol.* **9**, 390.
Remmer, H. (1962). *In* "Metabolic Factors Controlling Duration of Drug Action" (B. B. Brodie and E. B. Erdös, eds.), Vol. VI, p. 235. Macmillan, New York.

QUALITY-CONTROL EDUCATION IN THE COLLEGE OF PHARMACY

Thomas Medwick

College of Pharmacy,
Rutgers University,
University Heights Campus,
New Brunswick, New Jersey

I. Introduction

The periodic call for an awareness of a particular philosophical view is common to every area of education, including pharmacy. This work considers the concept of the quality control of drugs and its importance to all pharmacists and, consequently, to colleges of pharmacy. First, some thoughts about the pharmacy curriculum, in general, as an instrument in producing educated people are discussed. Then, the idea of quality control, its evolution, codification, and development is treated before the involvement of pharmacists is introduced. Finally, an attempt is made to survey the pharmacy curriculum to point out those many areas where particular knowledge important to the understanding of the science and practice of quality control lies. Suggestions are made as to types of laboratory or didactic practices which could be adopted to help demonstrate pertinent points. This writing is not meant to be exhaustive or final, but will achieve some success if the point that the pharmacist should be thoroughly educated in the pharmaceutical sciences is understood and if the pharmacist assumes his role in the establishment and maintenance of drug quality, an activity to which he is uniquely suited.

II. Educational Philosophy in Pharmacy

If one were asked to give a succinct definition of the graduate pharmacist of today, a reasonable try might yield something like "an educated person with an in-depth knowledge of drugs." This relatively simple statement, if accurate, assumes that colleges of pharmacy have taken on and successfully accomplished a difficult task comprising the education of the student as a person and also the education of the student about drugs.

The balance between the diverse elements of general and professional education requires considerable skill to maintain. As curricular change is contemplated and brought about, one must always remember that the general education elements of the curriculum need to be preserved in order to develop an educated person. It is extremely important that the pharmacy curriculum provide the opportunities for the student to choose from courses in English literature, drama, history, art appreciation, music appreciation, philosophy, psychology, and other arts and social-science activities. A fuller appreciation of life, people, and man's accomplishments including his own contribution to organized society can result from these studies, making the pharmacist an interesting, sensitive person. This background should not be diminished or sacrificed in the name of increased professional demands.

Since the knowledge of drugs requires competence in the sciences, a good foundation in fundamental courses in biology, chemistry, mathematics and physics is essential. Biology courses should include general biology, biochemistry, physiology, and microbiology, thereby forming a sound background for pharmacognosy, pharmacology, and specialized topics, such as biopharmaceutics and sterile techniques. Inorganic, organic, analytical, and selected topics in physical chemistry are necessary in order to be sure that medicinal chemistry, both inorganic and organic, and the analysis of drugs are understood. In addition, a good chemistry background is a requirement for dealing with many aspects of pharmaceutical systems and with molecular biology, important in the interpretation of drug action. Finally, since physics and mathematics lie at the root of both biology and chemistry, it is difficult to think of a curriculum as being complete without these disciplines.

In addition to arranging for the foundations of a liberal education as well as an extensive background in the sciences, each college of pharmacy faculty must be actively engaged in providing a proper professional education. This turns out to be a formidable job since the possibility exists that the pharmacy graduate may enter any one of a number of different areas of professional activity. The pharmacist may be found in industry, involved in research and development, manufacturing, or quality control, in the hospital, in the community, or in other activities, such as governmental regulatory work. Each of these areas of involvement, as will become apparent later on, finds the pharmacist concerned with the nature and use of drugs.

III. The Concept of Quality in Pharmaceuticals

The discussion which follows concerns itself with pointing out the omnipresent concepts of quality control which are to be found in the activities of the pharmacist. It must be recognized that the quality of drugs, its establishment and maintenance, should be a concept with which the pharmacist is continually concerned. To project and transmit this awareness, pharmacy faculty members must recognize its importance.

A. The Basis of Quality Control

When a drug is given to a patient, it is assumed that it is precisely the one needed, in an appropriate form, so that it may elicit the desired physiological response. This presupposes that the drug is (1) in a dosage form in which it is stable and biologically available; (2) produced in an environment which will not permit any foreign materials, viz. chemicals or biological systems, to be introduced; and (3) in a container which protects it from any potential changes which are possible from the environment. The three preceding statements broadly define the cardinal requirements of a good quality control scheme or a total quality control system. If one examines these goals it can be seen that the practice of pharmacy, in industry, the hospital, and the community are very much involved in their accomplishment.

The concept of quality control makes very good sense. Good scientific principles would dictate that a drug system be so designed that its integrity is protected. In any experiment, condition must be carefully controlled if reproducible results are to be expected. For a drug system, the variables would be the exact composition of the formulation, the presence or absence of any extraneous materials, and the conditions under which the drug was produced. However, in addition to scientific soundness, the case for quality control has a strong legal basis as well. The Federal Food and Drug Act of 1906 and the Federal Food, Drug and Cosmetic Act of 1938 established the "United States Pharmacopeia" and the "National Formulary" as official compendia. These books of standards strive to build monographs which define "official" drugs and dosage forms in a manner such that adherence to the described tests, procedures, and assays will produce a drug of desired quality. In addition to the regulation of official drugs, a class of drugs called "Nonofficial Drugs" is defined with a statement which requires that they meet the manufacturer's approved standards. Thus the Federal Food, Drug and Cosmetic Acts, provide a legal basis for quality control (FDA, 1970; Deno *et al.*, 1966).

It soon becomes apparent to anyone studying drug standards that the drug monograph can be effective as a quality-control instrument only if the entire history of the drug is carefully controlled. Only then can the small probability contaminant be guarded against. This concept of regulating the history of materials has long been recognized by the pharmaceutical industry and government and, by means of the Drug Amendments of 1962, has been legalized in the form of Good Manufacturing Practices (GMP) regulations, a collection of guidelines to be adhered to during the manufacture and production of drugs. From these brief statements, it can be seen that first the philosophical basis of drug quality (and inherently quality control) was established in the recognition of official compendia and their standards, and, for nonofficial drugs, in the expressed prohibition of deviation from approved manufacturer's standards. More recently, the practical implementation of this concept in the shape of formal GMP regulations has been provided (Quality Control Reports, 1971).

Since the quality of a drug must be maintained until taken by the patient, the very broad implication of quality control begins to become clearer. If the pharmacist is working in industry he must carry out his part of the quality assurance program, whether it be formulating a drug within a stable system, assaying the materials at some point, or being certain the labeling is correct. The pharmacist in the community and the hospital also has the definite responsibility to assure himself that the drug finally reaching the patient is correct from the point of view of identity, purity, and strength. One might legitimately question whether the pharmacist in the hospital and community can properly be part of the quality control system. When the educational background of the pharmacist is compared with that of the nurse and physician, two other candidates for this responsibility, it becomes rather apparent that the pharmacist is the only one of the three with the background to carry out this job. Neither the nurse nor physician is competent in this regard.

B. Quality Control in Pharmacy

Quality control as a professional activity of the pharmacist in industry is rather apparent. If the pharmacist is experimenting in formulations research, the final formula which he develops for a particular drug dosage form must provide for the drug's stability as well as ensuring that the drug will be biologically available. The pharmacist engaged in manufacturing must respect all the specific processes so that the laboratory and pilot plant experiences are realistically translated into large-scale operations capable of yielding "identical" batches of drugs. Analytical research involves him in the development of new and exact methods for the measurements of a drug. The pharmacist in quality-control activities is involved at all stages of the drug's life. The control laboratory assays components at the time of purchase and certifies their acceptability. During manufacture, appropriate in-process controls may be employed to monitor the progress of the production sequence. Inspection functions may be designed to check such activities as proper use of quarantine space for storage, adherence to record keeping procedures and use of check lists, and cleanliness practices including proper cleanup of machinery between runs and general housekeeping routines to prevent chemical cross-contamination and microbiological growth. Proper labeling must be ensured by appropriate controls. Packaging in containers designed to minimize decomposition must be respected. All of these activities as well as others which may be built into an effective quality-control system are provided for in the GMP regulations. The value of quality control in the industry is without question and is easily appreciated by the industrial pharmacist.

Quality control is extremely important to the pharmacist working in a hospital. If any small-scale manufacturing takes place, then the concepts inherent in the GMP regulations should be implemented. Purchasing of drugs by generic designation should be done intelligently (Feldmann, 1971). The manufacturer should be visited and his quality-control system evaluated. Further, an analytical data sheet should be required so that the laboratory behavior of the particular batch of material purchased is known, understood, and found acceptable, as Higuchi (1968) has suggested. Despite vigilant inspections by FDA inspectors and other governmental personnel, the ultimate responsibility for the nature of dispensed drugs rests with the pharmacist, whose education and professional license portends competence. The pharmacist, with a thorough knowledge of drugs, can make an invaluable contribution as a member of the hospital's Pharmacy and Therapeutics Committee.

The preceding points are only the beginning. If one visits a hospital and finds that a pharmacist is not involved in each step of the drug distribution system, a high level of reported medication errors should not be surprising. Great care must be exercised to be certain that mistakes are not made in moving the drug from the pharmacy or drug station to the bedside. Anderson (1962) has reported guidelines for drug safety in hospitals. Proper labeling must be enforced at all times. Dilution or reconstitution of medication must be carried out under a pharmacist's supervision to assure accuracy of calculation and proper volumetric technique. The stability of the resultant solution must be known (Latiolais *et al.*, 1967). Finally, the introduction of drug additives into intravenous solutions must be monitored by the pharmacist. Lack of knowledge of incompatibilities is an instance where ignorance of drug properties can make all well-intentioned quality-control efforts worthless (Carlin and Perkins, 1968). In this setting of hospital activities, the pharmacist must be completely involved with all aspects of drugs. The nurse and physician are not educated to deal with these situations.

Seemingly, the pharmacist in the community pharmacy is most remote from involvement with quality control of drugs, and yet this impression is misleading. If the current moves to change the anti-substitution laws are successful, then the community pharmacist will certainly have to be in a position to make an intelligent choice of drugs from manufacturers on the basis of scientific evaluation. In the manner indicated in the preceding section, inspection of a plant and the study of quality-control laboratory data would tell about the conditions under which the drug was manufactured and the finished drug's properties. Selection of drugs to be used when requested generically could then be made on an intelligent basis (Feldmann, 1971; Higuchi 1968).

In addition to this activity of drug selection based on quality control information, the community-based pharmacist can become involved in quality-control work within his own pharmacy to be certain that the drug protection sequence is carried out until the patient consumes the dosage form. First, proper storage of the pharmaceuticals must be practiced. If this is not indicated by the drug literature or is not apparent from the pertinent chemistry, they the manufacturer should be contacted. The date of receipt of a drug lot should be noted and expiration dates respected. Second, in the process of filling prescriptions, drugs should be handled in a manner which ensures against the introduction of any chemical or microbiological contamination. Counting of dosage units should be done on a clean, fresh surface each and every time. Prescriptions which require compounding should be double-checked for accuracy and any possible incompatibility. Dispensing containers should be stored carefully to prevent contamination and should not be re-used. Labeling procedures should be controlled and designed to prevent possibilities of mislabeling. Notations must be made on the prescription including calculations and data to permit exact duplication on any refill order, e.g., capsule size used, size of prescription container. The lot number of the drug dispensed should be recorded so that, in the unlikely prospect of a drug recall, any particular lot may be ascribed to a particular patient. Family medication records must be faithfully maintained. Finally, the pharmacy must be a model of cleanliness and order. A schedule of regular cleanups, implemented by a checklist, and inspected for compliance each time should be instituted. The responsible employees must be aware of the importance of this task.

The philosophy of quality control does not end until the drug is used. The pharmacist should inform his patron about proper drug storage. Keeping aspirin in a bathroom medicine cabinet, an area with periods of very high humidity, does not seem like good quality control if one knows some chemistry. Proper storage of biologicals such as insulin or of light-sensitive drugs is something about which community pharmacy patrons must be educated. If the quality-control chain is maintained by the manufacturer and the pharmacist only to be naïvely violated by the patron, the drug dosage form finally exposed to the receptor biological system (the human) is still substandard. In an era in which there is a strong awareness of clinical pharmacy, or patient orientation, efforts to have the patron handle his drugs intelligently seem most timely. Yet many of these practices have been carried out by some pharmacists long before a formalization of a new professional philosophy was suggested.

The community pharmacist must be very versatile to operate an economically solvent business while providing the various professional services involved in the filling of prescriptions, selling over-the-counter medication, and providing necessary counsel. The responsibilities involved are appreciated by few professionals in related fields and even fewer laymen. It is refreshing to see recognition of the pharmacist's activity by another practitioner. For example, Dr. Lester Coleman, a physician who is a syndicated medical writer for the lay press, recently wrote about a particular activity of the pharmacist, and the liberty of him (Coleman, 1971) *in extenso* is taken here.

> One of the great talents of the pharmacist, with his long background in chemistry, is to know how well certain drugs will mix with others, and how safe the combination will be.

If he is not completely satisfied, he will call the physician and discuss the problem of drug compatibility with him.

Far too often, the scientific training of the pharmacist is overlooked because of the commercial aspect of his profession. He plays an indispensable role in the health team.

IV. Quality Control in the Pharmacy Curriculum

The broad nature and variety of quality control practices require a diverse background which includes biology, chemistry, pharmacy, and statistics, as is depicted in Fig. 1. It must be apparent that a thorough knowledge of pharmaceutical systems is necessary if the variables to be controlled are to be recognized. The analytically related activities require specific knowledge of separation and measurement techniques and interpretation and treatment of data, including bioassay. Other operations which include proper housekeeping, good data recording, and use of statistical techniques are common to many areas of science but need to be emphasized in the quality-control system.

The following sections discuss the knowledge related to quality control and make suggestions as to didactic and laboratory activities which may be

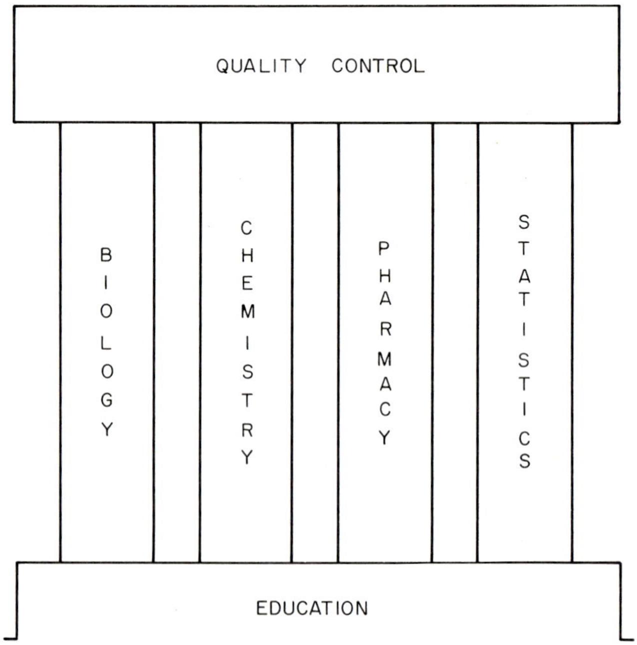

Fig. 1. *The dependence of quality control on biology, chemistry, pharmacy, and statistics.*

useful in treating particular topics. It is apparent that many of the proposals made here are in active use at various schools. For example, 36 out of 56 colleges responding to a recent survey (Rutgers University, 1971) include a discussion of quality-control systems in their curriculum, whereas 29 of 56 introduce GMP regulations. From the same survey, 48 of 56 colleges provide for a consideration of analytical data in assessing the acceptability of pharmaceutical dosage forms. Even though the present discussion may involve some practices and activities in current use, these writings hopefully will introduce some new ideas or treat a particular concept of quality control or related knowledge in a useful fashion.

Since quality control activities are so diverse, it appears rational to deal with this knowledge in a decentralized way, as it occurs in the appropriate discipline. The previously mentioned survey indicates that some aspects of quality control are covered in different parts of the curriculum in 28 of 56 colleges. When the student has advanced to the fourth or fifth year, the entire quality-control system may then be considered in a course dealing with the specific type of pharmaceutical practice involved, viz., industrial, hospital or community.

Current practices and literature should be incorporated continually into the curriculum. A convenient way to keep abreast of developments and advances in quality-control activities is by reading The Gold Sheets (Quality Control Reports), referred to previously in Section III,A. In addition, the proceedings or published reports of meetings which deal with specific quality-control subjects under the sponsorship of government, industry, or academic institutions are excellent sources of information. The volume which contains this work should be useful in this regard.

One of the major concerns in any quality-control program is the question of chemical and physical drug stability. Based on concepts developed in organic chemistry and applied to drugs in organic medicinal chemistry, the stability of drug systems must be studied using the methods of chemical kinetics with the benefit of predictions derived from accelerated stability programs (Lachman and De Luca, 1970). The stabilization of drugs and their protection from hydrolytic, auto-oxidative, and microbial degradation should be understood. The special techniques necessary in the manufacture, production, and control of sterile products must be included. Use of stability data in the establishment of storage conditions, packaging specifications, labeling statements, and expiration dates should be introduced and explained in terms of quality-control practices.

Papers presented at pertinent meetings such as that sponsored by the FDA and the University of Connecticut in 1967 dealing with drug stability, the environment, and containers (FDA University of Connecticut, 1967) and the more recent conclave which considered the dating of pharmaceuticals

(Windheuser and Blockstein, 1970) are good sources of information. An excellent exercise for the laboratory is the study of the stability of a well-behaved drug system. If an automated analytical system is available, the analytical measurement is greatly simplified, permitting more time for other work (Cullen *et al.*, 1968).

To understand the problems of physical stability and behavior related to physical factors, the physical properties of drugs and pharmaceutical dosage forms must also be covered in the curriculum. The nature of colloidal dispersions must be extended to pharmaceutical systems where the dispersing of solids and the prevention or diminution of physical instability, e.g., flocculation, sedimentation, and caking, is important. The methods for stability evaluation should be understood and used at some point in the laboratory. Liquid–liquid and semisolid dispersions, their properties, stability, and measurement of stability should be studied. A study of micrometrics makes the comprehension of the role of particle size in dosage form behavior possible. Undesirable properties such as the low density of powders which permits these solids to be dissipated as a dust during manufacturing and become a chemical contamination hazard, e.g., penicillin, may be cited. Tingstad (1964) provides a good discussion of the physical stability of pharmaceutical systems.

Processes studied in the manufacturing pharmacy course must be understood if the problems in producing reproducible batches of drug dosage forms are to be appreciated. The properties of tablets, the physics of the compression process, and the relationship of process variables to tablet properties could be included in the laboratory. Other unit processes including dissolution, heating, and mixing are topics to be studied. The difficulties in mixing could be exemplified by the problems experienced in product uniform digoxin tablets where content uniformity studies have shown that proper mixing of solids must be followed if formulations with small percentages of active component are expected to be uniform. The extension of this experience to the community pharmacy where a mortar and pestle is the mixing device gives renewed emphasis to the proper execution of a venerable technique.

Two other topics merit discussion at this point. Dissolution, as a process, and the rate of dissolution, a factor in drug availability, must be studied. An experiment measuring the rate of dissolution where it is a requirement in the monograph of one of the official dosage forms, e.g., indomethacin capsules (NF, 1970), could be included in a pharmacy laboratory course. Finally, the mode of operation of prolonged action dosage forms and the evaluation of their behavior must be included.

The concepts of biopharmaceutics must be adequately understood so that variations in dosage form properties designed to optimize biological availability can be appreciated. Control of drug absorption and the rate of the absorption process are examples of the pharmacokinetic aspects of drug formulation. But in addition to the *in vitro* elements, the *in vivo* factors which are known should be pointed out to alert the student to the role of the receptor system and biological variation in drug response. For example, it has been reported that in certain instances where patients are found to be unresponsive or limitedly responsive to spinal anesthetic, a bioassay of the anesthetic by means of rabbit corneal anesthesia shows proper anesthetic activity (VanDeripe and Yim, 1960).

The analytical concepts in the pharmacy curriculum must be dealt with strongly if the pharmacist is to understand and interpret analytical data as part of any quality-control activity. The classical methods must be considered as to their physicochemical basis. Gravimetric analysis should be viewed from the concepts of precipitate properties and generation. Calculation of titration curves from pertinent equilibria gives an insight into the distribution of species as a function of changing solution conditions and makes end-point detection a theoretically valid process. Both indicator and potentiometric end points should be included. Fundamental concepts of radiochemistry should be introduced. To reinforce these theoretical concepts, selected experiments should be carried out. An automatic recording titrator may be used to titrate carbonate or phosphoric acid; this instrumental setup removes the tedium of a manual procedure and allows calculation of pK values (Medwick and Kirschner, 1966). Connors (1967) has published a good experiment using nonaqueous titrimetry to follow the partition chromatographic separation of aminopyrine and antipyrine. The nonaqueous titrimetric analysis of aminophylline (Medwick and Schiesswohl, 1963) is a good example of solvent selection in the differentiation of two bases. Other experiments could be selected, such as the determination of calcium in calcium gluconate tablets by titration with EDTA (USP, 1970), or the oxidation–reduction Malaprade determination of glycols or polyhydric alcohols (USP, 1970).

Electrochemical techniques in addition to potentiometry, which is fairly common, should be treated at least on an introductory level. Coulometry, not yet used to any great extent in pharmaceutical analysis, may be considered when electron-transfer phenomena are studied. Similarly, polarography may be introduced and an experiment to demonstrate its nature or its application to pharmaceutical systems, e.g., hydrochlorothiazide tablets (USP, 1970), used in the laboratory. More advanced techniques, e.g., AC polarography, can be studied as an option or in an advanced course.

It is not possible to consider pharmaceutical analytical chemistry without an adequate treatment of spectroscopy. A physics course should include a study of light and its properties. This knowledge provides a good basis for the understanding of the quantum hypothesis, quantum numbers, discrete energy levels, the Aufbau principle, and molecular orbitals. The basis and value of UV and visible spectrophotometry must be included and may be applied to such determinations as the analysis of a binary mixture of sulfonamides (Englis and Skoog, 1943). Nuclear magnetic resonance (NMR) spectroscopy and infrared (IR) spectroscopy, introduced in many organic chemistry courses, could be applied to the identification of a number of different pharmaceutical compounds. Even if actual experimental work cannot be included the pharmacist should understand emission spectroscopy, X-ray diffraction, mass spectrometry, and atomic absorption spectrophotometry. The current cost of atomic absorption instruments, however, is at a level which is not prohibitive for most colleges and thus permits easy analysis of metals present at trace levels.

Since automated analysis has become so important in industrial pharmaceutical laboratories, it must be included in the curriculum. The fundamental principles should be emphasized and the techniques used in the laboratory, if possible. Professor Hans Veening of Bucknell University has conducted a successful one-week course in automated analysis for students from different science curricula (Comte *et al.*, 1971). This experience indicates the feasibility of such an activity and should encourage some pharmacy faculties to institute this topic. The convenience of automation in content uniformity determinations such as individual tablet analysis is easily appreciated. For example, barbiturate-containing tablets have been monitored by automated analysis (Hall and Meyer, 1970).

Although the general utility and value of separations to analytical chemistry is undeniable, the need for separations in the analysis of pharmaceutical dosage forms is most critical. It is current compendial practice to require a separation step with all tablet analyses for which the measurement is an UV spectrophotometric one. This step is designed to separate the active component from any UV absorbing excipients. Simple solvent extraction, generally used in organic chemistry laboratories, can be developed further and led into countercurrent distribution methods and the prediction of solute distribution. Chromatography, as a generalized separation scheme, should be set on a good theoretical basis. Similarities and differences between the types of chromatography are excellent summarizing criteria to be noted. The nature and size of the sample, the variables involved in the separation, and the important laboratory manipulations should be covered. Laboratory exercises should be included to permit some of the chromatographic methods to be used. The pharmacognosy laboratory is an excellent place for thin-layer chromatography to be used. Separations of plant extracts and mixtures of alkaloids demonstrate the technique well. Column chromatography can also be included, as has been mentioned in the instance of aminopyrine and antipyrine (Connors, 1967) separation. The advent and potential utility of high-pressure liquid chromatography requires its inclusion in any up-to-date curriculum. Finally, the use of gas chromatography may be illustrated with a number of different experiments, one of which is the determination of alcohol in a tincture (Jenkins *et al.*, 1967).

Since the preceding discussion deals with measurement and separation techniques largely from a basic point of view, even though the test object may be a pharmaceutical one, there must be an attempt to bring analysis to the point where it is directed to quality control. The monographs in the USP and NF serve this function well. If the concept of a monograph is approached from its role as a quality-control instrument for a finished pharmaceutical, then the specific parts of the monograph fit into place. In the laboratory the identification of a particular drug may be carried out by several different techniques, viz., chemical reaction, infrared scan and comparison with a known reference standard, or chromatographic mobility compared to a known standard. The role of reference standards as means by which interlaboratory differences may be obviated should be explained. The use of TLC to identify a drug and monitor possible contaminants may be carried out. Limits tests may be done so that the student gets to appreciate this type of analytical procedure. In a similar context, the use of fluorimetry, atomic absorption, and gas chromatography in trace-level analysis should be included. Finally, the calculation of assay results in terms of meeting standards may be included as problems in which a decision is made as to the rejection or acceptance of a particular batch of drug or chemical. As Smith (1965) has suggested, a case approach where the evolution of drugs is discussed brings home the importance of GMP in preserving the relevance of the monograph and all of the various specific steps.

A very important aspect of the quality control of pharmaceuticals is that of bioassay. Even though the majority of assays are chemical or physical in nature owing to their relative convenience, the ultimate measure of drug activity is the bioassay. A useful experiment would involve the comparison of a microbiological assay of an antibiotic with a convenient chemical procedure. The point to be demonstrated is that the chemical and biological responses are not identical. Assay of biologicals such as vaccines and antitoxins should be studied, since this type of measurement is very specific. Finally, the concepts of toxicity, LD_{50}, and the statistical nature of biological response must be mastered and demonstrated by experiment in the pharmacology course.

The course in microbiology must be relied upon to accomplish a specific goal. In addition to educating the student as to the nature of microbiological organisms, the manner in which microorganisms may be transferred must be discussed. With a knowledge and consciousness of this potential danger, cleanliness practices, personal hygiene habits, sterilization techniques, and all other attempts to eliminate microbial hazards are understandable and sensible. Laboratory means of establishing the presence and the identification of an organism should be included.

There is one remaining area of importance to quality-control practice, the proper maintenance and treatment of data. Throughout the curriculum stress should be placed on the keeping of adequate records. Invalid data destroys good work. Treatment of data by statistical methods and sampling should be considered on at least an introductory level. More sophisticated techniques can be covered in an elective course in statistics, available to those who choose to follow an industrial career. Lin and Lachman (1970) discuss statistical quality control and sampling. The use of computers cannot be ignored. Students should be aware of the advantages and capabilities of computers in solving problems such as those in statistics or in storing large amounts of information, such as patient profile records (Lordi and Felmeister, 1971). Able students should be encouraged to learn programming techniques.

On the basis of the results achieved from a curriculum which includes the topics discussed in the preceding section, it should be possible to discuss the quality-control system as an entity. The quality-control activities practiced in industry may be discussed in the manufacturing course and the practices used in the manufacturing laboratory should be examples of the GMP regulations. In the hospital pharmacy course, a logical place is available for the discussions involving quality-control practices and problems in the hospital. Practical experience will permit the student to observe the strengths and weaknesses of the hospital program in which he is involved. The points discussed in the preceding section, e.g., the nature of the drug distribution system, the labeling practices, and the way additives are introduced into i. v. solutions should be specifically cited for discussion and constructive criticism. The practices of a quality-control nature to be ideally followed in a community pharmacy seem to belong logically in a course in dispensing pharmacy. All aspects, e.g., general housekeeping, labeling, record keeping, dispensing techniques, may be logically discussed in small groups and applied in the laboratory. In addition, students with experience in community pharmacy can discuss actual practices, their strength and shortcomings, in order to give meaning to the quality-control ideas.

The preceding sections have touched on many topics and contain many suggestions. However, one point, in closing, must be clearly made. The purpose of these pages has been to create an awareness of quality control so that the student acquires the knowledge and understanding to think constructively about quality control in all its complications. No curriculum can possibly include every aspect of a topic but every curriculum must be designed to get the student to think. Quality-control systems, or whatever they are called, vary with the institution, be it industry, hospital, or community pharmacy. No one should expect a pharmacy graduate to be able to walk into an environment and know its quality-control practices a priori. This would involve clairvoyance, not yet part of most curricula. However, the pharmacy graduate should be expected to understand the local practices, think about them, and, with experience, improve upon them. Who but the pharmacist has the education and training to understand all aspects of drugs? Who, but he, is capable of maintaining drug quality? There is no other.

Acknowledgments

The author is grateful to Professors Nicholas Lordi and Bartley Sciarrone, Rutgers University, and Miss Evelyn Sarnoff, New York District of the Food and Drug Administration, for their useful suggestions and comments.

References

Anderson, R. D. (1962). *Amer. J. Hosp. Pharm.* **19**, 577.

Carlin, H. S., and Perkins, A. J. (1968). *Amer. J. Hosp. Pharm.* **25**, 271.

Coleman, L. (1971). *Jersey J.* August 26, p. 22. Jersey Journal, Jersey City, New Jersey.

Comte, R. F., Norregaard, A. N., and Veening, H. (1971). *J. Chem. Educ.* **48**, 110.

Connors, K. A. (1967). "Pharmaceutical Analysis," p. 341. Wiley, New York.

Cullen, L. F., Packman, D. L., and Papariello, G. J. (1968). *Ann. N.Y. Acad. Sci.* **153**, 525.

Deno, R. A., Rowe, T. D., and Brodie, D. C. (1966). "The Profession of Pharmacy," 2nd ed., pp. 215–219. Lippincott, Philadelphia, Pennsylvania.

Englis, D. T., and Skoog, D. A. (1943). *Ind. Eng. Chem., Anal. Ed.* **15**, 748.

FDA (1970). "Requirements of the United States Food, Drug and Cosmetic Act." Superintendent of Documents, US Govt. Printing Office, Washington, D.C.

FDA University of Connecticut (1967). "Drug Stability as Affected by Environment and Containers." FDA Bureau of Education and Voluntary Compliance, Washington, D.C.

Feldmann, E. (1971). *J. Amer. Pharm. Ass.* [N.S.] **11**, 379.

Hall, C. H., and Meyer, R. C. (1970). *Advan. Automat. Anal., Technicon Int. Congr.*, 1970 Abstracts, p. 21.

Higuchi, T. (1968). *In* "Development of Safer and More Effective Drugs" (S. W. Goldstein, ed.), p. 162. Amer. Pharm. Ass., Washington, D.C.

Jenkins, G. L., Knevel, A. M., DiGangi, F. E. (1967). "Quantitative Pharmaceutical Chemistry," 6th ed., p. 438. McGraw-Hill (Blakiston), New York.

Lachman, L., and De Luca, P. (1970). *In* "The Theory and Practice of Industrial Pharmacy" (L. Lachman, H. A. Lieberman, and J. L. Kanig, eds.), pp. 669–710. Lea & Febiger, Philadelphia, Pennsylvania.

Latiolais, C. J., Shoup, L. K., and Thur, M. P. (1967). *Amer. J. Hosp. Pharm.* **24**, 666.
Lin, S. and Lachman, L. (1970). *In* "The Theory and Practice of Industrial Pharmacy" (T. Lachman, H. A. Lieberman, and J. A. Kanig, eds.), pp. 719–735. Lea & Febiger. Philadelphia, Pennsylvania.
Lordi, N. G. and Felmeister, A. (1971). *Pharm. Alumni Rep.* **3**, 2. Rutgers College of Pharmacy Alumni Association, New Brunswick, New Jersey.
Medwick, T., and Kirschner, E. (1966). *J. Pharm. Sci.* **55**, 1296.
Medwick, T., and Schiesswohl, F. (1963), *J. Pharm. Sci.* **52**, 843.
NF (1970). "National Formulary," 13th ed., p. 369. Amer. Pharm. Ass. Washington, D.C.
Quality Control Reports. (1971). "The Gold Sheet" (W. Werble, ed.), January, Spec. Ed. F-D-C Reports, Inc., Washington, D.C.
Rutgers University (1971). "The Status of Chemistry in the Pharmacy Curriculum." Survey by Department of Pharmaceutical Chemistry, College of Pharmacy, New Brunswick, New Jersey.
Smith, P. F. (1965). *Amer. J. Pharm. Educ.* **29**, 686.
Tingstad, J. E. (1964). *J. Pharm. Sci.* **53**, 955.
USP (1970). "United States Pharmacopeia," 18th rev. ed., p. 93. Mack Publ. Co., Easton, Pennsylvania.
VanDeripe, D. R., and Yim, G. K. W. (1960). *Anaesthesia* **21**, 26.
Windheuser, J. J., and Blockstein, W. L., eds. (1970). "The Dating of Pharmaceuticals." University Extension, University of Wisconsin, Madison, Wisconson.

THE ROLE OF THE WORLD HEALTH ORGANIZATION IN THE QUALITY CONTROL OF BIOLOGICAL AND PHARMACEUTICAL PRODUCTS

A. G. Mathews

Commonwealth Serum Laboratories, Melbourne, Australia

The first positive steps towards the international control of drugs were taken just half a century ago, and it happened that drugs of biological origin were the first to come under international attention—for the obvious reason that such drugs are extremely variable unless subjected to very close control. Indeed, the oldest vaccine of all—smallpox vaccine—was for many years notoriously uncontrolled and variable, and even today the official requirements to which it is subject in most countries are strikingly less stringent than those for other analogous products.

I. Biological Products

A. International Biological Standards

The history of international control of biological drugs starts with the establishment of international standard preparations, and indeed, for a third of a century after the first such preparation—the International Standard for Diphtheria Antitoxin—was set up in 1922, the work of international organizations was directed almost solely to this purpose. Truly international efforts were slow in starting. The first few biological standards were established by a national body, the Statens Seruminstitut, Copenhagen: it was not until several years later than 1922 that this work was taken over by the then newly created Health Committee of the League of Nations (WHO, 1958). It is a tribute to the foresight of the Danish authorities that the specimen of diphtheria antitoxin chosen as a standard is still in use today, after half a century, and that the supply of this pioneer preparation is not likely to be exhausted during the half century to come. The preparation consists of a dried hyperimmune horse serum, and there is little doubt that its remarkable stability stimulated further efforts in the field of international control. It was truly a case of chance favoring the prepared corporate mind!

By the time the World Health Organization was established in 1948, the number of international biological standards distributed by the League of Nations had grown to 32, in the categories listed in Table I. WHO took over from the League of Nations the task of establishing, storing, and distributing international biological *standards*, of which there are now 79. In addition there are 63 international biological *reference preparations*. Also, in recent years, 62 international biological *reference reagents* have been established by WHO. Generally, these latter reagents are intended as reference materials for substances used in the diagnosis of disease and in the identification of microorganisms. Many leptospiral typing antisera are included among these reagents, and a recently established set of viral typing antisera is being

TABLE I

Numbers of International Biological Standards, Reference Preparations, and Reference Reagents in Various Categories

Category	Standards 1948	Standards 1970	Reference preparations, 1970[a]	Reference reagents, 1970[a]
Antibodies	12	38	11	62
Antigens	1	10	14	—
Antibiotics	1	17	23	—
Hormones, vitamins, and enzymes	14	13	5	—
Miscellaneous	4	1	10	—
Total	32	79	63	62

[a]None in 1948.

rapidly expanded. Table I gives a classification of the current international preparations, with comparative figures for 1948. All of the current standards and reference preparations are listed in Table II (WHO Expert Committee on Biological Standardization, 1971a).

In general, the main purpose served by the international standards and reference preparations is to provide a means of ensuring world-wide uniformity in expressing the potency of preparations used in the prophylaxis, therapy, or diagnosis of human and animal disease. Most such substances, at least at the time of their establishment, could not be characterized fully by chemical and physical means. The activity of an ill-characterized substance may be measured by biological assay, and the results may be best expressed as a ratio of its activity to the activity of a closely similar physical specimen, designated the international standard. In many cases, the defining of an international unit of activity for such a standard affords a convenient way of expressing the ratio, and this is what has been done for all international standards and for some of the international reference preparations. An international *standard* is usually established after an extensive collaborative assay has been carried out to determine the suitability of a lot proposed to serve as such. Many of the international *reference preparations*, however, have not been so extensively studied, or are used only indirectly in the assay of some prophylactic or therapeutic agent. But the distinction between international standards on the one hand and international reference preparations on the other is at best rather artificial and arbitrary.

With the progress of knowledge, certain biological substances that formerly required biological assay can now be characterized fully by chemical

TABLE II

List of Current International Biological Standards and Reference Preparations

Substance	Standards: First	Standards: Current[a]	Reference preparations: First	Reference preparations: Current[a]	Held by[b]
Antibodies					
Diphtheria antitoxin	1922				C
Tetanus antitoxin	1928	1969 (2)			C
Anti-dysentery serum (Shiga)	1928				C
Gas-gangrene antitoxin (*perfringens*) (*Clostridium welchii* type A antitoxin)	1931	1963 (5)			C
Gas-gangrene antitoxin (*Vibrion septique*)	1934	1957 (3)			C
Gas-gangrene antitoxin (*oedematiens*)	1934	1966 (3)			C
Staphylococcus α antitoxin	1934	1938 (2)			C
Antipneumococcus serum (type 1)	1934				C
Antipneumococcus serum (type 2)	1934				C
Gas-gangrene antitoxin (histolyticus)	1935	1951 (2)			C
Diphtheria antitoxin for flocculation test			1935	1956 (4)	C
Gas-gangrene antitoxin (*Sordelli*)	1938				C
Anti-A blood-typing serum	1950				C
Anti-B blood-typing serum	1950				C
Scarlet fever streptococcus antitoxin	1952				C
Antityphoid serum			1952		C
Anti-*Brucella abortus* serum	1952	1967 (2)			W
Anti-Q-fever serum	1953				C
Clostridium welchii (perfringens) type B antitoxin	1954				W
Clostridium welchii (perfringens) type D antitoxin	1954				W

[a]Entries in this column indicate, in parentheses, whether the current preparation is the 2nd, 3rd, 4th, etc., to have been established for the particular substance. The absence of an entry indicates that the first preparation is still current.

[b]C indicates: WHO International Laboratory for Biological Standards, Statens Seruminstitut, Copenhagen. W indicates: WHO International Laboratory for Biological Standards, Central Veterinary Laboratory, Weybridge, England. L indicates: WHO International Laboratory for Biological Standards, National Institute for Medical Research, London. U indicates: Rijks Instituut voor de Volksgezondheid, Utrecht, the Netherlands.

TABLE II (continued)

	Year of establishment				
	Standards		Reference preparations		
Substance	First	Current[a]	First	Current[a]	Held by[b]
Swine erysipelas serum (anti-N)	1954				W
Antirabies serum	1955				C
Syphilitic human serum	1958				C
Antistreptolysin O	1959				C
Antipoliovirus serum (type 1)	1962				C
Antipoliovirus serum (type 2)	1962				C
Antipoliovirus serum (type 3)	1962				C
Anti-yellow-fever serum			1962		C
Clostridium botulinum Type A antitoxin	1963				C
Clostridium botulinum Type B antitoxin	1963				C
Clostridium botulinum Type C antitoxin	1963				C
Clostridium botulinum Type D antitoxin	1963				C
Clostridium botulinum Type E antitoxin	1963				C
Anti-swine-fever serum	1963				W
Naja antivenin	1964				C
Antimeasles serum			1964		C
Clostridium botulinum Type F antitoxin	1965				C
Antismallpox serum	1965				C
Antistaphylococcal P–V leucocidin serum			1965		C
Rheumatoid arthritis serum			1965		C
Anti-Rh_0 (anti-D) Incomplete blood-typing serum	1966				C
Antirubella serum			1966	1970 (2)	C
Anti-Newcastle disease serum			1966		W
Anti toxoplasma serum	1967				C
Anticanine-distemper serum	1967				W
Anticanine-hepatitis serum	1967				W
Anti-*Mycoplasma gallisepticum* serum			1969		W

(continued)

TABLE II (continued)

List of Current International Biological Standards and Reference Preparations

	Year of establishment				
	Standards		Reference preparations		
Substance	First	Current[a]	First	Current[a]	Held by[b]
Human serum immunoglobulins IgG, IgA, and IgM			1970		C
Anti-nuclear-factor serum (homogeneous)			1970		C
Antigens					
Old tuberculin (OT)	1931	1965 (3)			C
Purified protein derivative of mammalian tuberculin	1951				C
Tetanus toxoid	1951				C
Diphtheria toxoid, plain	1951				C
Cardiolipin			1951	1967 (4)	C
Lecithin (beef heart)			1951	1953 (2)	C
Lecithin (egg)			1951	1970 (4)	C
Cholera vaccine (Inaba)			1953		C
Cholera vaccine (Ogawa)			1953		C
Purified protein derivative of avian tuberculin	1954				C
Schick test toxin (diphtheria)	1954				C
Diphtheria toxoid, adsorbed	1955				C
Pertussis vaccine	1957				C
Swine erysipelas vaccine	1959				W
Rabies vaccine			1960	1965 (2)	C
Smallpox vaccine			1962		C
Typhoid vaccine (acetone-inactivated)			1962		C
Typhoid vaccine (heat-phenol-inactivated)			1962		C
Poliomyelitis vaccine (inactivated)			1962		C
Newcastle disease vaccine (inactivated)	1963				W
Tetanus toxoid, adsorbed	1965				C
BCG vaccine			1965		C
Clostridium oedematiens (alpha) toxoid			1966		W
Influenza virus hemagglutinin (type A)			1967		C
Newcastle disease vaccine (live)			1967		W

TABLE II (continued)

	Year of establishment				
	Standards		Reference preparations		
Substance	First	Current[a]	First	Current[a]	Held by[b]
Antibiotics					
Streptomycin	1950	1958 (2)			L
Dihydrostreptomycin	1953	1966 (2)			L
Bacitracin	1953	1964 (2)			L
Chlortetracycline	1953	1970 (2)			L
Oxytetracycline	1955	1966 (2)			L
Polymyxin B	1955	1969 (2)			L
Tetracycline	1957	1970 (2)			L
Erythromycin	1957				L
Neomycin			1958		L
Kanamycin			1959		L
Viomycin			1959	1969 (2)	L
Ristocetin			1960		L
Gramicidin S			1962		L
Spiramycin			1962		L
Demethylchlortetracycline			1962		L
Triacetyloleandomycin			1962		L
Procaine penicillin in oil with aluminium monostearate			1962	1966 (2)	L
Nystatin	1963				L
Amphotericin B	1963				L
Vancomycin	1963				L
Oleandomycin	1964				L
Kanamycin B			1964		L
Ristocetin B			1964		L
Novobiocin	1965				L
Paromomycin			1965		L
Cefalotin			1965		L
Lincomycin			1965		L
Gramicidin			1966		L
Colistin methane sulfonate			1966		L
Tylosin	1966				W
Hygromycin B	1966				W
Capreomycin			1967		L
Rifamycin SV			1967		L
Colistin	1968				L
Rolitetracycline	1968				L
Gentamycin			1968		L
Lymecycline			1968		L
Methacycline			1969		L
Nisin			1969		W
Neomycin B			1970		L

(continued)

TABLE II (continued)

List of Current International Biological Standards and Reference Preparations

Substance	Year of establishment: Standards: First	Standards: Current[a]	Reference preparations: First	Reference preparations: Current[a]	Held by[b]
Hormones, vitamins, and enzymes					
Insulin, bovine and porcine, for bioassay	1925	1958 (4)			L
Oxytocin and vasopressin (antidiuretic hormone), bovine, for bioassay	1925	1957 (3)			L
Vitamin D_3	1931	1949 (2)			L
Prolactin, ovine, for bioassay	1939	1962 (2)			L
Serum gonadotrophin, equine, for bioassay	1939	1966 (2)			L
Chorionic gonadotrophin, human, for bioassay	1939	1963 (2)			L
Heparin	1942	1958 (2)			L
Corticotrophin, porcine, for bioassay	1950	1962 (3)			L
Thyrotrophin, bovine, for bioassay	1954				L
Growth hormone, bovine, for bioassay	1955				L
Hyaluronidase	1955				L
Human menopausal gonadotrophins (follicle-stimulating hormone and interstitial-cell-stimulating hormone), urinary, for bioassay			1959	1964 (2)	L
Vitamin B_{12}			1959		L
Streptokinase-streptodornase	1964				L
Erythropoietin, human, urinary, for bioassay			1965	1970 (2)	L
Growth hormone, human, for immunoassay			1968		L
Urokinase			1968		L
Blood coagulation factor VIII	1970				L
Miscellaneous					
Neoarsphenamine			1925	1940 (3)	L
Sulfarsphenamine			1925	1951 (3)	L
Digitalis	1926	1949 (3)			L
Oxophenarsine			1951		L
Dimercaprol			1952		L

TABLE II (continued)

Substance	Year of Establishment: Standards — First	Standards — Current[a]	Reference preparations — First	Reference preparations — Current[a]	Held by[b]
Opacity reference preparation			1953	1965 (3)	C
Mel B			1954		L
MSb			1954		L
Protamine			1954		L
Pyrogen			1958		L
Hemiglobincyanide			1967		U

or physical means (or have fallen into disuse), and so the international standards established for them have been discontinued. Among the 32 standards in use at the inception of WHO, those for vitamins B, C, and E, provitamin A, ouabain, estrone, estradiol monobenzoate, androsterone, and progesterone have been discontinued. Also, ten standards or reference preparations established by WHO since 1948 have been discontinued: these are for the following substances: vitamin A, tubocurarine, penicillin, penicillin K, phenoxymethylpenicillin, chloramphenicol, cholera antigen (Inaba), cholera antigen (Ogawa), and staphylococcus β antitoxin.

In some cases, where international biological standards have been discontinued, corresponding international chemical reference substances have been made available by WHO. This has been done in the case of substances which, although fully characterizable by chemical or physical means, are still sometimes more conveniently measured by biological assay or by physical tests in which direct comparison with a reference preparation eliminates some types of instrumental error. At the time of the second edition of the International Pharmacopoeia (WHO, 1967), about 40 chemical reference substances had been established, mainly steroids, cardiac glycosides, and semisynthetic penicillins. These are needed for assays and identification tests described in the Pharmacopoeia. Some of them (for example, the semisynthetic penicillins) are also used for microbiological tests. The chemical reference substances, and some discontinued biological standards which are available also from the Apotekens Central-laboratorium in Solna, Sweden, are listed in Table III.

In accordance with principles which were enunciated at an Intergovernmental Conference on Biological Standardization held at Geneva in 1935 and later adopted by the League of Nations, international biological

TABLE III

List of Current International Chemical Reference Substances[a]

p-Acetamidobenzalazine	Hydrocortisone acetate
Ampicillin	*o*-Iodohippuric acid
Ampicillin sodium	Lanatoside C
Ampicillin trihydrate	Methyltestosterone
Carbenicillin sodium	Meticillin sodium
Chloramphenicol	Nafcillin sodium
Cloxacillin sodium	Ouabain
Cortisone acetate	Oxacillin sodium
Deoxycortone acetate	Pheneticillin potassium
Dexamethasone	Prednisolone
Dexamethasone acetate	Prednisolone acetate
Digitoxin	Prednisone
Digoxin	Prednisone acetate
Ergometrine maleate	Progesterone
Ergotamine tartrate	Propicillin potassium
Estradiol benzoate	Riboflavine
Estrone	Testosterone propionate
Ethinylestradiol	Thioacetazone
Ethisterone	Tubocurarine chloride
Folic acid	Vitamine A acetate (solution)
Furosemide	Warfarin
Griseofulvin	
Hydrocortisone	

[a]Note. All of the substances listed are distributed by the WHO Centre for Chemical Reference Substances, Solna, Sweden. The list includes some discontinued international biological reference preparations and standards, which are still available.

standards and reference preparations are "freely distributed" in two senses—first that they are issued free of any charges and second that, as far as possible, they are issued to all institutions having a genuine need for them. Nevertheless, as has been emphasized recently by the WHO Expert Committee on Biological Standardization (1971b), the primary purpose of these preparations is the calibration of national standards in countries which have the facilities for establishing national standards: in other countries, lacking such facilities, the international preparations are often made available to manufacturers for use in calibrating their house standards, distribution being effected normally through the appropriate national health control authority. Use of the international preparations by research institutes can only be regarded as of secondary importance, although as many as possible of academic and research requests are met.

The reasons for carefully conserving stocks of the international biological preparations are sound: many of the substances are in short supply (such as hormones of human origin); it is difficult to prepare, dispense and dry large quantities of standards under the very uniform conditions that are desirable; study and assay of the preparations is often extremely laborious and time-consuming; and it is highly desirable that the preparations should not have to be replaced at unduly short intervals. Nevertheless, the result of this policy of conserving the international preparations is that manufacturers of biological drugs have to interpose at least one intermediate standard preparation—more usually, at least two intermediate preparations—between the internationally recognized standard and their own product. Thus, the opportunity for variation in the results of biological assays performed by different manufacturers in different countries is increased, compared with the situation which would exist if the international preparations could be prepared and distributed on a scale large enough to permit their use as manufacturers' working standards.

It is interesting to compare the system of distribution of international biological standard preparations with that applying to international chemical reference substances. The latter are distributed free of charge to national control authorities and to other nonprofit institutions: they are made available to manufacturers upon payment of a small fee. Thus, for non-biological drugs it *is* open to manufacturers to use internationally recognized preparations as their working house standards, the only obstacle, at present, being one of expense. So far, this obstacle has prevented the embarrassment which might otherwise have been caused by rapid exhaustion of the stocks of some of the chemical reference substances.

It is worth considering more deeply the role of these internationally recognized standards, reference preparations, reagents, and chemical substances in the improvement of pharmaceutical practice, particularly in the sphere of the manufacture of biological products. Indeed, it is difficult to overestimate the importance of international uniformity in the expression of dosages of complex medicinal products—uniformity that could not possibly have been achieved without the enormous amount of effort devoted to the establishment of international standards. The benefits include the direct and obvious ones, but very important also is the stimulus to research brought about by international cooperation in biological assays and in the collaborative study of the stability and purity of complex biological mixtures.

Time and again collaborative assays have revealed gross discrepancies between the results of assays conducted by ostensibly the same method in different laboratories, and these discrepancies are not always eliminated by expression of the results in terms of the activity of a reference preparation. Knowledge of the magnitude of such errors is useful, of course, as a warning against placing too much reliance on the results of an assay done in a single laboratory, and this knowledge could not be accumulated except by collaboration between different laboratories. But large discrepancies between laboratories are often a clear sign of some qualitative difference between the composition of the reference preparation and of the substance under test, and once the discrepancies have been revealed the need for further purification studies becomes obvious, and the presence of previously unsuspected active impurities may be revealed. Thus, as well as organizing international collaborative assays prior to the establishment of an international standard, WHO also often arranges collaborative post-assay studies, in which several commercial specimens of the biological drug are compared with the standard preparation in several laboratories in different countries. One typical example which may be cited is from the field of snake antivenins—a field which presents particularly difficult problems of biological standardization because of the extremely complex composition of snake venoms (and hence of the corresponding antisera), and because of the degree of variation between venoms from otherwise closely related species of snakes of a single genus. The International Standard for *Naja* antivenin was established by WHO in 1964 after an extensive collaborative assay, and since then a series of post-assay collaborative studies have been conducted, as a result of which it has been possible to assess the utility of a standard preparation in eliminating some—but by no means all—of the variability between assays of different specimens of *Naja* antivenin in different laboratories, using as reagents different specimens of cobra venoms (WHO Expert Committee on Biological Standardization, 1971c).

B. International Requirements

1. Establishment of Specifications

Turning away from the activities of WHO in the sphere of establishing material standard preparations of biological drugs, the role of WHO in drawing up specifications for biological drugs and requirements for their quality control will now be considered.

The activity of WHO in drawing up specifications for biological substances has developed strongly during the last 15 years, and has borne fruit in the form of a set of Requirements for Biological Substances. In one sense, this set of documents may be thought of as a supplement to, or a partial replacement for, the International Pharmacopoeia, which itself deals only in summary fashion with some biologicals, and omits others altogether. But the WHO Requirements for Biological Substances, taken as a whole, represent a great intensification of the degree of control attempted over complex substances in this particularly difficult field. The Requirements for Biological Substances which have been drawn up so far are indicated, in chronological order, in Table IV (WHO Expert Committee on Biological Standardization, 1971d).

Since 1952, when WHO interest in the establishment of international requirements for biological products began, various measures have been examined for attempting to achieve a greater degree of uniformity in the quality, safety, and potency of vaccines, antisera, etc. (WHO, 1958). Several conferences of heads of control laboratories were held and study groups of experts were set up to examine the requirements already in force in various countries for the control of substances of particular interest to WHO in relation to its mass immunization and mass prophylaxis schemes in developing countries. In these fields, as in all others, WHO efforts are

TABLE IV

Who Requirements for Biological Substances

Year adopted	No.	Subject
1958	1	General Requirements for Manufacturing Establishments and Control Laboratories (revised in 1965)
1958	2	Poliomyelitis Vaccine (inactivated) (revised in 1965)
1958	3	Yellow Fever Vaccine
1958	4	Cholera Vaccine (revised in 1968)
1958	5	Smallpox Vaccine (revised in 1965)
1959	6	General Requirements for the Sterility of Biological Substances
1961	7	Poliomyelitis Vaccine (Oral) (revised in 1965)
1963	8	Pertussis Vaccine
1963	9	Procaine Benzylpenicillin in Oil with Aluminium Monostearate (revised in 1966)
1963	10	Diphtheria Toxoid and Tetanus Toxoid
1965	11	Dried BCG Vaccine
1965	12	Measles Vaccine (Live) and Measles Vaccine (inactivated)
1966	13	Anthrax Spore Vaccine (Live—for Veterinary Use)
1966	14	Human Immunoglobulin
1966	15	Typhoid Vaccine
1967	16	Tuberculins
1967	17	Inactivated Influenza Vaccine
1969	18	Immune Sera of Animal Origin
1969	19	Rinderpest Cell Culture Vaccine (Live) and Rinderpest Vaccine (Live)
1969	20	*Brucella abortus* Strain 19 Vaccine (Live—for Veterinary Use)
1970	21	Snake Antivenins

directed preferentially toward problems that can be satisfactorily solved only through cooperation between several Member States. Among the first such study groups was one concerned with pertussis vaccine, but its efforts did not bear fruit directly and indeed it was not until 1963 that International Requirements for Pertussis Vaccine were adopted (No. 8 in the series). The first substance for which international requirements were formally adopted was yellow fever vaccine—as far back as 1945, under the aegis not of WHO but of the Standing Committee on Health of the United Nations Relief and Rehabilitation Administration. Yellow fever vaccine was one of the first substances for which WHO international requirements were set up in 1958.

Another substance for which international requirements were established at the same time was poliomyelitis vaccine (inactivated). The study group concerned with drawing up these requirements was also charged with revising the work of a slightly earlier group, which had, in 1957, drawn up General Requirements for Manufacturing Establishments and Control Laboratories. This document, in its revised form, also was adopted in 1958, and care was taken to formulate the International Requirements for Yellow Fever Vaccine and Poliomyelitis Vaccine (Inactivated) in such a way as to fit as closely as possible into the framework of the general requirements. All subsequent requirements for specific biologicals have also been drawn up within the framework of the general requirements.

2. *General Requirements for Manufacturing Establishments and Control Laboratories*

It is worth studying the general requirements in some detail, using the text as revised by a study group in 1965 (WHO Expert Committee on Biological Standardization, 1966a). For convenience, Part A of the requirements is reprinted in Appendix A to this chapter.

The general requirements are in two parts: Part A, General Requirements for Manufacturing Establishments; Part B, General Requirements for Control Laboratories.

The introduction to the general requirements stresses, very properly, that:

> The most important information concerning the safety of a biological substance is given by consistency of production, which is complementary to the tests applied to the final filled material. The approval of manufacturing methods, the maintenance of accurate records, and the inspection of production by the national control authority play a major part in creating confidence in the safety of the product.

The requirements themselves are arranged in the form of sections. A portion of each section is phrased in such a way that national control authorities can, if they wish, adopt the requirements as the basis of their own national regulations. Most sections also include paragraphs in the nature of comments or recommendations intended for the guidance of manufacturers and control laboratories, rather than for adoption as legal requirements.

The requirements for manufacturing establishments deal with the following: *staff*—qualifications, responsibilities, and organization; *buildings*—constructional materials, isolation of production areas, etc., and facilities for sterilization, for aseptic work, for work with animals, and for work at constant temperatures; *production control*—need for methods to be approved by the national control authority, precautions to ensure cleanliness, orderliness, and freedom from contamination, and precautions for the safe use of animals; *filling and containers*—requirements for aseptic rooms and aseptic techniques; *tests*—need for responsibility for testing to be separated from responsibility for production; *records*—keeping of complete written records of all stages of manufacture and testing, and complete histories of cultures; *samples*—submission of samples to the national control laboratory and retention of samples by the manufacturer; *labeling*—information required on leaflets and on labels of containers and packages; *distribution and shipping*—need to study complete sets of test results from a series of consecutive batches before release of a product; *storage and expiration date*—need to base expiration date on experimental data.

The requirements for national control laboratories deal with the following: *administration and personnel*—need for the control laboratory to be administered by the national control authority and to be staffed by experts; *buildings and equipment*—as for manufacturing establishments; *scope of activities*—licensing of manufacturers, inspection of their establishments, and testing of their products; establishment of national biological standards, or distribution of international standards; release and certification of batches of biologicals; and the fostering of research and training.

3. Requirements for Individual Biological Substances

The requirements for individual biologicals adopted so far fit into this general framework. As an example, the Requirements for Measles Vaccine (Live) may be considered (WHO Expert Committee on Biological Standardization, 1966b). Under the heading General Considerations there are discussions of the history of vaccination against measles, the antibody response in man and animals, the neurovirulence of measles virus, and the danger of adventitious viral agents.

Part A, Manufacturing Requirements, comprises ten sections with numerous subsections, and Part B, National Control Requirements, comprises two sections. A perusal of the contents of Part A will give some idea of the complexity of the manufacture and testing of a modern viral vaccine.

A study of these Requirements for Measles Vaccine (Live) will focus attention on several themes that recur throughout most of the WHO Requirements for Biological Substances so far promulgated. Thus, the product has an international name, in this instance *Vaccinum morbillorum vivum*, which can be used only if the product meets the international requirements. Second, nearly all the general requirements for manufacturing establishments are specifically stated to apply, together with a number of special requirements. Third, the production process is controlled in great detail and is based on a seed-lot system: that is, the vaccine harvest is removed from a seed lot by only a very few generations or passages, and each seed lot, destined to be the parent of a large number of vaccine harvests, is to be tested most exhaustively. Again, very great stress is placed on demonstrating that the final vaccine batches (as well as the seed lots and various intermediate stages) are free from all known or demonstrable adventitious agents. Last, great stress is placed on the importance of consistency of production. No batch may be released unless it is one of a series of consecutive satisfactory batches; specification of the length of the series is left to the national control authority. Five is the number specified in some countries. In these countries, a single failure would preclude issue of subsequent batches until a prescribed number of consecutive satisfactory batches had again been produced.

4. Legal, Commercial, and Scientific Significance

It may well be asked what force attaches to these international requirements. The general answer is that they are legally binding only if individual countries incorporate them into their national regulations. Some Member States have already done so, at least to the extent of modifying the relevant provisions of existing legislation. It is the hope that eventually every country will follow suit, thus ensuring a greater degree of uniformity of biologicals. However, even in countries that have not legally adopted them, the requirements still have considerable influence on manufacturers since they constitute a set of recommendations based on the best international expert advice. Moreover, it is clearly to a manufacturer's advantage to comply with the requirements voluntarily, so that he may promote the export of his products to other countries. Indeed, WHO is itself a very large purchaser of vaccines, chemotherapeutic agents, and chemoprophylactic agents for use in developing countries, and it may well insist on suppliers complying with the international requirements.

A common instance in which the requirements have great value is in agreements between countries governing the exchange of biological products. The requirements form a ready-made and authoritative basis for the supply of biological products under such contracts, and they are then, of course, legally binding. Again, it is in a manufacturer's interest to be prepared for such agreements by complying with the requirements in advance.

A wider form of agreement exists concerning the International Requirements for yellow fever vaccine, smallpox vaccine, and cholera vaccine. In these particular cases, a system has been established by international agreement whereby International Certificates of Vaccination are valid only for those travellers who have been vaccinated with products complying with the relevant international requirements, whether or not these have been adopted by national control authorities.

In the case of yellow fever vaccine, manufacturers are required to prepare protocols of production and testing of each batch and to submit the protocols to the WHO secretariat to provide evidence of compliance of the product with the international requirements. The medical officer who performs the vaccination must endorse each International Certificate of Vaccination with the name of the manufacturer and the batch number of the vaccine. In the case of smallpox vaccine, a similar endorsement system is obligatory, but protocols of production and testing do not have to be submitted to WHO. For cholera vaccine, neither a protocol system nor an endorsement system has been adopted.

Generally, it may be stated that the international requirements have to some extent facilitated international trade in certain important vaccines and chemotherapeutics, and they have helped WHO in that they are constantly referred to for acquiring products of uniformly high quality for use in mass campaigns for the eradication or control of communicable diseases. Most of all, they have stimulated manufacturers in all countries to try to adopt adequate measures for controlling their manufacturing processes and testing procedures, and they have stimulated much research directed to improving these practices.

C. Organization of WHO Activities in Biological Standardization

It may be appropriate at this stage to consider, briefly, the organizational aspects of the means used by WHO to achieve the objects discussed. The coordinating body in all this work is the WHO secretariat, with full-time officers and part-time consultants in Geneva, working in collaboration with laboratories in several countries.

The laboratories most deeply involved are the WHO International Laboratories for Biological Standards within the departments of biological standards of the Statens Seruminstitut, Copenhagen, the National Institute for Medical Research, London, and the Central Veterinary Laboratory,

Weybridge, England. Between them, these laboratories undertake the detailed work of organizing international collaborative assays and of holding and distributing the international biological standards and many of the international biological reference preparations and international biological reference reagents. The initiative for setting up biological standards and reference preparations usually comes from a WHO Expert Committee on Biological Standardization, which is convened annually in Geneva. It comprises recognized experts in the field, who serve without remuneration in their personal capacity and not as representatives of governments or other bodies, together with members of the WHO secretariat. This Expert Committee also establishes the international standards and reference preparations on the basis of the results of the international collaborative assays.

In earlier years, the Expert Committee on Biological Standardization took the view that its chief function was the provision of material standards, and that it was not the most appropriate body to initiate and consider the formulation of international requirements for biological substances. Thus, initially, the stimulus for writing international specifications for biologicals came from various other expert committees on particular diseases, and from discussions within the governing bodies of WHO. Consequently, the first seven sets of international requirements were drawn up by study groups appointed for the purpose, and the Expert Committee on Biological Standardization merely expressed agreement with the reports of the study groups. Gradually, the Expert Committee took a larger part in their formulation, and now the pattern is that the Expert Committee takes the initiative in requesting the WHO secretariat to draft new requirements. These drafts are submitted to members of the WHO Expert Advisory Panel on Biological Standardization and to other experts in the field for their written comments, and the revised drafts are then considered—and generally adopted—by the Expert Committee on Biological Standardization.

Needless to say, close liaison is needed between the WHO secretariat, the Expert Committee on Biological Standardization, and various other WHO committees—especially the Expert Committee on Specifications for Pharmaceutical Preparations, the work of which will be examined in detail in Section II of this article.

D. National Control Activities

It would be well to note yet another WHO biological program that has been intensified during the last decade. The program is intended to stimulate the interest of Member States in establishing national activities for the control of biological products where facilities for such national control are at present limited. This is particularly the case in the developing countries. The work is complementary to the WHO program for the development and improvement of the quality control of pharmaceuticals generally. When countries become conscious of the need for controlling biologicals, WHO helps, by advice and encouragement, in the establishment and development of national control laboratories.

Very recently, WHO advice in this regard has been codified in the form of a document entitled Development of a National Control Laboratory for Biological Substances (A guide to the provision of technical facilities) (WHO Expert Committee on Biological Standardization, 1970).

Adequate control of biological substances, however, exists in only a few countries of the world, and the majority of Member States of WHO have few facilities for testing, whether the products are manufactured within the countries or imported. It is the aim of the WHO program of biological standardization to change this state of affairs, but it is likely that many years will elapse before success is achieved.

E. Possible Future WHO Activities

It must not be thought that the activities of the WHO secretariat and the Expert Committee on Biological Standardization have solved all of the problems of safety and efficacy of vaccines, antisera, and endocrine products. The widespread use of international standards and reference preparations has led to a great reduction in the variability of assays of the same material attempted in different countries, but the variation has by no means been eliminated. This is due to the complex nature of most of the substances concerned, and of the reagents used in their assay. Such complexities of composition provide, of course, much scope for interactions with the variable responses of different strains of laboratory animals, kept under different environmental conditions. The consequent relatively poor level of control of biologicals is accentuated also by the fact that most of the WHO Requirements for Biological Substances rightly leave many decisions concerning details of production, assay, and safety testing of biologicals to the individual national control authorities.

To counteract deficiencies in international control, several projects are under consideration by WHO (Outschoorn, 1971). One improvement would be for international working standard preparations to be established, so that every manufacturer and control authority in the world could have the opportunity of using a single preparation as a standard of comparison in *routine* assays. This reform could be difficult to put into practice, but it would have the effect of elininating any variability introduced by qualitative differences between the present international standard and the wide assortment of national and house standards currently used for each biological product.

Another possible reform would be to adopt internationally acceptable protocols for recording the details of assays and safety tests performed by manufacturers or control authorities. This would at least provide an opportunity for pin-pointing possible causes of unexpected variations in results. A further contribution to standardization would be the compilation of a manual on biological laboratory techniques which, over an extended period, might come to be adopted by manufacturers and control authorities in most countries.

In the case of vaccines, a great need exists for studies on the correlation between the results of potency tests in the laboratory and the degree of protection conferred in the field. In most vaccines there is a great paucity of such data, and this sphere of research certainly offers opportunities for fruitful international collaboration.

For all of these possible developments, and similar ones in the more distant future, it would be of great value to have available the voluntary services of a reference and research group of laboratories, maintained by manufacturers and control authorities in various countries as part of their own organizations, but dedicated to international collaboration in a field promising rich rewards to public health.

II. Pharmaceutical Products Generally

A. The International Pharmacopoeia

Although some discussions on the possibility of compiling an international pharmacopeia were started as early as 1865, international agreement on the subject was not reached until 1929, when the representatives of 26 countries met at Brussells and allotted jointly to the League of Nations and the Belgian government the task of preparing the ground for such a compilation (WHO, 1958). Work began in earnest in 1937 by a Technical Commission of Pharmacopoeial Experts appointed by the Health Committee of the League of Nations, and much was accomplished before the work was interrupted by the World War. After the war, but before the formal creation of WHO, an Interim Commission appointed an Expert Committee on the Unification of Pharmacopoeias, charged with continuing the work.

This committee was replaced by an Expert Committee on the International Pharmacopoeia, which formally took over the entire project, the Belgian government relinquishing its special status in 1951.

The International Pharmacopoeia itself saw the light of day in two volumes and a supplement, all published by WHO (1951, 1955, 1959). In approving publication of the first volume, the World Health Assembly recommended to all Member States that the provisions of the International Pharmacopoeia be incorporated into national pharmacopoeias. This has been done in a few countries only. Some years later the International Pharmacopoeia was further supplemented by a volume entitled Specifications for Reagents Mentioned in the International Pharmacopoeia (WHO, 1963), and in 1967 a complete new edition of the whole work was published under the title Specifications for the Quality Control of Pharmaceutical Preparations—Second edition of the International Pharmacopoeia (WHO, 1967). By this time, the task of revising the International Pharmacopoeia had been entrusted to an Expert Committee on Specifications for Pharmaceutical Substances, with the aid, of course, of the WHO secretariat in Geneva.

The International Pharmacopoeia follows the same general form as most national and regional pharmacopeias. The second edition contains 555 monographs on drugs, including 162 newly introduced ones. The work does not include many drugs of biological origin, and those that are included are not subject to very strict controls, in recognition, no doubt, of the much more comprehensive control attempted in the series of WHO Requirements for Biological Products. The second edition also contains 69 appendixes, several of which deal with modern analytical methods such as infrared spectrophotometry, polarography, thin-layer chromatography, nonaqueous titration, and the Kofler method of identification.

In common with national pharmacopeias, each edition of the International Pharmacopoeia has tended to be somewhat out of date rather soon after publication, and it is difficult to bring out substantial addenda or supplements at sufficiently short intervals (a supplement comprising 112 pages of text has just been published (WHO, 1971a)). In accordance, therefore, with a resolution of the 1967 World Health Assembly, the Expert Committee on Specifications for Pharmaceutical Preparations is giving attention (Wallén, 1971) to a scheme whereby close collaboration with manufacturers and national control authorities may result in the issue of analytical data on new drugs very soon after their introduction, and in the publication of small addenda to the International Pharmacopoeia at short intervals. Development of such a scheme must necessarily be a long-term project, but the benefits to quality-control operations will be very substantial if it succeeds.

B. International Chemical Reference Substances

The impetus for setting up a collection of chemical reference substances came from the Expert Committee on Biological Standardization in 1952, at a time when it was decided that some of the international biological standards (such as that for vitamin A) were no longer needed for biological assays, although the need for a standard preparation continued for spectrophotometric assays. Four years later a WHO Centre for Chemical Reference Substances was established at the Apotekens Centrallaboratorium in Solna, Sweden. The collection now includes, as well as some of the discontinued international biological standards, some 40 reference preparations of pharmaceuticals described in the International Pharmacopoeia. They are intended mainly for use in spectrophotometric assays, chromatographic tests and assays, and infrared identification tests. A full list will be found in Table III. A set of 13 WHO melting point reference substances, covering a range of melting temperature from 69°C to 263°C, is also available from the Centre.

The work of the Centre is being expanded rapidly and much attention is being paid to determination of the purity of the current and proposed reference substances. The presence of small quantities of total impurities is being sought by the most sophisticated techniques, such as phase solubility analysis and differential scanning colorimetry. Special attention is given to those impurities which are liable to interfere with the official assays of the International Pharmacopoeia, and great care is taken to ensure that the substances are in the most appropriate isomeric and crystalline states.

Among the tasks awaiting the Centre is that of endeavouring to reduce the number of standard preparations which often come to be set up, by various authorities, for a single substance. This sometimes leads to confusion, and it is hoped that a closer collaboration between national control authorities and the Centre will lead to some desirable rationalization in this field.

C. Quality Control of Manufacturing Operations

1. Origin and Development of WHO Concern

Despite publication of the International Pharmacopoeia, by 1960 the rapid growth of international commerce in pharmaceuticals, and the poor control exercised over their export in some countries, led to increasing concern for protection of the consumers, especially those in the less-developed countries. As a result of several surveys by various groups of experts, WHO concern in the matter crystallized in 1963 with the passing of a resolution by the World Health Assembly, that steps should be taken to ensure that exported drugs comply with the same requirements as those imposed, in the country of manufacture, on drugs intended for domestic use. This topic has been debated in the Assembly every year since 1963, and WHO concern has deepened and broadened considerably each year (WHO, 1968; 1971b).

Thus, in 1964 the World Health Assembly urged exporting countries to provide testing facilities for importing countries. The following year all Member States were urged to subject both imported and locally produced pharmaceuticals to quality-control examination. Simultaneously, a WHO program was launched with the dual aims of assisting the establishment of control laboratories, and of formulating a set of principles for quality control. In 1966 this program was extended to include the study of a certification scheme and the official recognition of certain reference laboratories. The 1967 and 1968 Assemblies exhorted all parties to the utmost speed in all these reforms. A set of requirements for Good Practices in the Manufacture and Quality Control of Drugs having been drawn up and published by the WHO Expert Committee on Specifications for Pharmaceutical Preparations (1969a), the World Health Assembly in that year took the unusual step of recommending that all Member States adopt *and apply* this code, and also the certification scheme mentioned above. For good measure, the 1970 Assembly invited Member States to advise WHO of the steps that had been taken to implement the Good Practices code and the certification scheme.

2. Requirements for Good Practices in the Manufacture and Quality Control of Drugs

This document (which is reprinted as Appendix B to this article) is analogous to the WHO Requirements for Biological Substances No. 1 (General Requirements for Manufacturing Establishments and Control Laboratories), but whereas the latter applies only to biological products and is intended only as a guide to manufacturers and national control authorities, the Good Practices code applies to *all* drugs (very widely defined, and certainly including biological products) and has been recommended to Member States for adoption and application. Thus, as far as biologicals are concerned, the two documents supplement one another (except that the Good Practices code is stated therein not to be applicable to preparations for veterinary use).

The requirements for Good Practices in the Manufacture and Quality Control of Drugs are based on another document, entitled Principles of

Pharmaceutical Quality Control, published at the same time by the WHO Expert Committee on Specifications for Pharmaceutical Preparations (1969b). The principles most strongly emphasized are those of "building" quality into products from the very beginning of manufacture, and of ensuring adequate testing at every stage of manufacture, from the raw material to the finally packaged product.

The Good Practices code sets forth recommendations covering the following: *staff*—training and responsibilities; *accommodation for manufacturing operations* (*including operations in aseptic or especially clean environments*)—standards therefor; *equipment*—care, cleaning, and sterilization; *manufacturing premises*—sanitation and cleaning, according to a program drawn up in writing; *raw materials*—identification, storage, sampling, testing, and release or rejection, and records thereof; *manufacturing precautions*—cleanliness, identification of batches, freedom from all types of contamination, asepsis (where necessary), protective clothing, and health of personnel; *manufacturing procedures*—according to written instructions; *manufacturing records*—according to a complete batch-by-batch system; *labeling and packaging operations*—precautions in accounting for printed material used; *quality-control system*—the proper functions and operations thereof; regular voluntary inspections of overall manufacturing and control operations—schemes ancillary to whatever official inspections are required by law; *distribution of finished batches*—records; *recall procedures*—batches found to be faulty after issue; *complaints and reports of adverse reactions*—investigation and recording.

This code is certainly not intended to remain forever in its present text. Indeed, all Member States have been invited to comment on its provisions, and already parts of it have been reviewed by panels of experts, and some changes are likely to be made soon. Nevertheless, it seems certain that the main framework of the document will endure for a very long time, and will form the backbone of control legislation in many countries.

3. Certification Scheme on the Quality of Pharmaceutical Products in International Commerce

At the same time that the Good Practices code was recommended by the World Health Assembly to Member States for adoption and application, the Assembly also recommended adoption and application of schemes for certifying (1) manufacturers of drugs; (2) individual batches of drugs. Under scheme (1), the appropriate health authority of the exporting country would certify, on request, that a particular pharmaceutical manufacturer is authorized to manufacture and sell drugs and that regular inspections have shown that the WHO requirements for Good Practices in the Manufacture and

Quality Control of Drugs are applied in the manufacturing establishment. Under scheme (2), a certificate would be issued by the health authority of the exporting country, stating the name of the manufacturer of the batch, that the manufacturer is authorized to manufacture and sell the particular drug, and that all relevant details of manufacture and testing of the batch have been submitted to the health authority for examination.

These schemes are somewhat cumbersome, especially that dealing with certification of individual batches, and putting them into practice will present many complex problems. The comments of Member States have been sought, and their suggestions for improvements solicited, but it is likely that a considerable degree of refinement may be necessary, and that a long period may elapse before either scheme will make any notable direct contribution in the quality of pharmaceuticals reaching the less developed countries.

III. Other WHO Influences on the Pharmaceutical Industry

In the preceding sections of this article, the only aspects of WHO activities which have been chosen for discussion are those which have a direct bearing on the quality control of biological products and other pharmaceuticals. The discussion, has, therefore, omitted many pharmaceutical topics in respect of which WHO has exerted an influence on the industry. It may suffice to merely mention some of the main topics, namely: preclinical and clinical testing of new drugs for safety; international monitoring of drugs for adverse reactions or lack of efficacy; study of drugs as potential carcinogens; registration of nonproprietory names for new drugs.

In the field of biological products, the activities of the Expert Committee on Biological Standardization have been supported strongly by the work of several other Expert Committees, each concerned with some particular group of infectious diseases. But of course the influence has been mutual—much of the research work fostered by the Expert Committee on Biological Standardization has reacted to reinforce the work of the other committees, with consequent advances in the prophylaxis or chemotherapy of several diseases. From these advances have accrued substantial benefits, both for public health and for an important sector of pharmaceutical technology, quite outside the narrow field of quality control. Obviously the WHO secretariat is a vital link in all of these areas.

Especially in recent years, the secretariat has fostered the spread of good principles of production and quality control by organizing a series of regional conferences of representatives of manufacturers and control authorities. These conferences, which have dealt with a wide variety of biological or nonbiological drugs, represent just one further instrument for promoting the general WHO "effort to achieve the highest possible level of health throughout the world" by attention to "problems that can be satisfactorily solved through the cooperation of all or several countries."

Acknowledgments

I am indebted to the World Health Organization for permission to reprint the documents appended to this chapter, and to reproduce at length some passages from an earlier paper (Mathews, 1968). I am grateful to Dr. A. S. Outschoorn, Chief Medical Officer, Biological Standardization, WHO, Geneva, and to Dr. O. Wallén, Chief Pharmaceutical Officer, Pharmaceuticals, WHO, Geneva, for discussions on some aspects of WHO policies and for facilitating visits to the WHO International Laboratories for Biological Standards in Copenhagen, London, and Weybridge, and to the WHO Centre for Chemical Reference Substances in Solna. Discussions with members of the staffs of these institutions were most helpful and valuable. Thanks are due also to my colleagues, Dr. J. J. Graydon and Mr. V. F. Davey, for reading and helpfully criticizing the text.

Appendix A

WHO Requirements for Biological Substances—General Requirements for Manufacturing Establishments (WHO Expert Committee on Biological Standardization, 1966a).*

General Considerations

The procedures required for controlling biological substances during manufacture are different from the control procedures applied to final products by control authorities. Control at the manufacturing level is a matter of national concern, whereas control of final products, including imported products, by a control authority may have international as well as national implications.

The most important information concerning the safety of a biological substance is given by consistency of production, which is complementary to the tests applied to the final filled material. The approval of manufacturing methods, the maintenance of accurate records, and the inspection of production by the national control authority play a major part in creating confidence in the safety of the product.

The general requirements are applicable to all manufacturing situations.

*Reprinted from World Health Organ., Tech. Rep. Ser., **323**, Annex 1.

In an ideal situation the same control measures would be exercised by the governments of all countries. In such circumstances there would be no problem in the free exchange of biological substances between countries, and the control authority in any one would be faced only with the problem of controlling substances manufactured within its own jurisdiction. It is, however, essential to realize that it will be many years before such an ideal situation can possibly be brought about; in the interim it will continue to be necessary for the national control authority to deal not only with the substances manufactured within its own jurisdiction, but also with substances imported from other countries. . . .

Each of the following sections constitutes a recommendation. The parts of each section which are printed in large type have been written in the form of requirements so that, if a health administration so desires, these parts as they appear may be included in definitive national requirements. The parts of each section which are printed in small type are comments and recommendations for guidance.

Should individual countries wish to adopt these requirements as the basis for their national regulations concerning general requirements for the manufacture and control of biological products, it is recommended that a clause be included which would permit modifications, on the condition that it be demonstrated, to the satisfaction of the national control authority, that such modified requirements ensure a degree of safety and a potency of the products at least equal to those provided by the requirements formulated below. It is desirable that the World Health Organization should then be informed of the action taken.

The terms "national control authority" and "national control laboratory", as used in these requirements, always refer to the country in which the biological substance is manufactured.

Part A. General Requirements for Manufacturing Establishments

1. Personnel

Manufacturing shall be in charge of a person who has been trained in the techniques used in manufacturing biological substances and the scientific knowledge upon which the manufacture of these products is based. This person shall have sufficient authority to enforce discipline among employees, who shall include specialists with training appropriate to the products made in the establishment. The names and qualifications of such specialists, especially those responsible for signing a protocol, shall be registered with the national control authority.

Thus, in dealing with the problems of manufacture, a training is needed in some or all of the following fields: bacteriology, biometry, chemistry, medicine, pharmacy, pharmacology, veterinary medicine and virology.

The staff making control tests should be separate from the manufacturing unit and not responsible to the person in charge of production.

All staff engaged in manufacture, testing, and animal care should be vaccinated with appropriate specific vaccines, and should submit to a regular tuberculosis control.

2. *Buildings and Equipment*

2.1 *Buildings.* Laboratories, operating rooms, animal rooms and all other rooms and buildings used for the manufacture of biological products shall be so designed and constructed of such materials that the highest standards of cleanliness and sanitation can be maintained and freedom from dust, insects and vermin ensured. All such buildings shall be equipped with hot and cold running water and drainage. Adequate precautions shall be taken to avoid contamination of the drainage system with dangerous effluents and also to avoid airborne dissemination of pathogenic microbes and viruses. Staff changing rooms, etc., shall be provided as needed. All buildings and rooms shall be clean and sanitary at all times. If rooms intended for the manufacture of biological substances are used for other purposes, they shall be cleaned thoroughly and, if necessary, sterilized prior to resumption of manufacture of biological substances in them. Any persons not concerned with the production process who enter the production area for the purposes of inspection shall be supplied with sterile protective clothing.

Technical library facilities, including both books and journals, should always be available.

2.2 *Constant Temperature Rooms.* Adequate refrigerator space, as well as incubators or warm rooms, capable of being maintained at a uniform temperature within any required range shall be provided.

Refrigerators and incubators should maintain a uniform temperature in all parts of the interior and should preferably be equipped with recording thermometers and with appropriately placed alarm signals to ensure that an early repair can be effected in case of breakdown.

2.3 *Sterile Rooms.* Sterile transfer and processing rooms shall be of minimum size for their function and have low ceilings and smooth surfaces to permit thorough cleaning before each use.

These rooms should be essentially dust free and perferably supplied with filtered air at a pressure higher than that in adjacent rooms.

Staff working in these rooms shall be provided with a special changing room and wear sterile gowns.

2.4 Washing and Sterilization Equipment. Adequate facilities shall be available for washing apparatus. Steam autoclaves, dry-heat sterilizers, and bacterial retaining filters shall be available for sterilizing supplies, media and apparatus.

Autoclaves should preferably be equipped with recording thermometers. Other means of sterilization, including ultraviolet irradiation and chemical sterilization, have special applications and when appropriate should be used with proper controls.

2.5 Animal Quarters. Quarters for animals shall be designed in a manner and constructed of materials that permit maintenance in a clean and sanitary condition free from insects and vermin. Facilities for animal care shall include isolation units for quarantine of incoming animals, and vermin-free food storage. Provision shall be made for animal inoculation rooms which shall be separate from the post-mortem rooms.

There should be provision for the disinfection of cages, if possible by steam, and an incinerator for disposing of waste and of dead animals.

2.6 Apparatus. Instruments and apparatus shall be of high precision.

All instruments and apparatus should be calibrated and checked at regular intervals.

3. Production Control

3.1 Production Methods. Production methods shall be approved by the national control authority and written procedures shall be prepared for each product, describing each step in production and testing. Proposals for modifications shall be submitted for approval to the national control authority before their implementation. At any one time, manufacture of each biological product shall take place in a separate area using separate equipment. Only strains of micro-organisms or viruses used for the production of the particular biological product shall be permitted in the manufacturing area.

3.2 Cleanliness. Apparatus, equipment and materials used in manufacturing shall be clean and, if necessary, sterile and free from pyrogenic contamination.

3.3 Orderliness. All containers of biological substances, regardless of the stage of manufacture, shall be identified by securely attached labels.

3.4 Precautions against Contamination. All procedures with spore-forming micro-organisms or viruses shall be confined to separate areas with complete equipment used exclusively in those areas.

Separate facilities shall be provided for work with each virus and care shall be taken to prevent aerosol formation (especially by centrifugation and blending), which might lead to transfer of virus from one production unit to another.

Adequate staff shall be provided to avoid the necessity for staff to work in any one working day in areas in which different biological products are being manufactured.

Sequential manufacture of different products in the same area shall be allowed provided that the method of sterilization of the area between manufacture of the different products is shown to be satisfactory and has the approval of the national control authority.

Pathological specimens sent in for diagnosis shall be permitted only in separate areas not used for manufacturing biological substances.

Employees should stay in their own work areas, and wear protective clothing, including shoes, caps etc., which should remain in the area. Employees suffering from an infective illness should not be permitted to work until completely recovered.

Visitors should be as few as possible and they should not normally be permitted to enter sterile rooms.

3.5 Animal Care. Animals used for production purposes, or for test purposes, shall show no signs of communicable disease, and shall be adequately housed at all times. They shall be provided with a well-balanced diet, and be kept clean and sanitary. If the production process or test necessitates the use of animals of a particular species or strain, the animals used shall be approved by the national control authority.

Animals intended for use in production or in tests should be observed daily during a quarantine period of not less than one week. In some instances it is desirable to maintain the animal rooms constantly at the optimum temperature for the particular species and test, and it may also be necessary to maintain pure strains of test animals.

It is desirable to use specific pathogen-free (S.P.F.) animals for both production and testing of certain biological substances.

Animals or animal carcasses shall not be removed from the establishment if capable of transmitting disease.

Animals that die from infection are destroyed, preferably in an incinerator.

4. Filling and Containers

4.1 Filling Rooms. Filling shall be performed in rooms reserved for this purpose. These shall be sterile rooms equipped specifically for transferring measured quantities of finished biological substances from bulk containers to the final containers. Strict dust control measures and aseptic techniques shall be enforced to ensure that the product is not contaminated during the filling process.

These measures include, for instance, laying of dust by steam or spray, proper protective clothing for workers etc.

4.2 Filling Procedures. Filling operations shall be conducted in such a way as to avoid any contamination or alteration of the product. They shall take place in areas that are completely separate from those in which living micro-organisms, including viruses, are handled.

The filling process should be checked at least twice each year at the end of a working day by filling not less than 500 ampoules with a nutrient medium containing no antibiotics or bacteriostatic substances and incubating the complete batch of filled ampoules. Not more than 1% of the ampoules filled in this way should show signs of contamination and all contaminants should be identified.

4.3 Containers. The final container shall be sealed as soon as possible after filling. Closures shall be of material that does not have a deleterious effect upon the biological substances, and shall be designed to maintain a hermetic seal throughout the dating period.

5. Tests

All tests of a specific biological substance, requiring the use of living micro-organisms, shall be carried out in rooms separate from those used for production.

Preferably, all tests should be carried out in such separate rooms.

The descriptions of the tests necessary to establish the safety, purity and potency of each lot of a biological substance will be given in the requirements to be formulated for the particular biological substance.

6. Records

6.1 Production Protocols and Distribution Records. Records shall be permanent and clearly indicate all steps in processing, testing, filling and distribution. Written records shall be kept of all tests irrespective of their results. The records shall be of a type approved by the national control authority. They shall be retained throughout the dating period of a lot or batch of a biological product and be available at all times for inspection by the national control authority.

Records must make it possible to trace all steps in the manufacture and testing of a batch, and should include records of sterilization of all apparatus and materials used in its manufacture. Distribution records must be kept in a manner that permits rapid recall of any particular batch, if necessary.

6.2 Records of Cultures. Records shall be maintained of the complete passage history of all cultures kept in the establishment. Cultures shall be labelled and stored in a safe, orderly manner.

7. Samples

Samples from each lot shall be taken in a sufficient amount to satisfy the requirements for samples of the national control laboratory. Additional samples shall be retained throughout the dating period as reference material, in a manner which ensures the identity of the lot.

Manufacturers should retain sufficient additional samples to permit repetition of the control tests.

8. Labelling

All products shall be clearly identified by labels. The information given on the label on the container or the label on the package shall be determined by the national control authority.

The label on the container shall show at least:

the name of the product (i.e., the international name and/or the proper name);
the name of the manufacturer (and address if required);
the number of the final lot;
the recommended human dose and route of administration;
the condition of storage and expiry date.

The label on the package shall, in addition to the information shown on the label on the container, show at least:

the nature and amount of any preservative or added substance present in the product;
a description of any substance likely to cause any adverse reaction;
any contra-indications to the use of the product.

In addition, the label on the package or the leaflet in the package should indicate the stability under different storage conditions, contain instructions for the use of the product and give information about reactions that may follow administration of the product.

It is desirable to have an indication that the product fulfils the relevant requirements published in the WHO technical report series.

It is also desirable that the labels used remain permanently attached to the containers under all storage conditions and that an area of the container be left uncovered to allow inspection of the contents.

If the final container is not suitable for labelling (for example, a capillary tube), it should be in a labelled package.

9. Distribution and Shipping

9.1 Release for Distribution. A lot of a biological substance shall not be released until all the required tests have been performed, summarized and reviewed and until any other official control requirement is satisfied. These tests shall always include an identity test performed on the contents of a finished package from each filling, to confirm the accuracy of the labelling.

No new biological substance shall be released until consistency of production has been established.* In routine production, failure of a single batch to meet the requirements for safety shall be considered as a breakdown in production, and consistency shall be re-established to the satisfaction of the national control authority before any further batches are released.

9.2 Shipping. Biological substances shall be shipped with precautions to ensure that the product retains its potency upon arrival at its destination.

Rules cannot be laid down to cover all situations; this requires the continuous exercise of judgement.

10. Storage and Expiry Date

The statements concerning storage temperatures and expiry dates appearing on the label and the packing leaflet, as required in Part A, section 8, shall be based on experimental evidence and shall be submitted for approval to the national control authority.

10.1 Storage Conditions. Biological products shall be stored at all times at controlled temperatures within a range which ensures optimal stability.

During distribution, short periods at ambient temperatures may have to be permitted.

10.2 Expiry Date. The expiry date of a biological product shall be defined and fixed with the approval of the national control authority.

Appendix B

Good Practices in the Manufacture and Quality Control of Drugs (WHO Expert Committee on Specifications for Pharmaceutical Preparations, 1969a).†

1. General Considerations

In the pharmaceutical industry, overall control is essential to ensure that the individual consumer receives drugs of high quality. Haphazard operations cannot be permitted in the manufacture of substances that may be necessary to save life or to restore or preserve health.

*In some countries, consistency of production has to be established for the first five production batches.

†Reprinted from World Health Organ. Tech. Rep. Ser. **418**, Annex 2.

Difficulties will undoubtedly arise in establishing the necessary criteria for the manufacture of drugs that will meet established specifications and that can, therefore, be used with confidence. Recommended practices for the manufacture of drugs of desired quality are set forth below. Adherence to these practices, complementing the various control tests followed from the beginning to the end of the manufacturing cycle, will contribute substantially to the manufacture of consistently uniform batches of high-quality drugs.

The manufacturer must assume responsibility for the quality of the drugs he produces. He alone can avoid mistakes and prevent mishaps by exercising adequate care in both his manufacturing and control procedures.

The good practices outlined below should be considered as general guides; whenever necessary, they may be adapted to meet individual needs, provided the established standards of drug quality are still achieved. . . . They are intended to apply to the manufacturing practices (including packaging and labelling) used in the production of drugs in their finished dosage forms.

It not infrequently occurs that several firms co-operate in the production (including packing and labelling) of the finished dosage forms of drugs. It may also occur that a finished, packed, and labelled drug is repacked and/or relabelled, giving it a new designation. It should be pointed out that since such procedures constitute part of a manufacturing operation, they should be subject to the requirements proposed below. However, packing and labelling do not necessarily affect the quality of a drug, and in such cases it may suffice to ensure that adequate measures are taken as specified in applicable sections of this document.

The requirements set forth herein are not intended to apply to preparations for veterinary use, although equal attention should be given to quality in the manufacture of such preparations.

2. Definitions

For the purposes of this document, the following definitions are adopted.

Drug. Any substance or mixture of substances that is manufactured, sold, offered for sale, or represented for use in (1) the treatment, mitigation, prevention, or diagnosis of disease, an abnormal physical state, or the symptoms thereof in man or animal; or (2) the restoration, correction, or modification of organic functions in man or animal.

Manufacturing. All operations involved in the production of a drug, including processing, compounding, formulating, filling, packaging, and labelling.

Starting materials. All substances, whether active or inactive or whether they remain unchanged or become altered, that are employed solely for the manufacture of drugs.

Batch. A quantity of any drug produced during a given cycle of manufacture. The essence of a manufacturing batch is its homogeneity.

Batch number. A designation printed on the label of the drug, that identifies the batch and that permits the production history of the batch, including all stages of manufacture and control, to be traced and reviewed.

Quarantine. The status of a material that is kept in isolation and that is not available for use until released.

Quality control. All measures designed to ensure the uniform output of batches of drugs that conform to established specifications of identity, strength, purity, and other characteristics.

"Half-finished" product. Any material or mixture of materials that must undergo further manufacture.

Purity. The degree to which other chemical or biological entities are present in any substance.

3. Personnel

Experts responsible for supervising the manufacture and control of drugs should possess the qualifications of scientific education and practical experience required by national legislation. Their education should include the study of an appropriate combination of (*a*) chemistry (analytical chemistry, biochemistry, physical chemistry, etc.); (*b*) chemical engineering; (*c*) microbiology; (*d*) pharmaceutical sciences and technology; (*e*) pharmacology and toxicology; (*f*) physiology and histology; and (*g*) other related sciences. They should also have adequate practical experience in the manufacture and control of drugs. In order to gain such experience, a preparatory period may be required, during which they should exercise their duties under professional guidance. The scientific education and practical experience of experts should be such as to enable them to exercise independent professional judgement, based on the application of scientific principles and understanding to the practical problems encountered in the manufacture and control of drugs.

Such experts should preferably not have any interests outside the manufacturer's organization that (*a*) prevent or restrict their devoting the necessary time to their assigned responsibilities or (*b*) may be considered to entail a conflict of financial interest. Finally, they should be given full authority and the facilities necessary to carry out their duties effectively.

In addition to the experts noted above, an adequate number of technically trained personnel should be available to carry out the manufacturing and control operations in accordance with established procedures and specifications.

4. Premises

4.1 General. Drugs should be manufactured, processed, packaged, labelled, and tested in isolated areas, which should

(1) not be utilized for any other purpose;

(2) be well lighted and ventilated and, if necessary, heated and air conditioned so as to ensure the maintenance of a satisfactory temperature and relative humidity that will not adversely affect the drug during manufacture and storage, nor the accuracy and functioning of laboratory instruments;

(3) be suitable for their intended use (walls, ceilings, etc., should have smooth surfaces and be of such construction that they (*a*) do not crack or shed particles into the atmosphere, and (*b*) can be readily cleaned and, if necessary, disinfected); and

(4) provide adequate working space and adequate room for the orderly placement of equipment and materials, so as to (*a*) minimize or eliminate any risk of confusion between different drugs and their components, and (*b*) control the possibility of cross-contamination by another drug that is manufactured, processed, packaged, labelled, or held on the same premises.

Special rooms or areas should be provided for the storage of highly toxic drugs and narcotics, and the access of personnel to such rooms or areas should be restricted.

4.2 Special. For special purposes, such as the manufacture of drugs that can be sterilized in their final containers, separate enclosed areas must be provided. These areas should be essentially dust-free, preferably supplied with filtered air at a pressure higher than that in adjacent areas, and entered through an air-lock. The access of personnel to such areas should be restricted. The areas should, if feasible, be designed so as to preclude the possibility that products intended for sterilization could be mixed with, or taken to be, products already sterilized. This may conveniently be effected by the use of double-ended sterilization apparatus opening into separate and noncommunicating areas.

For the manufacture of drugs that cannot be terminally sterilized, a separate and enclosed area, specifically designed for this purpose, should be used.

Routine microbe counts for the air in the areas described above should be carried out during manufacturing operations. The results of such counts should be checked against established standards, and adequate records of the counts should be maintained.

5. Equipment

Manufacturing equipment should be designed and maintained in such a way as to

(1) be suitable for its intended use;
(2) facilitate thorough cleaning wherever necessary;
(3) exclude any contamination of drugs and their containers during manufacture; and
(4) minimize the risk of confusion or the omission of a processing step such as filtration or sterilization.

Operating conditions within apparatus used to sterilize products should be monitored by means of recording devices and/or indicators, which should be initially calibrated and checked at approved intervals by approved methods.

Manufacturing equipment and utensils should be thoroughly cleaned and, if necessary, sterilized, and maintained in accordance with specific written directions. When indicated, all equipment should be disassembled and thoroughly cleaned, to preclude the carry-over of drug residues from previous operations. Adequate records of such procedures should be maintained.

Equipment used for aseptic filling should be checked at suitable intervals by microbiological methods.* Adequate records of such tests should be maintained.

6. Sanitation

Manufacturing premises should be maintained in accordance with the sanitary standards issued by the appropriate health authority. They should be clean and free from accumulated waste, orderly, and free from vermin. A written sanitation programme should be available, indicating:

(1) areas to be cleaned, and cleaning intervals;
(2) cleaning procedures to be followed and, if necessary, equipment and materials to be used for cleaning; and
(3) personnel assigned to and responsible for cleaning operations.

Eating, smoking, and unhygienic practices should not be permitted in manufacturing areas.

*This may be accomplished by conducting normal filling operations using suitable sterile liquid bacteriological media or other media suitable for dry powder filling, as the case may be, or by using biological indicators that can demonstrate the adequacy of the sterilization process.

Sufficient clean, well-ventilated toilet facilities including facilities for hand washing and rooms for changing clothes, should be available near working areas for the use of manufacturing personnel.

7. Starting Materials

An inventory should be made of all starting materials to be used at any stage in the manufacture of drugs, and records should be kept of their origin, date of receipt, date of analysis, date of release by the quality control department, and their subsequent use in manufacture. All such materials must be

(1) identified, and their containers examined for damage;
(2) properly stored;
(3) properly sampled by the quality control department;
(4) tested for compliance with requirements (all materials should be marked to indicate that they are undergoing testing, and should, if possible, be "quarantined" until released by the quality control department); and
(5) released by the quality control department by means of written instructions.

Starting materials that are accepted or approved should be properly and conspicuously labelled as such, and should then be transferred, if necessary, to areas designated for the storage of such materials.

All rejected starting materials should be conspicuously identified as such, and should be destroyed or returned to the supplier as soon as possible.

8. Manufacturing Operations

Manufacturing operations and controls should be carried out under the supervision of experts, as specified in section 3.

8.1 Cleanliness. Before any manufacturing operation is begun, a check should be made to ensure that all apparatus and equipment to be used in the operation has been cleaned and/or sterilized (see section 5).

8.2 Equipment and Containers. The contents of all vessels and containers used in manufacture and storage between manufacturing stages must be identified by conspicuously placed and clearly legible labels, bearing the name and/or identification code of the processed materials and the necessary batch identification data. Such labels should, whenever practicable, be securely attached to the vessels and containers concerned. Similar labels should be attached to mechanical manufacturing equipment during its operation, listing the name and/or identification code of the manufactured product and, where necessary, its batch identification.

8.3 Precautions against Contamination. All manufacturing operations should be confined to separate areas intended for such purposes, with complete equipment used exclusively in those areas, or measures should be taken to ensure that neither contamination nor confusion can occur.*

Sterile operations must be performed in areas specially designed and constructed for their intended purpose, as indicated in section 4.2. Whenever the different operations are not physically separated, and there is a possibility that unsterilized and sterilized products might be confused, all containers of batches of products for sterilization should bear a clear indication of whether or not their contents have been sterilized.

All operations in which highly potent drugs, including antibiotics, are weighed, mixed, micronized, encapsulated, formed into tablets, placed in containers, etc. should be conducted in confined areas that are provided with adequate exhaust systems or that are maintained under appropriate pressure, so as to prevent one drug from spreading to and contaminating another. Adequate precautions should be taken to prevent the recirculation of contaminated air.

In manufacturing areas, clean working garments should be worn over, or in place of, street clothing.

Products that undergo sterile operations should be protected from contamination by either (*a*) using methods such as laminar-flow techniques, or (*b*) ensuring that personnel wear clean, sterile gowns, head coverings, masks, rubber gloves, and shoe coverings. Before dressing and entering sterile areas, personnel must wash their hands with a suitable disinfectant.

8.4 Manufacturing Personnel. No person known to be affected with a disease in a communicable form, or to be the carrier of such a disease, and no person with open lesions on the exposed surface of the body, should be engaged in the manufacture of drugs. Manufacturing personnel should undergo periodic health checks. In order to prevent any impairment of health caused by the handling of hazardous or potent products, manufacturing personnel should, whenever necessary, wear protective clothing, shoes, headgear, dust masks, etc., and such protective clothing should remain in the area in which it is used. In some instances, it may be necessary to restrict personnel to their immediate working areas.

8.5 Manufacturing Procedures and Written Instructions. Manufacturing procedures and written instructions for each drug must be prepared under

*It is usually advisable to avoid, whenever possible, the simultaneous manufacture of drugs that are similar in appearance in adjacent areas that are not physically separated.

the direct supervision of experts (see section 3) who have the necessary authority. They should contain at least the following information for each drug:

(1) name and presentation;
(2) a description or identification of the final container(s), packaging material(s), and labels and, where applicable, of the closure(s) to be used;
(3) the identity, quantity, and quality of each starting material to be used, irrespective of whether or not it appears in the finished drug (the permissible excess ("overage") that may be included in a formulated batch should be indicated);
(4) the theoretical yields to be expected from the formulation at different stages of manufacture and the permissible yield limits;
(5) detailed instructions for, and precautions to be taken in, manufacture and storage of the drug and of "half-finished" products; and
(6) a description of all necessary quality control tests and analyses to be carried out during each stage of manufacture, including the designation of persons or departments responsible for or charged with the execution of such tests and analyses.

8.6 Batch Manufacturing Records. Manufacturing records must provide a complete account of the manufacturing history of each batch of a drug, showing that it has been manufactured, tested, and analysed in accordance with the manufacturing procedures and written instructions described in section 8.5. A separate batch manufacturing record should be prepared for each batch of drug produced, and should include the following information:

(1) name and presentation;
(2) date of manufacture;
(3) batch identification;
(4) complete formulation of the batch (see section 8.5, point 3);
(5) the batch number (or analytical control number) of each component used in the formulation;
(6) the actual yield obtained at different stages of manufacture of the batch as compared with the theoretical yield (see section 8.5, point 4);
(7) a duly signed record of each step followed, precautions taken, and special observations made throughout the manufacture of the batch;
(8) a record of all in-process controls followed and of the results obtained;
(9) a specimen of the actual coded label used;
(10) identification of packaging materials, containers, and where applicable, closures used;

(11) signature of the expert responsible for the manufacturing operations, and the date of his signature; and

(12) a full analytical report showing whether the batch complies with the prescribed specifications for the drug (this report should be duly signed and dated, and endorsed by the expert responsible for quality control, to permit the batch to be released).

8.7 Maintenance of Batch Manufacturing Records. For reference purposes, all batch manufacturing records should be retained for a specified period.

9. Labelling and Packaging

Labelling and packaging materials, including leaflets, should be stored in such a way as to ensure that the correct labels, etc., are affixed to or accompany any given drug. Access to such materials should be restricted to authorized personnel.

Prior to packaging and labelling of a given batch of a drug, the manufacturing and control records specified in section 8.6 should show that the batch has been duly tested, approved, and released by the responsible quality control expert. Prior to being issued, all labels for containers, cartons, and boxes and all circulars, inserts, leaflets, etc. should be examined and released as satisfactory for use by the designated authority.

To prevent packaging and labelling errors, a known number of labels should be issued and properly coded. Such issuance should be made against a written, signed request that indicates the quantity and type of labels required. Upon completion of packaging and labelling, the number of labels actually used should be carefully compared with the number issued and coded. Destroyed and unused labels should also be checked.

All finished drugs should be identified by labels that should bear, clearly indicated, at least the following information:

(1) the name of the drug;

(2) a list of the active ingredients, showing the amount of each present, and a statement of the net contents;

(3) the batch number assigned by the manufacturer;

(4) the date of manufacture and/or the expiry date, as required (if desired, the date of manufacture may be given as a code);

(5) the name and address of the manufacturer;

(6) any special storage or handling precautions that may be necessary;

(7) indications and directions for use and any warnings and precautions that may be necessary.

10. The Quality Control System

Every establishment that manufactures pharmaceuticals should have a quality control department that is autonomous in the areas of responsibility assigned to it. It should control all starting materials, monitor the quality aspects of manufacturing operations, and control the quality and stability of drugs.

A quality control laboratory must also be available. The laboratory should:

(1) be adequately staffed and fully equipped for performing all quality control tests and analyses required during and after manufacture;*

(2) be supervised by a qualified expert (see section 3), who should have the final responsibility for approving or rejecting all materials tested;

(3) be promptly informed of all changes and modifications in the manufacturing procedures and written instructions (see section 8.5).

The quality control department should have the following principal duties:

(1) to prepare detailed instructions, in writing, for carrying out each test and analysis;

(2) to control and release each batch of starting material;

(3) to control and release "half-finished" products, if necessary;

(4) to control and release each batch of finished drug that is ready for distribution;

(5) to control and release packaging and labelling materials and the final containers in which drugs are to be placed;

(6) to evaluate the adequacy of the conditions under which starting materials, "half-finished" products, and finished drugs are stored;

(7) to evaluate the quality and stability of finished drugs and, when necessary, of starting materials and "half-finished" products;

(8) to establish expiry dates and shelf-life specifications, whenever necessary, on the basis of stability data; and

(9) to establish (and, when necessary, revise) control procedures and specifications.

In order to fulfil its responsibilities, the quality control department should take samples in sufficient quantities, according to established procedures,

*If animal tests are necessary, the animals should be given adequate quarters and care (for further information, see *Wld Hlth Org. Techn. Rep. Ser.*, 1966, No. 323, pp. 14, 16). The use of outside independent laboratories may be advisable for specialized and complex analytical and biological procedures that require the use of costly equipment and that can be performed only by technicians with specialized training. Such laboratories should be adequately staffed and fully equipped to perform such analyses.

and keep appropriate analytical records. The samples should be properly labelled, and portions should be kept for future reference.

The quality control department should maintain adequate analytical records concerning the control of each batch of drugs manufactured. Such records should include:

(1) a final evaluation of the product and a decision as to whether or not the analysed and controlled batch conforms to the established specifications;

(2) the source of the specifications used;

(3) the signature(s) of the person(s) who performed the quality control procedures; and

(4) a final review and dated endorsement by a duly authorized expert.

The quality control department should also be responsible for the full examination of returned drugs to determine whether such drugs should be released, reprocessed, or destroyed. Adequate records of the disposition of such drugs should be maintained.

11. Self-Inspection

In order to maintain strict adherence to all manufacturing procedures and prescribed controls, it may be advisable for a firm to designate an expert or a team of experts to conduct regularly scheduled inspections of its overall manufacturing and control operations. However, this should not be taken to mean that any firm electing to exercise self-inspection should be exempt from the official inspections required by the laws and regulations of the country in which it is located.

12. Distribution Records

Adequate records should be maintained of the distribution of a finished batch of a drug in order to facilitate prompt and complete recall of the batch if necessary.

13. Complaints and Reports of Adverse Reactions

Reports of injuries or adverse reactions resulting from the use of a drug should be forwarded to the appropriate authorities. Complaints regarding the quality of a drug, including any change in its physical characteristics, must be thoroughly investigated. If they prove well-founded, appropriate measures must be taken as soon as possible. The measures taken should be recorded and filed with the original complaint.

References

Mathews, A. G. (1968). *World Health Organ., Chron.* **23**, 3.
Outschoorn, A. S. (1971). Personal communication.
Wallén, O. (1971). Personal communication.
WHO (1951). "International Pharmacopoeia," 1st ed., Vol. I. WHO, Geneva.
WHO (1955). "International Pharmacopoeia," 1st ed., Vol. II. WHO, Geneva.
WHO (1958). "The First Ten Years of the WHO." WHO, Geneva.
WHO (1959). "International Pharmacopoeia," 1st ed., Suppl. WHO, Geneva.
WHO (1963). "Specifications for Reagents Mentioned in the International Pharmacopoeia." WHO, Geneva.
WHO (1967). "Specifications for the Quality Control of Pharmaceutical Preparations—Second Edition of the International Pharmacopoeia." WHO, Geneva.
WHO (1968). "The Second Ten Years of the WHO." WHO, Geneva.
WHO (1971a). "Specifications for the Quality Control of Pharmaceutical Preparations—Second Edition of the International Pharmaeopoeia." Supplement 1971. WHO, Geneva.
WHO (1971b). "Handbook of Resolutions and Decisions of the World Health Assembly and the Executive Board," 11th ed. WHO, Geneva.
WHO Expert Committee on Biological Standardization (1966a). *World Health Organ., Tech. Rep. Ser.* **323**, Annex 1.
WHO Expert Committee on Biological Standardization (1966b). *World Health Organ., Tech. Rep. Ser.* **329**, Annex 2.
WHO Expert Committee on Biological Standardization (1970). *World Health Organ., Tech. Rep. Ser.* **444**, Annex 3.
WHO Expert Committee on Biological Standardization (1971a). *World Health Organ., Tech. Rep. Ser.* **463**, Annexes 3 and 4.
WHO Expert Committee on Biological Standardization (1971b). *World Health Organ., Tech. Rep. Ser.* **463**, 8–9.
WHO Expert Committee on Biological Standardization (1971c). *World Health Organ., Tech. Rep. Ser.* **463**, 19 and 60–61.
WHO Expert Committee on Biological Standardization (1971d). *World Health Organ., Tech. Rep. Ser.* **463**, Annex 2.
WHO Expert Committee on Specifications for Pliarmaceutical Preparations (1969a). *World Health Organ., Tech. Rep. Ser.* **418**, Annex 2.
WHO Expert Committee on Specifications for Pharmaceutical Preparations (1969b). *World Health Organ., Tech. Rep. Ser.* **418**, Annex 1.

AUTHOR INDEX

Numbers in italics refer to the pages on which the complete references are listed.

SUBJECT INDEX